Accounting Technician

INTERMEDIATE STAGE
NVQ/SVQ 3

Unit 6

Recording and Evaluating Costs and Revenues

TEXTBOOK

FOULKS LYNCH
PUBLICATIONS

British Library Cataloguing-in-Publication Data

A catalogue record for this book is available from the British Library.

Published by:

Foulks Lynch Ltd
4, The Griffin Centre
Staines Road
Feltham
Middlesex
TW14 0HS

ISBN 0 7483 5948 6

© Foulks Lynch Ltd, 2003

Printed and bound in Great Britain by Ashford Colour Press Ltd.

Acknowledgements

We are grateful to the Association of Accounting Technicians for permission to reproduce extracts from the Standards of Competence for Accounting.

CONTENTS

INTRODUCTION

This is the new edition of the AAT NVQ/SVQ Textbook for Unit 6 – *Recording and Evaluating Costs and Revenue*.

Tailored to the new Standards of Competence, this Textbook has been written specifically for AAT students in a clear and comprehensive style.

This book takes a very practical approach, with the inclusion of numerous examples and activities to help you practise what you have learnt. Self test questions and key terms at the end of each chapter reinforce your knowledge.

STANDARDS OF COMPETENCE

A unit of competence (for example, Unit 1 *Recording Income and Receipts*) is made up of elements which contain all the essential information to define the standard and how it can be achieved. These elements consist of **performance criteria**, **range statements** and **knowledge and understanding**.

Performance criteria: These are the tasks you need to do to complete each element.

Range statements: These are the methods to use to complete the performance criteria.

Knowledge and understanding: These statements are the underpinning requirements to be able to complete the tasks.

Listed below are the elements, performance criteria, knowledge and understanding and range statements. These have been referenced to the chapters in the book where they are covered.

Unit 6: Recording and Evaluating Costs and Revenues

Unit commentary

This unit is concerned with how organisations record, analyse and report current and future costs and revenue data for use within the organisation. You will need to know that organisations build up costs and revenues in different ways. The way costs are recorded vary with the type of industry as well as the measurement rules chosen by the organisation. You have to understand the meaning and consequence of these different ways of recording costs and revenues and be able to apply them in relevant circumstances.

There are three elements. The first element focuses on direct costs and revenues, the second on overheads. You will need to apply both types of cost to the reporting of the organisation's expenses. In addition, you will need to apply both types of costing to the recording and analysing of unit and departmental costs. The third element is concerned with using cost and revenue information to help organisations make decisions. You will need to know about cost behaviour and apply it appropriately to managerial decisions for both short- and long-term planning purposes.

Elements contained within this unit are:

Element: 6.1   Record and analyse information relating to direct costs and revenues

Element: 6.2   Record and analyse information relating to the allocation, apportionment and absorption of overhead costs

Element: 6.3   Prepare and evaluate estimates of costs and revenues

Knowledge and understanding

To perform this unit effectively you will need to know and understand:

The business environment	*Chapter*
1 The nature and purpose of internal reporting (Elements 6.1, 6.2 & 6.3)	10
2 Management information requirements (Elements 6.1, 6.2 & 6.3)	10, 11

Element 6.1 Record and analyse in formation relating to direct Costs and revenues

Performance criteria

Chapter

In order to perform this element successfully you need to:

A	Identify direct costs in accordance with the organisation's costing procedures	2, 3, 4
B	Record and analyse information relating to direct costs	2, 3
C	Calculate direct costs in accordance with the organisation's policies and procedures	2, 3, 4
D	Check cost information for stocks against usage and stock control practices	2
E	Resolve or refer queries to the appropriate person	2, 3, 4

Range statement

Performance in this element relates to the following contexts:

Direct costs:

• Materials	2
• Direct labour costs	3

Stocks:

• Raw materials	2
• Part-finished goods	2
• Finished goods	2

Element 6.2 Record and analyse information relating to the allocation, apportionment and absorption of overhead costs

Performance criteria

In order to perform this element successfully you need to:

A	Identify overhead costs in accordance with the organisation's procedures	4, 5
B	Attribute overhead costs to production and service cost centres in accordance with agreed bases of allocation and apportionment	5
C	Calculate overhead absorption rates In accordance with agreed bases of absorption	5
D	Record and analyse information relating to overhead costs in accordance with the organisation's procedures	4, 5
E	Make adjustments for under and over recovered overhead costs in accordance with established procedures	5
F	Review methods of allocation, apportionment and absorption at regular intervals in discussions with senior staff and ensure agreed changes to methods are implemented	5
G	Consult staff working in operational departments to resolve any queries in overhead cost data	5

Range statement

Performance in this element relates to the following contexts:

Overhead costs:

• Fixed	4
• Variable	4

Element 6.3 Prepare and evaluate estimates of costs and revenues

Range statement

Performance in this element relates to the following contexts:

ASSESSMENT

Unit 6 is assessed by both **Skills Testing** and **Examination**. If you take the examination, you may also need to provide further evidence of your competence in this unit in your portfolio.

Examination

The examination will be three hours long (plus 15 minutes reading time) and will include practical tests linked to the performance criteria and questions focusing on knowledge and understanding.

Section 1: This will assess your competence in elements 6.1 and 6.2. Tasks may include:

- methods of stock control and pricing of materials, including First In First Out, Last In First Out and Weighted Average Cost.
- preparing cost accounting entries for material, labour and overhead costs of the organisation
- calculating direct labour costs
- allocating and apportioning indirect costs to responsibility centres, including direct and step-down methods
- calculating departmental absorption rates using different absorption bases
- calculation product cost using absorption and marginal costing.

Section 2: This will assess your competence in element 6.3. Tasks may include:

- separating variable and fixed costs and the effect of changing capacity levels
- preparing estimates of future income and costs
- short-term planning tasks involving cost-volume-profit analysis for a single product
- product mix decisions using limiting factor analysis
- long-term planning tasks using net present value and payback techniques
- preparing a report.

Skills testing

Skills testing when your approved assessment centre (AAC) is a workplace

You may be observed carrying out your accounting activities as part of your normal work routine. You need to collect documentary evidence of the work you have done in an accounting portfolio.

Skills testing when your AAC is a college

This will use a combination of:

- documentary evidence of activities carried out at work, collected in a portfolio
- realistic simulations of workplace activities
- projects and assignments.

Skills testing when you don't work in accountancy

Don't worry – you can prove your competence using one of AAT's simulations, or from case studies, projects and assignments.

Portfolio building

Your portfolio is where you will keep all of your **evidence** to show your competence. It should contain different types of evidence from a range of sources.

Rules of evidence

Evidence must be:

- Valid – clearly related to the standards being assessed
- Authentic – must be your own work
- Current – make sure it is as recent as possible
- Sufficient – all performance criteria need to be met

Sources of evidence

- Prior achievement
- Performance in the workplace
- Performance in specially set activities
- Questioning: oral, written or by computer

Portfolio contents

For Unit 6, ensure your portfolio contains the following:

- Title page (your name, contact details and what you are studying)
- Your CV
- Information about your organisation (name and address, type of business, staff numbers, organisation chart if you have one)
- Job description
- Summary of your previous and current work experience (if appropriate)
- Witness statements from supervisors at work listing performance criteria and details of the job undertaken (these need to be on headed paper, be signed by your supervisor and have their job title on it)
- Evidence that you have performed all of the necessary performance criteria, including printout of classroom or workplace documents relating to direct costs: identification, records, calculations and analysis; cost information for stocks: raw materials, part-finished goods and finished goods; overheads: identification, records, calculations, analysis, adjustments for over/under recovery, allocation, absorption and apportionment; estimates of future incomes and costs; written reports.
- Evidence that you possess the underpinning knowledge and understanding (this could be written answers to questions set in class or a statement from your tutor outlining the oral questioning you received)
- Evidence grid (from the AAT's student record)
- Index to evidence

Chapter 1

INTRODUCTION TO COST ACCOUNTING

In this chapter the basic principles of cost accounting and why it exists will be introduced. Much of the chapter concentrates on the terminology that will be encountered throughout cost accounting studies and in particular on the different classifications and definitions of costs.

The chapter also concentrates on the distinction between direct and indirect costs which is fundamental to the new revised standards.

CONTENTS

1   Cost accounting

2   Costing methods

3   Direct and indirect costs

4   Fixed and variable costs

5   Summary and illustration of cost classification

6   Cost behaviour

7   Cost prediction

KNOWLEDGE AND UNDERSTANDING

		Reference
1	Analysis of the effect of changing activity levels on unit costs	Item 13
2	The identification of fixed, variable and semi-variable costs and their use in cost recording, cost reporting and cost analysis	Item 15

LEARNING OUTCOMES

At the end of this chapter you should have learned the following topics.

• Classification of costs as direct or indirect and according to their function or activity group

• The terminology of cost centres and cost units

• Identification of costs as fixed, variable, semi-fixed or semi-variable

1 COST ACCOUNTING

The financial accounts record transactions between the business and its customers, suppliers, employees and owners e.g. shareholders. The managers of the business must account for the way in which funds entrusted to them have been used and, therefore, records of assets and liabilities are required as well as a statement of any increase in the total wealth of the business. This is done by presenting a balance sheet and a profit and loss account at least once a year.

However, in performing their task, managers will need to know a great deal about the detailed workings of the business. This knowledge must embrace production methods and the cost of processes, products etc.

Cost accounting involves the application of a comprehensive set of principles, methods and techniques to the determination and appropriate analysis of costs to suit the various parts of the organisation structure within a business.

Definition   Cost accounting is the establishment of budgets, standard costs and actual costs of operations, processes, activities or products; and the analysis of variances, profitability or the social use of funds'.

Management accounting is a wider concept involving professional knowledge and skill in the preparation and particularly the presentation of information to all levels of management in the organisation structure. The source of such information is the financial and cost accounts. The information is intended to assist management in its policy and decision-making, planning and control activities.

2 COSTING METHODS

2.1 COST UNITS

At this stage, it is helpful to consider cost accounting procedures in relation to a single aim:

> to find the cost of the output/product of the business

Definition   A **cost unit** is a unit of product or service in relation to which costs are determined.

The physical measure of product or service for which costs can be found, is a cost unit. In a printing firm, the cost unit would be the specific customer order. For a paint manufacturer, the unit would be a litre (or a thousand litres) of paint.

The cost per cost unit is important for a variety of reasons:

(a)   making decisions about pricing, acceptance of orders, and so on

(b)   measuring changes in costs and relative levels of efficiency

(c)   stock valuation for financial reporting

(d)   planning future costs (budgeting and standard costs).

The process of finding unit costs involves analysis, classification and grouping of costs. In the remainder of this section, we will introduce the main terms encountered in cost accounting.

2.2 EXAMPLES OF COST UNITS

Industry or activity	Cost unit
Manufacturing industries	
Brewers	Barrel/hectolitre
Brick-making	1,000 bricks
Coal mining	Tonne
Paper	Ream
Sand and gravel	Cubic metre
Service industries	
Hospitals	(a) Bed occupied
	(b) Out-patient
Professional service e.g. accountants	Chargeable man-hour
Individual departments	
Personnel departments and welfare	Employee
Materials storage/handling	(a) Requisition units issued/received
	(b) Material movement values issued/ received

2.3 COST CENTRES

Definition   A **cost centre** is a production or service location, function, activity or item of equipment for which costs are accumulated.

A **cost centre** is a small part of a business in respect of which costs may be determined and then related to cost units. Terminology varies from organisation to organisation, but the small part of a business could be a whole department or merely a sub-division of a department. A number of departments together would comprise a function. Thus a cost centre could be a location, function or item of equipment or a group or combination of any of these.

It is important to recognise that cost centre costs are necessary for control purposes, as well as for relating costs to cost units.

The terms **direct** and **indirect** may be used in relation to a cost centre. For example, a supervisor's salary would be a direct charge to the cost centre in which he is employed, whereas rent would need to be shared between a number of cost centres. Both of these items are, of course, indirect as regards specific cost units.

2.4 BASIC COSTING METHODS

Two fundamental types of business activity exist - where the cost unit is unique, e.g. a job made to the customer's specification; or where cost units are identical or basically similar, e.g. cans of paint. Consequently basic costing methods fall into two categories:

(a)   specific order costing

(b)   operation costing.

Specific order costing is applicable where the work consists of separate contracts, jobs or batches, each of which is authorised by a specific order or contract. The type of business applicable to operation costing is where standardised goods or services are produced by repetition. The crucial test in deciding if operation costing is appropriate is whether unit costs are found by dividing cost for a period by the units produced in that period.

ACTIVITY 1

Give some examples of business activities where each of specific order costing and operation costing would be appropriate.

For a suggested answer, see the 'Answers' section at the end of the book.

2.5 FURTHER ANALYSIS OF COSTING METHODS

In subsequent studies these two basic costing methods are further sub-divided into major costing methods, so that **job, batch** and **contract** costing are three types of application of the more general **specific order** costing.

Operation costing can be split into **process** and **service** costing.

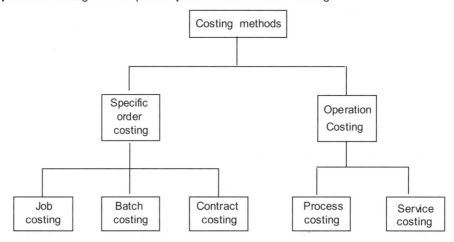

3 DIRECT AND INDIRECT COSTS

Classification is a means of analysing costs into logical groups so that they may be summarised into meaningful information for management.

Management will require information concerning a variety of issues, each of which may require different cost summaries, for example costs may be required for a particular department, or for a product. For this reason there are many different classifications of cost which may be used - these are explained below.

3.1 ELEMENTS OF COST

The initial classification of costs is according to the **elements** upon which expenditure is incurred:

(a)   Materials

(b)   Labour

(c)   Expenses.

Within cost elements, costs can be further classified according to the **nature** of expenditure. This is the usual analysis in a financial accounting system, e.g. raw materials, consumable stores, wages, salaries, rent, rates, depreciation.

3.2 DIRECT AND INDIRECT COSTS

Definition   A **direct cost** is expenditure which can be economically identified with and specifically measured in respect to a relevant cost object.

Definition   **Prime cost** is the total cost of direct material, direct labour and direct expenses.

Definition   An **indirect cost** is expenditure on labour, materials or services which cannot be economically identified with a specific saleable cost unit. Indirect costs are also referred to as overheads.

Definition   **Overheads** are the total of the indirect costs.

Summary

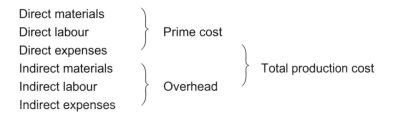

To ascertain the total production cost of a cost unit, indirect costs are allocated to cost centres and cost centre costs are shared over (absorbed by) cost units. The subject of allocation and absorption of overhead costs is explained later.

ACTIVITY 2

Consider direct and indirect costs and note down in particular the types of factors that are likely to influence whether a cost is treated as direct or indirect in relation to a cost unit.

For a suggested answer, see the 'Answers' section at the end of the book.

3.3 FUNCTIONAL ANALYSIS OF COST

(a)   Direct costs are usually regarded as being solely related to manufacturing, and so are not classified into any other function.

(b)   Indirect costs (overheads) are usually categorised into the principal activity groups:

   (i)   production

   (ii)   administration

   (iii)   selling

   (iv)   distribution

   (v)   research.

This unit is concerned with the identification, allocation and absorption of **production** overheads.

4 FIXED AND VARIABLE COSTS

In the previous section, materials, labour and expenses costs were classified as either direct or indirect costs according to whether or not they could be directly attributed to a cost unit.

In this section a different classification of costs will be considered that is also useful to the cost accountant. This classification is known as analysis of costs by behaviour and considers whether a cost varies with the level of production or if it remains constant whatever the level of production.

4.1 FIXED COSTS

Definition   **Fixed costs** are costs which tend to be unaffected by fluctuations in the level of activity in the organisation.

A fixed cost is therefore one that will tend to be at the same level whatever the production levels of that organisation.

Examples

Examples of fixed costs might include the following:

* the rental of a factory as this will not alter whether 200 units are produced or 20,000 units

* the insurance of the machinery as again the amount that the machinery is used will not affect the insurance cost

* the managing director's salary is a fixed labour cost as this will be paid whatever the level of production in the organisation

* the rental element of the telephone bill, rather than the call charges, as this remains constant however many calls are made and however much the organisation produces.

4.2 VARIABLE COSTS

Definition   **Variable costs** are those that tend to vary with the level of activity of the organisation.

Therefore, if the business produces more products a variable cost will tend to increase. If the business produces twice as many products then the variable costs will tend to double.

Examples

Examples of variable costs might include the following:

* the cost of the materials used in the product. If twice as many products are made then twice as much of the material will be required

* the cost of the labour for production workers. Again, if twice as many products are produced then the labour cost is likely to be twice as high as either the hours worked are doubled or the number of employees is doubled

* power for running the machines will vary according to the amount of time they are in use which itself will vary with the amount of production

* the oil used to lubricate the machines will again vary with the amount of use of the machines and therefore production.

ACTIVITY 3

A factory produces double glazed window units. The factory is rented and the annual rental is £100,000 per annum. The cost of the materials, labour and expenses for a window unit is estimated at £250.

Identify the fixed and variable costs and estimate each of those costs for production levels of 500 units and 2,000 units.

For a suggested answer, see the 'Answers' section at the end of the book.

5 SUMMARY AND ILLUSTRATION OF COST CLASSIFICATION

We have seen the major ways in which costs can be defined and analysed. We shall now summarise this by a series of examples to reinforce this analysis.

The main thrust of the syllabus is to classify costs into direct and indirect and we shall keep this as our main classification in what follows, giving examples of each type and stating whether they are fixed or variable.

5.1 DIRECT COSTS

(a) **Direct materials**

Examples	Bricks for a house
	Steel used in building a car
	Wood used in building a fence
Fixed or variable	Variable

(b) **Direct labour**

Examples	Machine minder in print factory
	Lathe operator in furniture factory
	Paint sprayer in car repair shop.
Fixed or variable	Variable

(c) **Direct expenses**

Examples

There are very few examples of direct expenses. Remember that it has to be economically viable to attach the costs to a cost unit. Thus electricity or other power used to run a machine could be allocated to a specific unit produced by the machine, but it will generally be difficult to do and such costs would rarely be treated as direct expenses.

Royalties or licence fees paid for the right to use designs or patents are the only real examples of direct expenses.

Fixed or variable	Variable

5.3   INDIRECT COSTS

(a)   **Indirect materials**

Examples	Small nuts and bolts used in assembly of products.
	Paint used in painting small items.
	(in theory both the above could be allocated to specific cost units but in practice it is not economic to do so and they will be treated as indirect and not costed directly to the product).
Fixed or variable	Variable

(b)   **Indirect labour**

Examples	Supervisor of machine minders in print factory
	Mechanic servicing several lathes in furniture factory
	Painter, painting the outside of a factory.
Fixed or variable	Fixed

(c)   **Indirect expenses**

Examples	(Most expenses will be treated as indirect.)
	Rent and rates
	Electricity
	Freight costs.
Fixed or variable	Fixed

6   COST BEHAVIOUR

6.1   TOTAL COST

It has been shown that production cost comprises three elements - materials, wages and expenses; it can also be noted that production cost includes both fixed and variable segment elements. It is useful to look at the way costs behave in response to changes in production volume.

Definition   **Cost behaviour** is the variability of input costs with activity undertaken.

Example

	Production	
	500 units	*1,000 units*
	£	£
Sales (@ £3 per unit)	1,500	3,000
Total costs	1,000	1,500
	———	———
Profit	500	1,500
	———	———
Average unit cost	£2.00	£1.50
Average unit profit	£1.00	£1.50

Total costs have increased by only 50% although production has doubled. This is because some costs will not rise in relation to the increase in volume.

Suppose the output is a single product and the only costs are:

(a)   rental of a fully equipped factory, £500 pa

(b)   raw materials, £1 per unit.

Solution

Then the way these two costs react to producing varying numbers of widgets is as follows:

(a)   **Factory rental – a fixed cost**

Although production rises, the same rent is payable.

Definition   A **fixed cost** is a cost which is incurred for an accounting period, and which, within certain output or turnover limits, tends to be unaffected by fluctuations in the levels of activity (output or turnover).

Graph showing relationship between rent and output

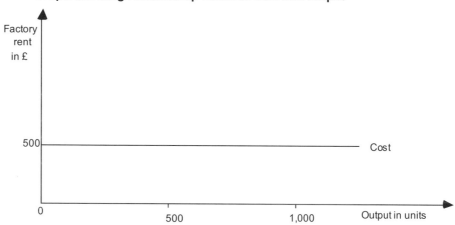

This may be also shown by plotting the average fixed cost per unit on a graph.

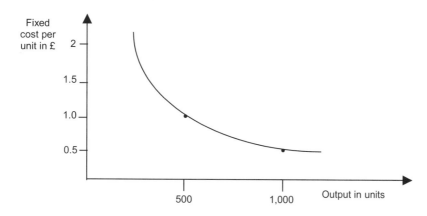

Conclusion   As output increases, unit fixed costs decline.

This only changes if a new or larger factory is rented.

(b)   **Raw materials – a variable cost**

Every unit of production has a raw material cost of £1; therefore, the cost varies directly with the level of production.

Definition   A **variable cost** is a cost which varies with a measure of activity.

Graph showing relationship between raw materials, costs and output

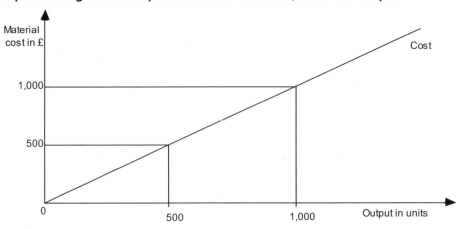

Conclusion   In the case of variable costs unit cost remain constant irrespective of the level of output (provided there are no discounts for bulk purchases).

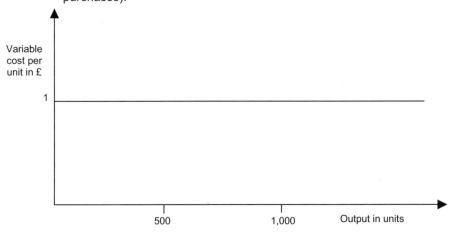

6.2 CONTRIBUTION

If the two types of cost are segregated, the operating statement can be presented in a different way:

	Production in units		
	1 unit	*500 units*	*1,000 units*
	£	£	£
Sales	3	1,500	3,000
Variable costs - Raw materials	1	500	1,000
Contribution	2	1,000	2,000
Fixed costs - Factory rent	500	500	500
Profit/(loss)	(498)	500	1,500

The revised presentation is based on the concept that each unit sold **contributes** a selling price less the variable cost per unit. Total contribution provides a fund to cover fixed costs and net profit.

Definition	**Contribution** is the sales value less variable cost of sales.	
Thus:	Sales – Variable cost of sales	= Contribution
	Contribution – Fixed costs	= Net profit

Note that unit contribution is a constant number unless prices or the specification for variable costs change.

Conclusion As output increases total unit costs gravitate towards the unit variable cost:

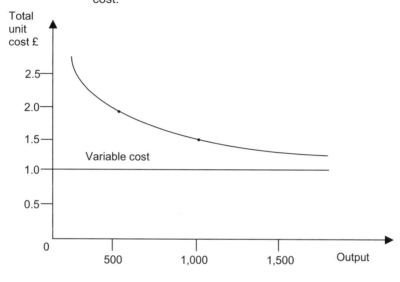

ACTIVITY 4

A company manufacturing widgets has estimated that the variable cost of making and selling widgets is £6.75 per unit. Its fixed costs are £560,000 each month.

Task

Calculate the unit costs of making and selling widgets, at monthly sales volumes of:

(a)   100,000 units

(b)   120,000 units

(c)   140,000 units

(d)   160,000 units.

Suggest what the implications might be for the company of increasing its monthly output from 100,000 units to 160,000 units, with no change in total fixed costs.

This activity covers performance criterion C in element 6.3.

For a suggested answer, see the 'Answers' section at the end of the book.

6.3   RELEVANT RANGE OF ACTIVITY

The analysis of cost behaviour is only appropriate when considering the kind of movement in activity which could reasonably be expected, i.e. within the relevant range of volume (output) levels. A number of simplifying assumptions are, therefore, usually made.

6.4   COSTS WHICH CHANGE PER UNIT

When buying items such as tyres, it is normal to obtain special prices for larger orders. Thus, the more tyres ordered, the lower the price paid for each tyre.

Graph showing relationship between the total cost of tyres and the output of cars

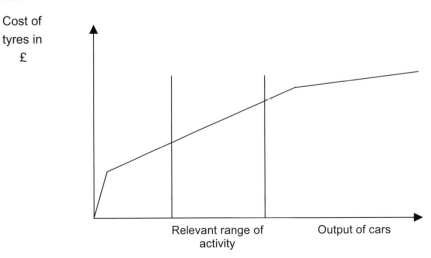

However, in practice it is likely that only relatively limited changes in the level of production will be considered. This is described as the **relevant range of activity**, and within that range unit prices are likely to be constant.

6.5 STEP COSTS

Some costs rise in a series of steps, e.g. renting additional factory space.

If the steps are large, the concept of the relevant range of activity usually applies i.e. only occasionally is a new factory considered and therefore one can assume the cost to be fixed for the relevant range.

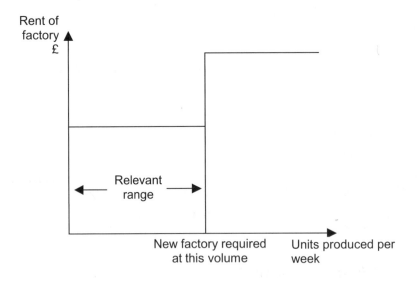

Further examples of a step cost would be depreciation when additional machinery is purchased and also extra supervisory costs if an additional shift is introduced.

6.6 SEMI-VARIABLE COSTS (ALSO REFERRED TO AS SEMI-FIXED COSTS)

Definition   A semi-variable cost is a cost containing both fixed and variable components and which is therefore partly affected by a change in the level of activity.

An example is maintenance costs: even at zero output **standby** maintenance costs are incurred. As output rises so do maintenance costs.

Graph showing relationship between machine maintenance costs and output

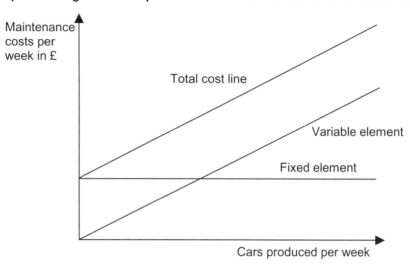

7 COST PREDICTION

An understanding of cost behaviour is essential to predict costs associated with a given level of activity. This analysis is not available from traditional cost analysis, and alternative approaches must be used.

We shall briefly examine four main approaches:

(a)   the engineering approach

(b)   the account analysis approach

(c)   the high-low method

(d)   scatter charts.

In all of these approaches the assumption is made that the linear model of cost behaviour is valid,

and therefore the relation between costs, y, and activity, x, is the form:

$y = a + bx$

Where   y = total costs

               x = activity level

               a = fixed costs

               b = unit variable (or marginal) cost

These four approaches are considered below.

7.1 THE ENGINEERING APPROACH

This approach is based on building up a complete specification of all inputs (e.g. materials, labour, overheads) required to produce given levels of output. This approach is therefore based on technical specification, which is then costed out using expected input prices.

This approach works reasonably well in a single product or start-up situation - indeed in the latter it may be the only feasible approach. However, it is difficult to apply in a multi-product situation, especially where there are joint costs, or the exact output mix is not known.

7.2   THE ACCOUNT ANALYSIS APPROACH

Rather than using the technical information, this approach uses the information contained in the ledger accounts. These are analysed and categorised as either fixed or variable (or semi-fixed or semi-variable). For example, material purchase accounts would represent variable costs, office salaries fixed cost. Since the ledger accounts are not designed for use in this way, some reorganisation and reclassification of accounts may be required.

You should note that this is the approach used in many examination questions.

There are several problems with this approach:

(a)   Inspection does not always indicate the true nature of costs. For example, factory wages would normally be a fixed cost, with only overtime and/or bonuses as the variable element.

(b)   Accounts are by their nature summaries, and often contain transactions of different categories.

(c)   It rests on historic information which may not be suitable for predicting the future.

7.3   HIGH LOW (OR RANGE) METHOD

This method is based on an analysis of historic information on costs at different activity levels.

Example

The data for the six months to 31 December 20X3 is as follows:

Month	Units	Cost
		£
July	340	2,260
August	300	2,160
September	380	2,320
October	420	2,400
November	400	2,300
December	360	2,266

The variable element of a cost item may be estimated by calculating the additional cost between high and low volumes during a period.

Six months to 31/12/X3	Units produced	Inspection costs
		£
Highest month	420	2,400
Lowest month	300	2,160
Range	____	____
	120	240
	____	____

The additional cost per unit between high and low is $\dfrac{£240}{120 \text{ units}}$ = £2 per unit

which is used as an estimate of the variable content of inspection costs. Fixed inspection costs are, therefore:

$$£2,400 - (420 \times £2) \quad = \quad £1,560 \text{ per month}$$

$$\text{or} \quad £2,160 - (300 \times £2) \quad = \quad £1,560 \text{ per month.}$$

 FOULKS LYNCH
PUBLICATIONS

i.e. the relationship is of the form y = £(1,560 + 2x).

The limitations of the high low method are:

(a)   Its reliance on historic data, assuming that (i) activity is the only factor affecting costs and (ii) historic costs reliably predict future costs.

(b)   The use of only two values, the highest and the lowest, means that the results may be distorted due to random variations in these values.

ACTIVITY 5

Use the high-low points method to calculate the fixed and variable elements of the following cost:

	Activity	£
January	400	1,050
February	600	1,700
March	550	1,600
April	800	2,100
May	750	2,000
June	900	2,300

For a suggested answer, see the 'Answers' section at the end of the book.

7.4   SCATTER CHARTS

If the data from the example was plotted on a graph, the result would be a scatter-chart of inspections costs.

Scatter chart showing the relationship between total inspection costs and output

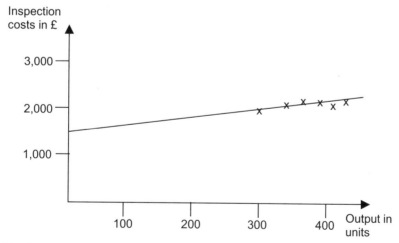

The **line of best fit** (a line which passes through the plotted points to equalise the number of points on each side and the aggregate distance from the line) may be drawn as accurately as possible by inspection. The point at which that line cuts the vertical axis indicates the fixed cost (about £1,460 in the illustration).

Scatter charts suffer from the general limitations of using historic data referred to above. In addition, their problem is that the estimate of the best linear relationship between the data is subjective. Finally, it should be noted that this can only be converted into a mathematical relationship by actual measurement.

ACTIVITY 6

Plot the data points from the previous activity on a scatter graph and draw a line of best fit to find the fixed cost. Measure the gradient of the line to determine the variable cost.

For a suggested answer, see the 'Answers' section at the end of the book.

CONCLUSION

This chapter was an important introduction to much of the terminology involved in dealing with costs and cost accounting. In order to understand cost accounting processes it is vital that an understanding is gained of the different types of costs and the different possible classifications and groupings of those costs.

SELF TEST QUESTIONS

		Paragraph
1	What is cost accounting?	1
2	What is a cost unit?	2.1
3	What are indirect costs?	3.6
4	What is a fixed cost?	4.2
5	What is the effect on variable cost per unit of output increasing?	6.3
6	What are step costs?	6.7

KEY TERMS

Cost accounting – the establishment of budgets, standard costs and actual costs of operations, processes, activities or products; and the analysis of variances, profitability or the social use of funds.

Cost unit – a unit of product or service in relation to which costs are determined.

Cost centre – a production or service location, function, activity or item of equipment for which costs are accumulated.

Direct cost – expenditure which can be economically identified with and specifically measured in respect to a relevant cost object.

Prime cost – the total cost of direct material, direct labour and direct expenses.

Indirect cost – expenditure on labour, materials or services which cannot be economically identified with a specific saleable cost unit. Indirect costs are also referred to as overheads.

Overheads – the total of the indirect costs.

Fixed costs – costs which tend to be unaffected by fluctuations in the level of activity in the organisation.

Variable costs – costs that tend to vary with the level of activity of the organisation.

Semi-variable costs – costs which exhibit the characteristics of both variable and fixed costs in that whilst they increase as output increases they will never fall to zero even at zero output level.

Cost behaviour – the variability of input costs with activity undertaken.

Fixed cost – a cost which is incurred for an accounting period, and which, within certain output or turnover limits, tends to be unaffected by fluctuations in the levels of activity (output or turnover).

Contribution – the sales value less variable cost of sales.

Chapter 2

ORDERING AND ISSUING MATERIALS

The three main categories of cost that will be incurred by an organisation are the costs of materials, labour and overheads. In this chapter and the next we look at the cost of materials. To begin with, we examine the ways in which physical stocks of materials are controlled and the documentation associated with movements of stocks (from suppliers to stores, stores to production departments etc). In the next chapter we will concentrate on the control of materials costs and usage through variance analysis.

CONTENTS

KNOWLEDGE AND UNDERSTANDING

		Reference
1	Recording of cost and revenue data in the accounting records.	Item 4
2	Methods of stock control and valuation including First In First Out, Last In Last Out and Weighted Average cost.	Item 5
3	Relationship between the materials costing system and the stock control system	Item 19
4	The sources of information for revenue and costing.	Item 27

PERFORMANCE CRITERIA

		Reference
1	Identify direct costs in accordance with the organisation's costing procedures	A (element 6.1)
2	Record and analyse information relating to direct costs	B (element 6.1)
3	Calculate direct costs in accordance with the organisation's policies and procedures	C (element 6.1)
4	Check cost information for stocks against usage and stock control practices	D (element 6.1)

LEARNING OUTCOMES

At the end of this chapter you should have learned the following topics.

Methods of stock control

- The periodic review system

- The reorder period

- The reorder quantity

- The fixed reorder level (two bin) system

- The reorder level

- The reorder quantity

Purchasing procedures and documentation

- Purchase requisition

- Purchase order

- Delivery note

- Goods received note
- Purchase invoice
- Bin card
- Stock ledger account
- Goods requisition note
- Goods returned note
- Part deliveries

Pricing issues from stores

- Determine price of issues in accordance with company's policy
- Value closing stock
- Reconcile stock per stock ledger account with physical stock and account for differences
- Identify the organisation's pricing policy - transfer price at actual or standard cost
- Check pricing of issues against the organisation's pricing policy for internal issues
- Identify the organisation's usage and stock control practices
- Check individual issues against organisation's stock control practices
- Reconcile issues made to organisation's overall usage
- Identify and report unusual issues

1 MATERIAL COSTING

The study of material costing can be considered as being divided into four sub-topics:

(a) Stock control.

(b) Purchasing procedures and documentation.

(c) Pricing of materials issued and stock valuation.

(d) Classification of materials cost.

The first three topics are covered in this chapter and the last topic is addressed in the next chapter.

Each of these sub-topics is introduced in the following paragraphs.

1.1 STOCK CONTROL

Stock holding represents a major cost to a company but running out of material may halt the production line. An important decision for a company is therefore when to order stock and in what quantity.

1.2 PURCHASING PROCEDURES AND DOCUMENTATION

Materials are purchased either because they are required by the production department or because the stock level of the item concerned is low and needs to be replenished. The ordering and receipt of the goods are two separate functions so as to minimise the risk of fraud. Goods are usually received into stores and issued to the production department when required. A formal system of purchasing procedures is required and full documentation of each stage ensures that mistakes are minimised and correct authorisation levels are used.

1.3 PRICING OF MATERIALS ISSUED AND STOCK VALUATION

There are basically two valuation bases which may be used:

(a) the actual price paid

(b) an estimated price.

The use of the actual price is not as administratively convenient and easy as it may sound, and for this reason an estimated value may be used. The actual value may be based on FIFO, LIFO or weighted average pricing. The estimated value is known as the standard cost. The different valuation methods are explained later in this text.

1.4 CLASSIFICATION OF MATERIAL COST

One of the purposes of cost recording is to calculate the cost of a single unit of product or service provided by the organisation; such a single unit is known as the cost unit.

In order to facilitate the calculation of unit costs, individual costs are analysed into logical groups; this is known as cost classification. Material costs are an example of such a logical group.

Material costs can be further analysed into those which can be economically identified with a single cost unit, such as the components used to repair a particular car; these are known as direct costs. Other material costs e.g. lubricating oil for production machinery cannot be identified with a single cost unit; these are known as indirect costs.

The technique for estimating standard material costs is considered in the next chapter.

2 METHODS OF STOCK CONTROL

Most organisations will find that it is necessary for the smooth running of their operations to hold some amount of the materials used in the organisation in stock.

The problem that the organisation will face is how much stock of each type of material is required.

2.1 STOCK HOLDING PROBLEMS

The problem associated with the holding of stock is that a high enough level of stock must be held in order to meet the requirements of production departments whilst also minimising the amount of working capital tied up in the stock.

If insufficient stock levels are maintained then the business runs the risk of not being able to provide manufacturing departments with the materials they require when they require them.

On the other hand if too high levels of stock are held then this will be expensive to the business in terms of the amounts of money tied up in the stock.

2.2 APPROACHES TO STOCK CONTROL

There are various approaches that an organisation can take to stock control. The stock levels can either be reviewed at set intervals of time and a suitable order then placed or alternatively each time the stock holding falls to a particular level then an order will be placed for new stocks.

These two approaches to stock control are known as a periodic review system and a re-order level system respectively. The more detailed operation of these systems will be considered in the following paragraphs.

3 PERIODIC REVIEW SYSTEM

3.1 INTRODUCTION

Definition A **periodic review system** of stock control is one where the stock levels are reviewed at fixed time intervals e.g. every four weeks.

At each review the amount of stock to be ordered will be that required to bring the stock levels up to a predetermined level.

Example

A company reviews the level of one line of stock every four weeks. An order is placed at each review and the new stock is received almost immediately. The company policy is that the amount ordered is the number of units required to bring the total stock holding to 40 units.

At the last review there were four units of the item in stock. How many units would the replacement order be for?

Solution

40 – 4 units = 36 units

3.2 STOCK-OUTS

Definition A **stock-out** is a situation where goods are required from stock but there are not enough of those items in stock at the time.

A periodic review system runs the risk of stock-out if more than the expected number of units of the item are required in the period between reviews.

Example

In the previous example at each review the stock level is brought up almost immediately to 40 units when the next order is placed. Therefore, if only 38 units are required in the next four week period there will be enough stock to satisfy that demand.

However, if 45 units of that item are in fact required during the next four weeks then the stores will not be able to provide five of those units as they are not in stock.

3.3 BUFFER STOCK

The risk of such stock-outs can be reduced by the holding of buffer stock.

Definition **Buffer stock** is an additional amount of stock that can be held with the intention of reducing or eliminating the risk of stock-outs.

In the example being used suppose that the expected usage of that particular item in a week is 10 units, which will total 40 units in the four week review period. If the stock level is brought up to 40 units every four weeks when the replacement order is made then if the actual usage is the same as that expected, 40 units, the amount of stock remaining at the end of the four week period will be zero.

However, if the actual usage is more than 10 units per week there will be stock-outs.

This could be prevented by holding say five units of buffer stock. In this case each time an order is placed it will be for an amount which will bring the total number of units of that item up to 45 units.

ACTIVITY 1

If the buffer stock in the example is to be five units and the number of units of the item remaining at the last review was seven then how many units would have been ordered?

For a suggested answer, see the 'Answers' section at the end of the book.

4 RE-ORDER PERIOD

The re-order period or review period will depend upon the expected usage of the item, the maximum amount of the item that the organisation wishes to hold and any buffer stock that is required.

Example

A business expects to use 100 units of an item each week and does not hold any buffer stock. The maximum number of units of this item that the business wishes to keep in stock is 500. What is the periodic review period for this item of stock? What would be the review period if the business wishes to hold a buffer stock of 100 units?

Solution

If the stock level is brought up to 500 units when each order is placed and no buffer stock is to be kept then the stock level will be reviewed when it is expected to be zero. This will take place every five weeks (500 units/100 units).

Alternatively, the business may keep a buffer stock of 100 units. In this case the review would take place when it was expected that there would be 100 units left in stock, the buffer stock. This would take place after 400 units (500 units – 100 units) had been expected to be used.

If 100 units are expected to be used each week then the stock level will be reviewed every 4 weeks (400 units/100 units).

5 RE-ORDER QUANTITY

Definition   The **re-order quantity** is the number of units of stock ordered.

In all of the examples used so far it has been assumed that when an order is placed the items of stock are received virtually immediately. Therefore, the re-order quantity is simply the amount necessary to take the stock levels from their level at the review date to the required level for the business.

5.1 LEAD TIME

In most practical instances there will be a delay between the placing of the order and the receipt of the goods. This is known as the lead time.

Definition   The **lead time** is the interval of time between the placing of a replenishment order and the receipt of the goods.

The expected lead time and the expected usage of materials in that period must also therefore be considered when determining the re-order quantity.

Example

A car manufacturing company reviews its stock levels every four weeks and then places an order for enough tyres to bring the stock level up to 1,000 tyres. The company expects to use 200 tyres each week.

If the stock level at the last review was 250 tyres what would be the re-order quantity:

(a)   If the new order of tyres is expected to be received immediately after the order is placed?

 **FOULKS LYNCH** PUBLICATIONS

(b) If the new order of tyres is expected to take one week to arrive after the order is placed?

Solution

(a) Re-order quantity

1,000 units – 250 units = 750 units

(b) In this example not only are 750 tyres required to take the current stock level to 1,000 tyres but during the week that it will take to receive the tyres a further 200 will be used.

If the stock level is to be 1,000 when the new order is received then the re-order quantity must be

750 units + 200 units = 950 units

6 FIXED RE-ORDER LEVEL SYSTEM

In a periodic review system of stock control the orders were placed at particular fixed time intervals. Under a fixed re-order level system orders are placed whenever stocks fall to a particular level.

The fixed re-order level system may be operated using either:

(a) the visual control method (or two-bin system)

(b) calculated control levels.

6.1 TWO-BIN SYSTEMS

Under this system the existence of two bins is assumed, say A and B. Stock is taken from A until A is empty. A new order is then made to replenish bin A. During the lead time stock is used from B. The standard stock for B is the expected demand in the lead time, plus any buffer stock. When the new order arrives, B is filled up to its standard stock and the rest placed in A. Stock is then drawn as required from A, and the process repeated.

6.2 SINGLE BIN APPROACH

The same sort of approach is adopted by some firms for a single bin. In such cases a red line is painted round the inside of the bin, such that when sufficient stock is removed to expose the red line, this indicates the need to re-order. The stock in the bin up to the red line therefore represents bin B, that above the red line bin A.

6.3 CALCULATED CONTROL LEVELS

This system uses past data concerning the usage of the item and the supplier lead time to determine stock quantity levels at which action should be taken. These are explained in the following paragraphs.

7 RE-ORDER LEVEL

7.1 INTRODUCTION

Definition   The **re-order level** is the level of stockholding at which a replenishment order is placed.

If it is assumed that no stock-outs are allowed then the re-order level (ROL) is

Maximum demand in the maximum lead time.

If the maximum lead times that are likely to occur and the maximum rate of stock usage can be predicted then it is possible to calculate a ROL which will avoid stock-outs giving a minimum stock level of zero.

Example

A company operates a fixed re-order level of stock control and wishes to set the re-order level for a new material, JK6, that it is now using in its production. It is company policy to ensure that they do not run out of any required materials.

It is estimated that 100 tonnes of JK6 will be the maximum amount used in a day in manufacturing and that the maximum delay between placing an order and receiving the materials will be three working days.

What is the re-order level for JK6?

Solution

Re-order level = 100 tonnes × 3 days = 300 tonnes

7.2 THE MINIMUM STOCK LEVEL

Definition   **Minimum** stock level usually corresponds with buffer stock.

If stock falls below that level, emergency action to replenish may be required.

An alternative explanation is to describe it as the level below which stocks would not normally be expected to fall. This can be calculated as:

Re-order level − (Average usage per day × Average lead time (days))

ACTIVITY 2

Calculate the minimum stock level from the following data:

Re-order level	3,600 units
Average lead time	5 days
Maximum lead time	7 days
Maximum usage	500 units per day
Minimum usage	300 units per day

For a suggested answer, see the 'Answers' section at the end of the book.

---

8   RE-ORDER QUANTITY

8.1 INTRODUCTION

Definition   The **re-order quantity** is the amount of the item of stock to be ordered each time the re-order level is reached.

As in the periodic review system of stock control the re-order quantity will be determined by the maximum amount of stock that is to be held, the estimated lead time and estimated usage in the lead time.

Under the periodic review system the level of stock when the order was placed would be likely to be different at each review date and therefore so would the re-order quantity.

However, under a re-order level system orders are always placed when stock is at the same level therefore the re-order quantity will be the same amount each time an order is placed.

Example

An item of stock in a business is always re-ordered when stock levels fall to 30 units. The amount of stock that the company wishes to hold immediately after the delivery is 250

units. If the lead time is estimated to be one week and the usage of these items is 25 units each week what is the re-order quantity?

Solution

	Units
Maximum stock	250
Current stock	30
	220
Usage in lead time	25
Re-order quantity	245

8.2 MAXIMUM STOCK LEVEL

Definition The maximum level of stock would represent the peak holding i.e. buffer stocks plus the re-order quantity.

The maximum level may be referred to as the level above which stock should not normally rise. It is given by:

Re - order level + Re - order quantity - (Mimimum usage per day × minimum lead time (days))

ACTIVITY 3

Z Limited places an order of 500 units, to replenish its stock of a particular component whenever the stock balance is reduced to 300 units. The order takes at least four days to be delivered and Z Limited uses at least 50 components each day. What is the maximum stock level?

For a suggested answer, see the 'Answers' section at the end of the book.

9 THE ECONOMIC ORDER QUANTITY (EOQ)

The economic order quantity is derived from a model which recognises that apart from the cost of the stock item itself (i.e. the purchase price) there are costs of holding stock and costs of ordering stock. The EOQ model seeks to minimise the total of all these costs.

9.1 HOLDING COSTS

The costs of holding stock are such costs as insurance, heating and lighting the warehouse, warehouse person's wages etc. These costs can be attributed to individual units so that it is possible to quote these costs as an average cost per unit stored. Also interest costs on the working capital tied up in stock can be a substantial holding cost.

Example

A company holds on average 5,000 electric toasters in stock at any time throughout the year. Each toaster costs the company £20 to buy, and costs the company £0.50 per annum to store - the cost being the apportioned cost of insurance, heating etc. In addition, the company borrows money at 10% pa.

What is the total annual holding cost?

Solution

			£
Cost of storage	5,000 × £0.50	=	2,500
Interest costs	5,000 × £20 × 10%	=	10,000
			———
Total holding cost per year			12,500
			———

9.2 ORDERING COSTS

Placing an order for stock costs money. Filling in the paperwork, receiving the goods into stock, checking quantities, paying invoices etc, all cost a certain amount of money per order.

These costs can be expressed as a total cost per order placed.

9.3 MINIMISING THE TOTAL COSTS OF HOLDING AND ORDERING STOCK

If a company sells 50,000 toasters a year, it has a choice of ordering a large number at a time placing only a few orders a year, or ordering a small amount at a time but placing many orders a year. Clearly there is a trade-off as the following example illustrates.

Example

A company uses 30,000 units of a particular stock item a year. It costs £200 to place an order and costs the company £1.20 to hold a unit of stock throughout the year. Illustrate the costs of ordering and holding stock at various different order levels.

Solution

A	B	C	D	E	F
No of orders per year	Annual ordering costs £(A × 200)	Order size 30,000 ÷ A	Average stock C ÷ 2	Stockholding costs per annum £(D × £1.20)	Total inventory cost £(B + E)
	£	units	units	£	£
4	800	7,500	3,750	4,500	5,300
6	1,200	5,000	2,500	3,000	4,200
8	1,600	3,750	1,875	2,250	3,850
10	2,000	3,000	1,500	1,800	3,800
15	3,000	2,000	1,000	1,200	4,200

To minimise total inventory costs (column F), make between eight and fifteen orders a year, i.e. order size should be between 3,750 and 2,000 units a time. A more accurate solution could be achieved by calculating costs at nine, ten, eleven, twelve, thirteen and fourteen orders per year.

ACTIVITY 4

It has been estimated that a computer bureau will need 1,000 boxes of printer paper next year. The purchasing officer of the bureau plans to arrange regular deliveries from a supplier, who charges £15 per delivery.

The bureau's accountant advises the purchasing officer that the cost of storing a box of printer paper for a year is £2.70. Over a year, the average number of boxes in storage is half the order quantity (that is the number of boxes per delivery).

FOULKS LYNCH
PUBLICATIONS

The ordering cost is defined as the delivery cost plus the storage cost, where the annual costs for an order quantity of x boxes will be:

Delivery cost: Number of deliveries × Cost per delivery = $£\dfrac{1,000}{x} \times 15$

Storage stock: Average stock level × Storage cost per box = $£\dfrac{x}{2} \times 2.70$

Calculate the delivery cost, storage cost and ordering cost for order quantities of 50, 100, 150, 200 and 250 boxes.

This activity covers performance criterion C in element 6.1.

For a suggested answer, see the 'Answers' section at the end of the book.

A more accurate answer can be calculated using the model:

$$\text{Re-order quantity} = \sqrt{\frac{2 \times Co \times D}{Ch}}$$

Where Co = order cost per order

D = annual demand

Ch = holding cost per item per year

Example

Using the information from the above activity the order cost per order is £15, annual demand is 1,000 boxes and the holding cost per item per year is £2.70. Calculate the economic order quantity.

Solution

$$EOQ = \sqrt{\frac{2 \times Co \times D}{Ch}}$$

$$= \sqrt{\frac{2 \times 15 \times 1000}{2.70}}$$

$$= \quad 105.4 \text{ Units}$$

ACTIVITY 5

PP Manufacturing purchases a raw material Y for use in its products. The cost of placing an order is £50 and holding costs are estimated to be 10% of cost. The purchase price of each unit is £575 and the annual demand is expected to be 5,000 units. Calculate the economic order quantity.

For a suggested answer, see the 'Answers' section at the end of the book.

10   JUST-IN-TIME SCHEDULING

Over the past few years firms (particularly in Japan) have been trying to reduce their stock levels by adopting a 'just-in-time' system.

At first sight the term 'just-in-time' stock policy would seem to be precisely what an 'ideal stock control system' sets out to achieve: a reorder level selected so that, just as the last unit of stock is used up, a fresh consignment arrives. As such, this is not inconsistent with the use of economic quantity policies. However 'just-in-time' has another interpretation.

A just-in-time production (and stock) system consists of a series of small factory units each delivering to one another in successive stages of production and eventually to the final

---

assembly plant. Each factory unit might work to a lead time of one day i.e. each unit delivers to the next unit the exact quantity it needs for the following day's production. It is used widely in the Japanese automobile industry where it is referred to as 'Kanban'.

The system was developed by Toyota who managed to achieve very low stock levels by relying on 'dedicated' suppliers who would deliver on time, as often as two or three times a day, defect-free components. The system has been tried in Britain with mixed results.

In order that such a system can be successfully adopted, the following are required:

(a)   stable, high volume

(b)   co-ordination of the daily production programmes of the supplier and the consumer

(c)   co-operation of the supplier who will ensure that the staff will make up for any problems of machine breakdowns or unforeseen defects in components

(d)   suitably designed factory layout for the consumer (each production line needs its own delivery bay rather than the factory having a single warehouse delivery area)

(e)   a convenient, reliable transport system and the supplier being in close proximity to the consumer

(f)   part ownership of the supplier by the consumer will help, particularly in fostering a suitable attitude to the job in hand.

The relative costs and benefits of such a policy are:

(a)   warehousing costs have been almost eliminated, sub-contracted to the supplier

(b)   the quality control function has been made the responsibility of the supplier

(c)   problems of obsolescence, deterioration, theft, cost of capital tied up and all other costs associated with holding stock have been avoided. (However, the production and unloading facilities may have to be specially designed or redesigned.)

In Britain it might not be possible to obtain suppliers as reliable as can be found in Japan. The accounting effects of JIT are discussed later in the text.

11   PURCHASING PROCEDURES AND DOCUMENTATION

Materials can often form the largest single item of cost for a business so it is essential that the material purchased is the most suitable for the intended purpose.

11.1   CONTROL OF PURCHASING

When goods are purchased they will require to be ordered, received by the stores department, recorded, issued to the manufacturing department that requires them and eventually paid for. This process will entail a great deal of paper work and strict internal controls.

The key elements of this internal control will be full documentation of all transactions in and movements of materials and appropriate authorisation of all requisitions, orders, receipts and payments.

11.2   CONTROL OF PURCHASING PROCEDURE

If control is to be maintained over the purchasing of materials it is necessary to ensure the following:

•   only necessary items are purchased

•   orders are placed with the most appropriate supplier after considering price and delivery details

- the goods that are actually received are the goods that were ordered, in good condition and in the correct quantity

- the price paid for the goods is that which was agreed when the order was placed.

In order to ensure that all of this takes place requires a lot of documentation and a system of checking and control.

11.3 OVERVIEW OF PROCEDURES

It will be useful to have an overview of the departments concerned in the purchasing process.

Production department - (the user of the goods)	Orders from the stores department using a goods requisition note
Stores department	Requisitions goods from the purchasing department using a purchase requisition
Purchasing department	Orders goods from external supplier using a purchase order
External supplier	Delivers goods to stores department
Stores department	Issues goods to production department.

There are many variations of the above system in practice, but it is a fairly typical system and does provide good control over the purchasing and issuing process.

12 PURCHASE REQUISITION

It is important that an organisation controls the goods that are ordered from suppliers. Only goods that are genuinely necessary should be ordered. Therefore, before any order for goods is placed a purchase requisition must be completed.

12.1 REQUISITIONING DEPARTMENT

Materials can be grouped into those items which are used regularly and which are held in stock, and those which are purchased as a need for them arises. In the case of these latter types of material the purchasing procedure will commence when the production department requests the stores department to obtain the goods. The production department authorises the stores department using a goods requisition note. In the case of stock items the stores will recognise the need to obtain the item. In either case the purchase requisition will usually come from the stores department. During the process of controlling the levels of stock the storekeeper should notice when re-order levels for various items of stock have been reached and then fill out a purchase requisition for that item.

12.2 AUTHORISATION

As only those purchases that are genuinely necessary should be made it is important that each purchase requisition is authorised by the appropriate person. This will usually be the storekeeper or store manager.

12.3 PROCEDURE

When the purchase requisition has been completed it should be sent to the purchasing department in order that the purchase order may be placed.

Example

On 15 April the storekeeper of an organisation wishes to order 400 more litres of oil for the machinery. The code for the type of oil that is to be purchased is L04. Delivery is to be made directly to the stores department by 2 May.

Draw up the purchase requisition.

Solution

PURCHASE REQUISITION					
Date: 15 April					Number: 6843
Purpose: General machinery maintenance					
Quantity	Material code	Job code	Delivery details		Purchase order details
			Date	Place	
400 litres	L04	-	2 May	Stores	
Origination department: Stores					
Authorisation: Storekeeper					

Note that the purchase requisition must have the following elements:

- be dated

- be consecutively numbered

- include the purpose for which the materials are required, showing any relevant job code where necessary

- include a detailed description of the precise materials required

- show when and where the goods are required

- include space to record the eventual purchase order details

- be authorised by the appropriate person in the department placing the purchase requisition.

13 PURCHASE ORDER

Purchase orders will be placed with suppliers by the purchasing department. The choice of supplier will depend upon the price, delivery promise, quality of goods and past performance of the supplier.

13.1 PURCHASE REQUISITION

The person placing the order must first check that the purchase requisition has been authorised by the appropriate person in the organisation.

13.2 PURCHASE PRICE

Once the supplier of the goods has been chosen the purchase price of the goods must be determined. This will either be from the price list of the supplier or from a special quotation

of the price by that supplier. The price agreed will be entered on the purchase order together with details of the goods being ordered.

13.3 AUTHORISATION

The purchase order must then be authorised by the appropriate person in the organisation before being despatched to the supplier.

Example

The purchase requisition for 400 litres of oil L04 has been received by the purchasing department.

<table>
<tr><td colspan="6" align="center">PURCHASE REQUISITION</td></tr>
<tr><td colspan="3">Date: 15 April</td><td colspan="3">Number: 6843</td></tr>
<tr><td colspan="6">Purpose: General machinery maintenance</td></tr>
<tr><td rowspan="2">Quantity</td><td rowspan="2">Material code</td><td rowspan="2">Job code</td><td colspan="2">Delivery details</td><td rowspan="2">Purchase order details</td></tr>
<tr><td>Date</td><td>Place</td></tr>
<tr><td>400 litres</td><td>L04</td><td>-</td><td>2 May</td><td>Stores</td><td></td></tr>
<tr><td colspan="6">Origination department: Stores

Authorisation: Storekeeper</td></tr>
</table>

From looking at the various possible suppliers' price lists Rowson Supplies Ltd has been chosen. They agree to deliver the oil at a price of £1.50 per litre.

Complete the purchase order in the proforma below.

<table>
<tr><td colspan="5" align="center">PURCHASE ORDER</td></tr>
<tr><td colspan="2">To:</td><td colspan="3">Number: 81742
Date:
Purchase requisition number:</td></tr>
<tr><td colspan="5">Please supply in accordance with attached conditions of purchase:</td></tr>
<tr><td>Quantity</td><td>Description/ code</td><td>Delivery date</td><td>Price £</td><td>Per</td></tr>
<tr><td></td><td></td><td></td><td></td><td></td></tr>
<tr><td colspan="5">Your quotation:
Authorisation:</td></tr>
</table>

Solution

PURCHASE ORDER				
To: Rowson Supplies Ltd		Number: 81742		
		Date: 15 April		
		Purchase requisition number: 6843		

Please supply in accordance with attached conditions of purchase:

Quantity	Description/ code	Delivery date	Price £	Per
400 litres	L04	2 May	1.50	litre

Your quotation: £600 (400 litres $\times$ £1.50)

Authorisation: Purchasing Manager

13.4 PURCHASE ORDER PROCEDURE

A copy of the purchase order is sent to the goods receiving department as confirmation of expected delivery. The goods receiving department therefore know that goods are due and can alert appropriate management if they are not received. A copy is also sent to the accounts department to be matched to the supplier's invoice.

14 DELIVERY NOTE

A delivery note is sent by the supplier to accompany the goods being delivered. This must include all of the details of the goods being delivered. The delivery note will be signed by the person receiving the goods as evidence that the goods arrived.

ACTIVITY 6

Rowson Supplies Ltd is delivering 200 metres of chipboard quality D35 to French Productions Ltd. The delivery takes place on 30 July 20X3 and is in response to a purchase order from French Productions number 7374. The purchase invoice for these goods is also included and is numbered FP 832.

Draw up the delivery note.

For a suggested answer, see the 'Answers' section at the end of the book.

15 GOODS RECEIVED NOTE

15.1 GOODS RECEIVED

When goods are received by the organisation they will usually be taken to a central goods receiving department or stores department rather than being delivered directly to the part of the organisation that will use the goods. This is because it enables the receipt of goods to be controlled.

The goods receiving department will have details of all purchase orders placed. It is important that the goods that arrive actually agree in all detail to those ordered before they are accepted on behalf of the organisation.

15.2 CHECKING OF GOODS

When the goods are received the goods receiving department will firstly check what the goods are. They will be identified and counted and the supplier and purchase order to which they relate will be identified.

15.3 DELIVERY NOTE

The details of the delivery note will then be checked to the actual goods and to the purchase order.

15.4 GOODS RECEIVED NOTE

Finally when the goods received department are satisfied with all of the details of the delivery the details will be recorded on a goods received note.

Example

From the previous example Rowson Supplies Ltd is delivering 200 metres of chipboard quality D35 to French Productions Ltd. The delivery takes place on 30 July 20X3 and is in response to a purchase order from French Productions Ltd number 7374. The purchase invoice for these goods is also included and is numbered FP 832. The goods are delivered by HP Deliveries Ltd and the wood is packaged in 10 lots of 20 metre bundles.

The wood was received by the stores department and required by manufacturing department C2. Two of these bundles were checked to ensure that they did measure 20 metres in total by the Stores Manager who was happy that they did.

Draw up the goods received note.

Solution

<table>
<tr><td colspan="4" align="center">GOODS RECEIVED NOTE</td></tr>
<tr><td>Supplier:</td><td>Rowson Supplies Ltd</td><td>Number:</td><td>8737</td></tr>
<tr><td></td><td></td><td>Date:</td><td>30 July X3</td></tr>
<tr><td>Carrier:</td><td>HP Deliveries Ltd</td><td>Purchase</td><td></td></tr>
<tr><td></td><td></td><td>order no:</td><td>7374</td></tr>
<tr><td>Date of delivery:</td><td>30 July 20X3</td><td></td><td></td></tr>
</table>

Description	Code	Quantity	Number of packages
Chipboard	D35	200 metres	10

Received by:	Stores
Required by:	C2
Accepted by:	Stores Manager
Date:	30 July 20X3

INSPECTION REPORT

Quantity passed	Quantity rejected	Remarks
200 metres	-	-

Inspector:	Stores Manager
Date:	30 July 20X3

Note the following details of the goods received note (GRN):

- the supplier, carrier and date of delivery are noted

- it carries a pre-printed consecutive serial number

- the details of the purchase order to which the goods relate are noted

- details of all aspects of the actual goods received are recorded

- details of the personnel involved in receiving and checking the goods are recorded.

15.5 GOODS RECEIVED NOTE PROCEDURE

The GRN is evidence that the goods that were ordered have been received and therefore should be, and can be, paid for. The GRN will, therefore, be sent to the accounts department to be matched with the supplier's invoice.

As evidence of the actual receipt of the goods the GRN is also used as the base document for entering receipts of materials in the stores records (see later in this chapter).

16 PURCHASE INVOICE

The purchase invoice for goods details the amount that the receiver of the goods must pay for them and the date that payment is due. The purchase invoice might be included when the goods themselves are delivered or alternatively might be sent after delivery.

16.1 PAYMENT PROCEDURE

If the purchase invoice is sent with the goods then it will be forwarded to the accounts department from stores together with the evidence that the correct goods have been received. If the invoice is sent after delivery then it is likely to be sent directly to the accounts department.

In either case the person responsible for payment must check that the details of the goods received note agree to the delivery note and the purchase order to ensure that what was ordered was received and what was received is what is being paid for and the price charged is that agreed.

16.2 AUTHORISATION

Once it has been checked that the details of the purchase invoice agree with the goods that were actually received then the invoice can be authorised for payment by the appropriate person in the organisation.

ACTIVITY 7

From information which follows, taken from a previous example, draw up the purchase invoice.

Rowson Supplies Ltd has delivered 200 metres of chipboard quality D35 to French Productions Ltd. The delivery takes place on 30 July 20X3 and is in response to a purchase order from French Productions Ltd number 7374. The purchase invoice for these goods is also included. It is also dated 30 July 20X3 and is numbered FP 832. This shows that the price for the goods was £4.35 per metre.

Rowson Supplies' terms are that payment should be made within 30 days of the invoice.

Draw up the purchase invoice for these goods.

For a suggested answer, see the 'Answers' section at the end of the book.

17 BIN CARDS

17.1 STORES RECORDS

As was noted earlier in this section the goods received note is the source document used to write up the receipts of goods in the stores records.

Obviously the storekeeper must know at any time how much of any item he has in stock. This is done by use of a bin card.

Definition A **bin card** is a simple record of receipts, issues and balances of stock in hand kept by storekeepers.

The bin card is a duplication of the quantity information recorded in the stores ledger (see later in this chapter) but storekeepers frequently find that such a ready record is a very useful aid in carrying out their duties.

Example

From the information which follows, taken from a previous example, write up the bin card.

Rowson Supplies Ltd has delivered 200 metres of chipboard quality D35 to French Productions Ltd. The delivery takes place on 30 July 20X3 and is in response to a purchase order from French Productions Ltd number 7374. The purchase invoice for these goods is also included. It is also dated 30 July 20X3 and is numbered FP 832. This shows that the price for the goods was £4.35 per metre.

The GRN number is 8737.

The maximum stockholding for this type of wood is 3,000 metres and the minimum level 1,000 metres. The re-order level is 1,400 metres and the re-order quantity is 200 metres.

Solution

BIN CARD								
Description Chipboard			Location Stores			Code D35		
Maximum 3,000m Minimum 1,000m Recorder level 1,400m Reorder quantity 200m								
Receipts			*Issues*			*Current stock level*	*On order*		
Date	*GRN Ref*	*Quantity*	*Date*	*Issue Ref*	*Quantity*		*Date*	*Ref*	*Quantity*
30/7/X3	9737	200m							

The bin card does not carry value columns.

Note: that the maximum, minimum, re-order level and re-order quantity information all relates to stock control that was studied earlier in this chapter.

The card shows the orders outstanding as well as the actual stock level and receipts and issues. This information can be used to confirm the correct operation of the stores system (e.g. order requisition when minimum stock level is reached).

18 STOCK LEDGER ACCOUNT

As was seen in the previous section the bin card gives information to the storekeeper about the amount of each type of material that there is in the stores and on order.

The accounting function of the organisation will also require this information and this is given by the stock ledger account (also referred to as a stores ledger account or a stores record card). The stock ledger account is, therefore, very similar to the bin card. The difference is that the bin card is kept by the storekeeper and the stock ledger account by the accounts department.

ACTIVITY 8

From the information which follows write up the stock ledger account.

Rowson Supplies Ltd has delivered 200 metres of chipboard quality D35 to French Productions Ltd. The delivery takes place on 30 July 20X3 and is in response to a purchase order from French Productions Ltd number 7374. The purchase invoice for these goods is also included. It is also dated 30 July 20X3 and is numbered FP 832. This shows that the price for the goods was £4.35 per metre.

The GRN number is 8737.

This activity covers performance criterion B in element 6.1.

For a suggested answer, see the 'Answers' section at the end of the book.

19 GOODS REQUISITION NOTE

19.1 MATERIALS REQUISITION

Materials issued to production departments from the stores department are controlled by a goods requisition note (also referred to as a stores requisition). This document authorises the storekeeper to release the goods.

Example

The factory of a company requires 200 tonnes of a particular metal coded TT4 from the stores department for product A.

Draw up a goods requisition note for this material.

Solution

<table>
<tr><td colspan="3" align="center">GOODS REQUISITION NOTE</td></tr>
<tr><td colspan="2">Requiring department: Factory
Required for: Product A</td><td>Number: 4027
Date: 3 March X3</td></tr>
<tr><td align="center">Code</td><td align="center">Description</td><td align="center">Quantity</td></tr>
<tr><td align="center">TT4</td><td>Metal</td><td align="center">200 tonnes</td></tr>
<tr><td colspan="2">Authorised by: Factory Manager</td><td>Received by......................</td></tr>
</table>

20   GOODS RETURNED NOTE

When unused materials are returned from user departments to the stores the transaction will be recorded on a document similar to the materials requisition but usually printed in a different colour. This will be a goods returned note. It will be completed by the user department that is returning the goods and signed by the storekeeper as evidence that the goods were returned to stores.

These returns must also be recorded in the bin card and stock ledger account.

20.1 PHYSICAL CHECK

When the goods are returned the details on the goods returned note must be checked to the actual goods themselves.

Example

The factory returns 24 litres of oil (code L09) that is not currently required on 25 June 20X3. The goods returned note is authorised by the factory manager and the oil is accepted by the storekeeper. The bin card and stores ledger card were written up on the same day.

Write up the goods returned note.

Solution

GOODS RETURNED NOTE			
Date Returned	Description	Code	Quantity
25 June X3	Oil	L09	24 litres

Released by: Factory Manager

Accepted by: Storekeeper

Bin card entered: 25 June 20X3

Stores ledger card entered: 25 June 20X3

21   ACCOUNTING RECORDS

Earlier in this chapter the bin card and stock ledger account were introduced and written up to reflect receipts of goods. The two documents are almost identical as they are providing the same information although to two different parties. The bin card is the storekeeper's record and the stock ledger account the accountant's record.

21.1 ISSUES OF GOODS

The bin card and the stock ledger account must also reflect issues of goods and show the balance of goods remaining in stock.

21.2 GOODS ON ORDER

The bin card also shows details of the amount of the goods that are on order but have not yet been received. This, therefore, gives a full picture of the position regarding that particular line of stock.

Example

There have been the following receipts and issues of a new material used by a company during the month of March 20X3.

Receipts

Date	GRN No.	Quantity
13 Mar	0743	30 kg
17 Mar	0752	100 kg
28 Mar	0799	40 kg

Issues

Date	Materials requisition No.	Quantity
18 Mar	FC197	25 kg
20 Mar	FA530	100 kg
30 Mar	FC198	35 kg

On 24 March an order was placed for a further 80 kg of the material and this had not been received by the end of the month.

Write up the bin card for this new material.

Solution

BIN CARD									
Description			Location				Code		
Maximum		Minimum		Recorder level			Reorder quantity		

Receipts			Issues			Current stock level	On order		
Date	GRN Ref	Quantity	Date	Issue Ref	Quantity		Date	Ref	Quantity
March			March				March		
13	0743	30 kg				30 kg			
17	0752	100 kg				130 kg			
			18	FC197	25 kg	105 kg			
			20	FA530	100 kg	5 kg	24		80 kg
28	0799	40 kg				45 kg			
			30	FC198	35 kg	10kg			

22 PART DELIVERIES

When a purchase order is placed with a supplier then it is hoped that the supplier will supply all of the items ordered by the agreed date for delivery. However, in practice this may not always be the case. For some reason a supplier may only deliver part of the amount that has been ordered.

22.1 DELIVERY NOTE

When the goods arrive from the supplier they will be accompanied by a delivery note. This delivery note will be compared to the purchase order for the goods. If the delivery note is for less than the amount that had been ordered then it will become clear at this point that this is only a part delivery and the remainder of the order is outstanding.

22.2 GOODS RECEIVED NOTE

A goods received note will be completed to show the goods received. The normal procedure would be to match the goods received note, delivery note and purchase order and then to send them to the accounts department to await the purchase invoice.

However, if only part of the goods have been delivered then the transaction is not yet complete and a further delivery will be due. A record must be made so that the further delivery can be matched to the original order.

22.3 CONTACT SUPPLIER

Comparison of the delivery note, goods received note and purchase order will indicate the amount of the order that has not yet been received. A reason for the goods not having been delivered must be sought by contacting the supplier and a date for delivery of the remainder should be agreed.

22.4 DOCUMENTATION

Finally the documentation relating to the part delivery will be filed as an outstanding amount. This will be the delivery note, goods received note and purchase order showing the amount still to be received and the date that it is due.

23 PART ISSUES

When the stores receive a goods requisition note then normally the full amount of those goods will be issued to the requisitioning department. However, on some occasions there may not be enough of that particular material in stock to satisfy the entire requisition.

23.1 STORES REQUISITION

For the goods that are actually issued a stores requisition must be completed and filed with the goods requisition as an outstanding amount. The amount of the requisition that has not been issued should be highlighted.

23.2 STOCK-OUT

If there is not enough of a material to issue the full amount of a requisition then this is known as a stock-out. It may be necessary to alter the re-order level of these goods or the review period for the stock line in order to reduce the risk of any stock-outs in future.

23.3 PURCHASE REQUISITION

As the materials were requisitioned by a user department they are obviously required by that department and therefore stores must immediately fill out a purchase requisition so that a purchase order may be placed. If the goods are required urgently then this must be made clear to the purchasing department on the purchase requisition as this may affect the choice of supplier.

23.4 RECEIPT OF NEW ORDER

As soon as the new order for the material has arrived the remainder of the original requisition must be issued to the user department. A stores requisition for these goods will be filled out and filed with the original requisition.

24   PURCHASING PROCEDURES

In the last paragraphs the documentation and related procedures for purchasing goods were considered. These procedures are summarised below.

24.1 SUMMARY

Purchase requisition

- filled out by stores
- authorised
- sent to purchasing department.
- Purchase order
- filled out by purchasing department
- supplier chosen by purchasing department
- price of goods calculated from price list
- authorised
- sent to supplier.

Delivery note

- provided by supplier with delivery
- received together with goods by stores department
- compared to actual goods
- goods checked and counted
- delivery note and goods checked to purchase order.

Goods received note

- a document provided by stores department for their own use
- goods checked and counted
- written up and signed
- matched with delivery note and purchase order
- sent to accounts to await purchase invoice.

Bin card

- written up from goods received note.

Stock ledger account

- written up from goods received note.

Purchase invoice

- checked to purchase order, delivery note and goods received note and authorised for payment
- payment made.

25 INTERNAL ISSUES PROCEDURES

The documentation and procedures for internal issues of goods have been discussed in the previous paragraphs. In the same way as for purchasing procedures these can be summarised.

25.1 SUMMARY

Stores requisition note

- filled out by user department
- authorised
- sent to stores.

Goods returned note

- filled out by returning department
- actual goods checked against goods returned note by stores
- signed as evidence of receipt.

Bin card

- written up from stores requisition note and goods returned note.

Stock ledger account

- written up from stores requisition note and goods returned note.

26 PRICING OF MATERIALS ISSUED

If materials were purchased exactly as required for production, the cost of a particular consignment could be immediately attributed to a specific job or production order. Frequently, however, materials are purchased in large quantities at different prices and issued to production in smaller lots.

When materials are issued from stores to manufacturing or production departments then in order to determine the cost of these materials a number of questions must be answered. Which materials were these? What was their original cost?

It is often impossible to answer these questions exactly, and assumptions must be made in order to estimate the original cost of the materials.

Example

The stock ledger of a business shows that at 31 January there are 100 kg of material GHJ available. 60 kg are to be issued from stores to the factory on 1 February.

The 100 kg in stores were purchased as follows:

4 January	50 kg	@	£10 per kg
20 January	50 kg	@	£12 per kg

Solution

The issue of 60 kg must be priced in order to charge the factory with the cost of the material. Should they be priced at £10 per kg or £12 per kg or a mixture of the two? This depends entirely on the method of pricing issues that the organisation uses.

The obvious alternatives are:

(a) price 50 kg at £10 and 10 kg at £12

(b) price 50 kg at £12 and 10 kg at £10.

Other possibilities would be to use the average cost (100 kg cost £1,100, so average cost is £11 per kg), or a standard cost.

ACTIVITY 9

In November 1,000 tonnes of 'grotom' were purchased in three lots:

3 November	400 tonnes at £60 per tonne
11 November	300 tonnes at £70 per tonne
21 November	300 tonnes at £80 per tonne

During the same period four materials requisitions were completed for 200 tonnes each, on 5, 14, 22 and 27 November.

In order to calculate the actual material cost of each requisition the cost accountant would need to identify physically from which consignment(s) each issued batch of 200 tonnes was drawn. Such precision is uneconomic as well as impractical, so a conventional method of pricing materials is adopted.

The main possible methods that will be examined are:

(a)   first-in-first-out (FIFO) price

(b)   last-in-first-out (LIFO) price

(c)   weighted average price.

Calculate the price of the issue on 5, 14, 22 and 27 November using the three different methods.

For a suggested answer, see the 'Answers' section at the end of the book.

27 VALUATION OF CLOSING STOCK – SUMMARY

Closing stock is the amount of physical stock that a business has at the end of an accounting period. This must be valued in some way.

The method of pricing of issues also affects the value that is put on this closing stock.

27.1 FIRST-IN-FIRST-OUT

Under the FIFO method of pricing materials issued, each issue is charged at the cost of the earliest purchase. Therefore, any stock remaining at the end of the period must be priced at the most recent purchase price.

27.2 LAST-IN-FIRST-OUT

Under the LIFO method of pricing issues, each issue is charged at the most recent purchase price. This means that any remaining stock must be valued at the earliest purchase prices.

27.3 WEIGHTED AVERAGE

Under the weighted average method of pricing issues, all issues are priced at the weighted average price at the date of issue. Similarly the stock at the end of the period is priced at the weighted average at that date.

Example

Continuing with the information from the example of Grotom:

Calculate the value of closing stock under the four pricing methods considered in the example.

Solution – First-in-first out

Definition   Closing stock is valued at the price of the most recent purchase.

The closing stock of 200 tonnes is therefore valued at £80 per tonne, £16,000, the price of the 21 November purchase.

Solution – Last-in-first-out

Definition   The closing stock is valued at the earliest purchase price.

The closing stock of 200 tonnes is therefore valued at £60 per tonne, £12,000, the price of the earliest purchase on 3 November.

Solution – Weighted average

Definition   The closing stock is valued at the weighted average price at the end of the period.

The closing stock of 200 tonnes is valued at the weighted average price at the end of November, £73 per tonne, £14,600.

ACTIVITY 10

You are given the following information about one line of stock held by Tolley plc:

		Units	Unit cost
			£
Opening stock	1 January	50	7
Purchase	1 February	60	8
Sale	1 March	40	
Purchase	1 April	70	9
Sale	1 May	60	

Assuming that there are no further transactions in the month of May value the closing stock at 31 May using a FIFO valuation method.

This activity covers performance criterion B in element 6.1.

For a suggested answer, see the 'Answers' section at the end of the book.

27.4 CONCLUSION

Note that in a period when prices are rising the cost of recent purchases will usually be greater than that of earlier purchases. This means that the closing stock valuation will tend to be higher if FIFO is used than if LIFO is used. The closing stock valuation using weighted average price will be somewhere between these two.

28 STOCK TAKING

28.1 BIN CARD

The bin card for each line of goods will provide information to the stock keeper about the amount of that item that is meant to be in stock.

28.2 PHYSICAL STOCK

The only way to check whether this is the amount actually in stock is to count the number of items of that particular type of stock. This is known as a physical stock take.

Stock takes will take place at varying intervals usually on a rotational basis.

28.3 DIFFERENCES

When the stock is actually counted then it will be compared to the balance shown on the bin card. If there is a difference between the amount of the item shown on the bin card and the actual amount held in stores then the reasons for this difference must be investigated.

28.4 REASONS FOR DIFFERENCES

There are a number of possible explanations for differences between the bin card balance and the actual stock:

- errors may have been made in entering items on the bin card or calculating the balance shown

- goods received or issues made may have been omitted from the bin card

- items of stock may have been stored in the wrong position in stores and were, therefore, not counted

- items of stock may have been stolen.

28.5 ACTION TO BE TAKEN

Once the reasons for the difference have been identified then the appropriate action must be taken.

If errors had been made when writing up the bin card or items omitted then the bin card must be corrected.

If items of stock were stored in the wrong place then they must be moved and a new total of actual stock calculated.

If items of stock have been stolen then this must be accounted for as an expense of the business and action taken to prevent this happening again.

29 CHECK PRICING OF ISSUES

29.1 ORGANISATION'S PRICING POLICY

As has been discussed in previous paragraphs there are a variety of different methods that an organisation can use to price the issues of goods from stores to user departments. The particular method that the organisation chooses will be the pricing policy.

29.2 CHECKING OF ISSUES

At various intervals it will be necessary to carry out checks to ensure that the pricing policy of the organisation is adhered to. If the policy is one of the methods of approximating cost then it will be necessary to ensure that the correct calculations are carried out under FIFO, LIFO or weighted average cost assumptions (see earlier paragraph).

If the organisation's policy is to use standard cost to price issues then it will be necessary to ensure that the correct standard cost is used for each material and that it is updated each time the standard costs of the organisation are updated.

30 USAGE AND STOCK CONTROL PRACTICES

30.1 INTRODUCTION

Most organisations will attempt to minimise the costs of holding stocks of materials and will also wish to reduce the risk of stock-outs to an acceptable level. There are a number of alternative stock control practices that could be used in order to meet these ends.

(a) **Periodic review system**

One method of stock control is to review the level of each line of stock at a set time interval. At each review the calculations are made to determine the size of the order that must be placed in order to bring the stock level back to some pre-determined figure.

(b) **Fixed re-order level system**

An alternative stock control practice is to place an order for a pre-determined amount of replacement stock whenever stock levels fall to a particular level.

Once an organisation has determined its approach to stock control then it will be able to decide whether to adopt a version of the periodic review system or the fixed re-order level system.

If a periodic review system is chosen then the period between reviews must be determined together with the amount that the stock level is to be made up to each time an order is placed.

If a fixed re-order level system is chosen then the re-order level and re-order quantity must be determined.

These details of the organisation's policy will be recorded on the bin card for each line of materials.

30.2 INDIVIDUAL ISSUES AND OVERALL USAGE

For any given level of product output the manager should be able to estimate the amount of materials that should have been used for that output.

The amount of materials issued during the period, with adjustments for any stocks held by the user departments themselves at the beginning and the end of the period, should be approximately equal to the overall material usage indicated by the amount of output.

30.3 UNUSUAL ISSUES

Unusual issues might include particularly large issues or more frequent issues of a material than usual. Alternatively an issue of a material in a normal quantity to a department or area of the organisation that does not usually require such materials might also be viewed as unusual.

Requisitions for material must always be authorised by the appropriate manager within the organisation. If requisitions are received that are not properly authorised or authorised by the wrong person then the materials must not be issued and the requisition should be returned to the requisitioning department.

The stores manager is the person responsible for the issue of materials to other departments. It is he, or his staff, who are familiar with the normal routine of materials issues and it is they who should be able to identify any issues that are out of the ordinary.

If the stores manager is concerned that requisitions are being made for unusual issues then this must be reported immediately to appropriate senior management for any required action to be taken.

CONCLUSION

STOCK CONTROL

There are two main approaches to stock control; a periodic review system and a re-order level system. In a periodic review system stock levels are reviewed at fixed time intervals and the amount of stock ordered is that required to bring the stock levels up to a pre-determined level. Re-order level systems may use visual control methods, such as the two bin system, or calculated control levels to determine when stock should be ordered. If

this method is used the re-order quantity is always the same as the order is always placed at the same level.

The Economic Order Quantity model is a method of determining the re-order quantity which minimises the total of the stock holding and ordering costs.

PURCHASING PROCEDURES AND DOCUMENTATION

A typical system of purchasing procedures was described which allows control to be maintained over material purchasing. Standard documentation is an important feature of a purchasing system which allows for the tracking of material movements and authorisation in accordance with the organisation's procedures.

PRICING OF MATERIALS ISSUED AND STOCK VALUATION

Material issues can be priced using a method related to the actual cost such as FIFO, LIFO or weighted average. Alternatively an estimate, standard cost, can be used. The method of pricing material issues will determine the valuation of closing stock.

SELF TEST QUESTIONS

		Paragraph
1	What is the periodic review system?	3.1
2	What is buffer stock?	3.3
3	What is lead time?	5.1
4	How do you calculate the minimum stock level?	7.2
5	How do you calculate the maximum stock level?	8.2
6	What is just-in-time scheduling?	10
7	What information will typically be included in a purchase requisition?	12.3
8	What is the purpose of a goods received note?	15.1
9	What is a bin card?	17.1

KEY TERMS

Periodic review system of stock control – one where the stock levels are reviewed at fixed time intervals e.g. every four weeks.

Stock-out – a situation where goods are required from stock but there are not enough of those items in stock at the time.

Buffer stock – an additional amount of stock that can be held with the intention of reducing or eliminating the risk of stock-outs.

Re-order quantity – the number of units of stock ordered.

Lead time – the interval of time between the placing of a replenishment order and the receipt of the goods.

Re-order level – the level of stockholding at which a replenishment order is placed.

Minimum stock level – usually corresponds with buffer stock. If stock falls below that level, emergency action to replenish may be required.

Re-order quantity – the amount of the item of stock to be ordered each time the re-order level is reached.

Maximum level of stock – represents the peak holding i.e. buffer stocks plus the re order quantity.

Bin card – a simple record of receipts, issues and balances of stock in hand kept by storekeepers.

First-in-first-out – Closing stock is valued at the price of the most recent purchase.

Last-in-first-out – closing stock is valued at the earliest purchase price.

Weighted average – closing stock is valued at the weighted average price at the end of the period.

Chapter 3

DIRECT LABOUR

In this chapter we look at the second major cost element incurred in producing goods or services: the cost of labour. We begin by looking at the ways in which labour times are recorded and controlled. In the next chapter we will examine the control of labour costs through variance analysis.

CONTENTS

KNOWLEDGE AND UNDERSTANDING

		Reference
1	Recording of cost and revenue data in the accounting records	Item 4
2	Methods for payments and calculation of labour	Item 6
3	Relationship between the labour costing system and the payroll accounting system	Item 20
4	The sources of information for revenue and costing data	Item 27

PERFORMANCE CRITERIA

		Reference
1	Identify direct costs in accordance with the organisation's costing procedures	A (element 6.1)
2	Record and analyse information relating to direct costs	B (element 6.1)
3	Calculate direct costs in accordance with the organisation's policies and procedures	C (element 6.1)

LEARNING OUTCOMES

At the end of this chapter you should have learned the following topics.

- Draft an employee's personnel record

- Draft an employee's record of attendance

- Describe procedures for recording an employee's daily attendance (e.g. a clock card)

- Distinguish between salaried employees, payment by results and time rates

- Calculate overtime in accordance with the company's policies

- Calculate bonuses in accordance with the company's policies

- Draft a time sheet suitable for salaried employees, payment by results and time rates

- Draft a cost card suitable for continuous production involving payment by results or time rates

- Draft a cost card suitable for costing particular jobs involving payment by results or time rates

- Outline the procedures and security requirements for payment to employees by cash or transfer to employee's bank account

- Distinguish between direct and indirect labour costs

1 EMPLOYEE PERSONNEL RECORDS

When an employee joins an organisation it is necessary to record a number of details about him and the details of his job and pay. This is done by the personnel department in the individual employee's personnel record.

1.1 PERSONNEL RECORD DETAILS

The type of details that might be kept about an employee are as follows:

- full name, address and date of birth
- personal details such as marital status and emergency contact name and address
- National Insurance number
- previous employment history
- educational details
- professional qualifications
- date of joining organisation
- employee number or code
- clock number issued
- job title and department
- rate of pay agreed
- holiday details agreed
- bank details if salary is to be paid directly into bank account
- amendments to any of the details above (such as increases in agreed rates of pay)
- date of termination of employment (when this takes place) and reasons for leaving.

Example

Jonathan Minor started to be employed by your organisation on 1 July 2001 as an engineer in the maintenance department of the organisation. He was born on 22 January 1983 and this is his first job after training at college for an HND in engineering.

His employee code and clock number are M36084 and his agreed rate of pay is £375.60 per week. He is to be paid in cash.

Complete the employee personnel record for Jonathan.

Solution

PERSONNEL RECORD CARD				
PERSONAL DETAILS				**EMPLOYMENT DETAILS**

Surname: MINOR
 	
Other names: JONATHAN
	Address: 24 Hill St
	               Reading
			Emergency Jane MINOR
			contact: 24 Hill St
			               Reading
				Previous Employment History

				Employer: Date:
Date of birth: 22/1/83	Nationality: British		Sex: M	(1)
Marital status: Single		Dependents: None		(2)
National Insurance Number: WE 22 41 79 J9				(3)
EDUCATIONAL DETAILS				(4)
Degree: -		Btec/HND: Engineering		**TRAINING DETAILS**
A levels: 2	O levels: 0	GCSE: 7	CSEs: 0	Course attended: Date:
University attended: -				
College attended: Reading				
Schools attended (with dates):	Reading High (1994-1999) Reading Junior (1987-1994)			
JOB DETAILS				**OTHER DETAILS**
Date of joining: 1/7/01		Clock Number: M36084		Bank account:
Job title: Engineer		Department: Maintenance		Date of termination:
Rate of pay:		Overtime: $1\frac{1}{2}$ times basic		
Date £		Holiday: 15 days		Reason for leaving:
1/7/01 375.60 pw		Pension Scheme: Joined: 1/7/01		

2   EMPLOYEE RECORD OF ATTENDANCE

On any particular day an employee may be at work, on holiday, absent due to sickness or absent for some other reason. A record must be kept of these details for each day.

2.1   HOLIDAY

An employee will usually have an agreed number of days holiday per year. This will usually be paid holiday for salaried employees but may well be unpaid for employees paid by results or on time rates.

It is important for the employer to keep a record of the days of holiday taken by the employee to ensure that the agreed number of days per year are not exceeded.

2.2   SICKNESS

The organisation will have its own policies regarding payment for sick leave as well as legal requirements for statutory sick pay. Therefore, it will be necessary to keep a record of the number of days of sick leave each year for each employee.

2.3   OTHER PERIODS OF ABSENCE

A record will need to be kept of any other periods of absence by an employee. These might be perfectly genuine such as jury service or training courses or alternatively unexplained periods of absence that must be investigated.

2.4 SOURCE OF INFORMATION

This information about an employee's attendance will come from various sources such as clock cards, time sheets and cost cards. These will all be examined in more detail later in the chapter.

ACTIVITY 1

In the first three months of the year the time records of an organisation show that Thomas Yung (employee number Y4791) had the following days off work:

January	2 days sick leave
	5 days holiday
February	4 days holiday
	3 days training
March	2 days sick leave

The total working days in these three months were 21, 18 and 21 respectively.

Record these details in Thomas's attendance record.

For a suggested answer, see the 'Answers' section at the end of the book.

3 PROCEDURES FOR RECORDING DAILY ATTENDANCE

If the organisation is to keep a record of days worked and days absent for one reason or another then it must have a system for recording an employee's arrival and departure from work.

3.1 CLOCK CARDS

Definition   A **clock card** is a document on which is recorded the starting and finishing time of an employee for ascertaining total actual attendance time.

A clock card is usually some form of electronic or computerised recording system whereby when the employee's clock card is entered into the machine the time is recorded. This will give the starting and finishing time for the day and also in some systems break times taken as well.

3.2 USE OF CLOCK CARDS

Clock cards are used as a source document in the calculation of the employee's earnings. The following example shows how the times would be mechanically or electronically recorded and used to calculate the number of hours worked.

Note too the foreman's signature to confirm the accuracy of the record.

3.3 EXAMPLE OF A CLOCK CARD

Works number:		Name:			
		Lunch			
Week ending	In	Out	In	Out	Hours
Monday					
Tuesday					
Wednesday					
Thursday					

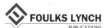

Friday					
Saturday					
Sunday					
FOREMAN'S SIGNATURE					

4 METHODS OF PAYMENT OF EMPLOYEES

There are two main alternative methods of calculating the pay or remuneration of employees. These are to pay either for the time spent at work (time related pay) or for the work produced (output related pay).

4.1 TIME RELATED PAY

Employees paid under a time related pay method can be split into two types, salaried employees and time rate employees.

4.2 SALARIED EMPLOYEES

Salaried employees are those whose pay is agreed for a fixed period of time whatever hours that they work in that period.

This might be expressed as an annual salary such as £18,000 per year or as a weekly rate such as £295.50 per week.

The organisation will have a set number of hours as the standard working week, such as 37.5 hours, and will expect salaried employees to work for at least that number of hours.

They may also work for more than the set number of hours and their employment agreement will specify any overtime payments that are to be made for additional hours worked (see later in the chapter).

4.3 TIME RATE EMPLOYEES

Time rate employees are paid for the actual number of hours of attendance in a period, usually a week. A rate of pay will be set for each hour of attendance.

Therefore, it is obviously extremely important that accurate records are kept of the actual number of hours of attendance by each employee.

Example

An employee is paid £5.50 per hour and is expected to work at least a 48 hour week. What would he be paid for a standard 48 hour week?

Solution

48 hours × £5.50 = £264.00

ACTIVITY 2

An employee is paid £5.86 per hour and works 31.5 hours in a particular week. What would be the employee's wage for that week?

For a suggested answer, see the 'Answers' section at the end of the book.

5 PIECEWORK

Piecework is also known as payment by results or output related pay. This is a direct alternative to time related pay.

Definition **Piecework** is where a fixed amount is paid per unit of output achieved irrespective of the time spent.

Example

If the amount paid to an employee is £3 per unit produced and that employee produces 80 units in a week how much should be paid in wages?

Solution

80 units × £3 = £240

5.1 ADVANTAGES OF PAYMENT BY RESULTS

As far as an employee is concerned the payment by results means that he can earn whatever he wishes within certain parameters. The harder that he works and the more units that he produces then the higher will be his wage.

From the employer's point of view higher production or output can also be encouraged with a system of differential piecework (this will be considered later in the chapter).

5.2 PROBLEMS WITH PAYMENT BY RESULTS

There are two main problems associated with payment by results. One is the problem of accurate recording of the actual output produced. The amount claimed to be produced determines the amount of pay and, therefore, is potentially open to abuse unless it can be adequately supervised.

The second problem is that of the maintenance of the quality of the work. If the employee is paid by the amount that is produced then the temptation might be to produce more units but of a lower quality.

Conclusion Payment methods for employees will either be time related or output related. Time related methods will either be salaried employees or time related employees and the output related method will be some sort of piecework payment.

6 VARIATIONS OF PIECEWORK

As was discussed earlier in the chapter, payment by results or piecework is a method of payment of employees for the amount of work they actually do, the number of units they produce.

6.1 BASIC PIECE RATE

Basic piece rate payments are a set amount for each unit produced e.g. £2.60 per unit. However, such systems are rare in practice and there are two main variations that could be viewed in a similar way to a bonus.

6.2 PIECE RATE WITH GUARANTEE

A piece rate with guarantee operates to give the employee some security if the employer does not provide enough work in a particular period. The way that the system works is that if an employee's earnings for the amount of units produced in the period are lower than the guaranteed amount then the guaranteed amount is paid instead.

Example

Jones is paid £3.00 for every unit that he produces but he has a guaranteed wage of £28.00 per eight hour day. In a particular week he produces the following number of units:

Monday	12 units
Tuesday	14 units

Wednesday	9 units
Thursday	14 units
Friday	8 units

Calculate Jones's wage for this week.

Solution

Total weekly wage

	£
Monday (12 × £3)	36
Tuesday (14 × £3)	42
Wednesday (guarantee)	28
Thursday (14 × £3)	42
Friday (guarantee)	28
	——
	176
	——

ACTIVITY 3

Continuing with the example of Jones above, what would be his weekly wage if the guarantee were for £140 per week rather than £28 per day?

For a suggested answer, see the 'Answers' section at the end of the book.

6.3 DIFFERENTIAL PIECE-WORK

Definition A **differential piece-work system** is where the piece rate increases as successive targets for a period are achieved and exceeded.

This will tend to encourage higher levels of production and acts as a form of bonus for payment by results for employees who produce more units than the standard level.

ACTIVITY 4

Payment by results rates for an organisation are as follows:

Up to 99 units per week	£1.50 per unit
100 to 119 units per week	£1.75 per unit
120 or more units per week	£2.00 per unit

If an employee produces 102 units in a week how much will he be paid?

For a suggested answer, see the 'Answers' section at the end of the book.

7 OVERTIME

If an employee works more than the number of hours set by the organisation as the working week then this is known as overtime. In many organisations employees that work overtime are paid an additional amount per hour for those extra hours that they work.

7.1 OVERTIME PREMIUM

If more hours are worked than the basic number of hours per week or month then usually an overtime premium is payable for the additional hours.

The overtime payment may be expressed as an actual amount per hour e.g. £5.50. Alternatively, it may be expressed as a percentage or fraction of the basic hourly rate.

Example

The basic hourly rate of an employee is £5.20. Any overtime is paid at 200% of his normal hourly rate.

What is the amount paid for each hour of overtime?

Solution

£5.20 × 200% = £10.40

7.2 CALCULATION OF THE OVERTIME PAYMENT

The overtime rate is only paid for the hours worked over the basic hours. The basic hours are paid at the basic rate.

ACTIVITY 5

An employee's basic week is 40 hours at a rate of pay of £5 per hour.

Overtime is paid at 'time and a half'. This means that the payment for the hours of overtime is one and a half times the basic hourly rate.

What is the wage cost of this employee if he works for 45 hours in a week?

For a suggested answer, see the 'Answers' section at the end of the book.

7.3 SALARIED EMPLOYEES

If an employee's pay is expressed as a weekly, monthly or annual salary rather than an hourly rate of pay then any overtime payment will still normally be expressed in terms of a percentage of the basic hourly rate. It is, therefore, necessary to convert the salary into an effective hourly rate based upon the standard working week of the organisation.

ACTIVITY 6

An employee is paid an annual salary of £19,500. The standard working week for the organisation is 38 hours per week and the employee is paid for 52 weeks of the year. Any overtime that this employee works is paid at time and a half.

What is the hourly rate for this employee's overtime?

For a suggested answer, see the 'Answers' section at the end of the book.

8 BONUSES

Bonuses may be paid to employees for a variety of reasons. An individual employee, a department, a division or indeed the entire organisation may have performed particularly well and it is felt by the management that a bonus is due to some or all of the employees.

8.1 BASIC PRINCIPLE OF BONUSES

The basic principle of a bonus payment is that the employee is rewarded for any additional income or savings in cost to the organisation. This may be for example because the employee has managed to save a certain amount of time on the production of a product or a number of products. This time saving will save the organisation money and the amount saved will tend to be split between the organisation and the employee on some agreed basis. The amount paid to the employee/employees is known as the bonus.

8.2 TYPE OF EMPLOYEE

The typical bonus payable will often be dependent upon the method of payment of the employee. The calculation and payment of bonuses will differ for salaried employees, employees paid by results and employees paid on a time rate basis.

9 SALARIED EMPLOYEES – BONUSES

Salaried employees are paid a predetermined salary or wage every week or every month. It may also be the organisation's policy to pay employees a bonus each month, quarter or annually.

9.1 REASON FOR BONUS

In general a bonus will be paid to employees if the organisation as a whole has performed well in the latest period. Some of the profits from this above average performance will be shared with the employees in the form of a bonus. This is known as a profit sharing bonus.

In some organisations bonuses may be determined on a departmental or divisional basis. If a particular department or division performs well then the employees in that department or division will receive some sort of bonus.

9.2 CALCULATION OF BONUS

The calculation of the amount of bonus to be paid to each individual will depend upon the policy of the organisation. The policy may be to assign the same amount of bonus to each employee or alternatively to base the amount of each individual employee's bonus on the amount of their salary.

9.3 FLAT RATE BONUS

Definition   A **flat rate bonus** is where all employees are paid the same amount of bonus each regardless of their individual salary.

The principle behind such a payment is that all of the employees have contributed the same amount to earning the bonus no matter what their position in the organisation or their salary level.

Example

Suppose that a small business made a profit of £100,000 in the previous quarter and the managing director decided to pay out £20,000 of this as a flat rate bonus to each employee. The business has 50 employees in total including the managing director earning a salary of £48,000 per annum and Chris Roberts his secretary who earns £18,000 per annum.

How much would the managing director and Chris Roberts each receive as bonus for the quarter?

Solution

Total bonus	£20,000
Split between 50 employees (£20,000/50) = £400 per employee	
Managing director's bonus	£400
Chris Roberts's bonus	£400

9.4 PERCENTAGE BONUS

The alternative method of calculating the bonus due to each employee is to base it upon the annual salary of each employee.

Definition   A **percentage bonus** is where the amount paid to each employee as bonus is a set percentage of that employee's annual salary.

The principle behind this method of calculating the bonus payable is to give a larger bonus to those with higher salaries in recognition that they have contributed more to the earning of the bonus than those with a lower salary.

ACTIVITY 7

Using the earlier example again, a small business made a profit of £100,000 in the previous quarter and the managing director decided to pay out £20,000 of this as a bonus to each employee. The business has 50 employees in total including the managing director earning a salary of £48,000 per annum and Chris Roberts his secretary who earns £18,000 per annum.

The bonus for each employee is to be calculated as 1.6% of each employee's annual salary.

How much would the managing director and Chris Roberts each receive as bonus for the quarter?

For a suggested answer, see the 'Answers' section at the end of the book.

10   TIME RATE EMPLOYEES – BONUSES

Employees paid on a time rate basis are paid a certain amount per hour regardless of the amount produced in that hour. Therefore, industrious and lazy employees are remunerated equally.

10.1 PRINCIPLE OF A BONUS SCHEME

The principle of a bonus or incentive scheme for time rate remunerated employees is to encourage them to achieve additional output in the time they work.

10.2 BASIS OF BONUS SCHEMES

The basis of bonus schemes in these instances is to set a predetermined standard time (or target time) for performance of a job or production of a given amount of output. If the job is completed in less than the standard time or more than the given output is achieved in the standard time then this will mean additional profit to the employer.

This additional profit will then be split between the employer and the employee in some agreed manner.

Example

It is expected that it will take 90 minutes for an employee to make a product. If the employee makes the product in 60 minutes what is the saving to the employer if the employee's wage rate is £5.00 per hour?

Solution

Time saving = 30 minutes

At a wage rate of £5.00 per hour the cost saving is £2.50.

Conclusion   This employee's efficient work has saved the organisation £2.50. The basis of a bonus scheme for time rate workers is that a proportion of this £2.50 should be paid to the employee as a bonus. The manner in which the proportion is calculated must now be considered.

11 INDIVIDUAL BONUS SCHEMES

Definition   **Individual bonus schemes** are those that benefit individual workers according to their own results.

The time savings made by the employee are measured by comparing the actual time taken on production to the time allowed for that production under the pre-set standards of performance.

11.1 PAYMENT TO EMPLOYEE UNDER A BONUS SCHEME

The employee is paid a basic time rate for his hours worked plus a bonus based upon the time that he saved compared to the standard time.

There are many methods of splitting the time saved between the employer and employee in order to calculate the employee's bonus and two popular schemes are the Halsey scheme and the Rowan scheme. These differ only in the proportion of the time savings that are attributed to the employee as his bonus.

11.2 HALSEY SCHEME

Under a Halsey bonus scheme the employee and the employer split the benefit of the time saving equally between themselves.

The formula that is used to calculate this is:

$$\text{Bonus} = \frac{(\text{Time allowed} - \text{Time taken}) \times \text{Rate per hour}}{2}$$

Example

Employee's basic rate	£4.80 per hour
Allowed time for job A	1 hour
Time taken for job A	36 minutes

What is the total amount that the employee will earn for job A?

Solution

		£
Basic rate	$\frac{36}{60} \times £4.80$	2.88
Bonus	$\frac{60-36}{2} \times \frac{£4.80}{60}$	0.96
Total payment for job A		3.84

11.3 ROWAN SCHEME

Under a Rowan scheme the proportion of the time saving paid to the employee is based on the ratio of time taken to time allowed.

The formula to calculate this is:

$$\text{Bonus} = \frac{\text{Time taken}}{\text{Time allowed}} \times \text{time saved} \times \text{hourly rate}$$

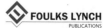

ACTIVITY 8

Employee's basic rate	£4.80 per hour
Allowed time for job A	1 hour
Time taken for job A	36 minutes

What is the total amount that the employee will earn for job A if the bonus is calculated based upon a Rowan scheme?

For a suggested answer, see the 'Answers' section at the end of the book.

11.4 OTHER METHODS OF CALCULATING BONUSES

The Halsey and Rowan schemes are examples of how time saving bonuses can be calculated. However, it is not necessary to use one or other of these schemes. An organisation can determine its own method of splitting the time saving between the employee and employer.

ACTIVITY 9

Employee's wage rate	£5.00 per hour
Time allowed for job	40 minutes
Time taken for job	25 minutes

The company's policy is to calculate the bonus payable to the employee as 35% of the time saved on the job. What is the bonus on this basis?

For a suggested answer, see the 'Answers' section at the end of the book.

12 GROUP BONUS SCHEMES

Definition A **group bonus scheme** is where the bonus is based upon the output of the workforce as a whole or a particular group of the workforce. The bonus is then shared between the individual members of the group on some pre-agreed basis.

12.1 ADVANTAGES OF A GROUP SCHEME

A group scheme has a number of advantages over individual schemes:

- 'group loyalty' may result in less absenteeism and lateness

- it is not necessary to record the output of each individual worker, therefore it is an easier system to operate and control

- in a production line situation where the speed of the output is determined by the speed of the production line then a group scheme is more appropriate than an individual scheme.

Example

Ten employees work as a group. The standard output for the group is 200 units per hour and when this is exceeded each employee in the group is paid a bonus in addition to the hourly wage.

The bonus percentage is calculated as follows:

$$50\% \times \frac{\text{Excess units}}{\text{Standard units}}$$

Each employee in the group is then paid as a bonus this percentage of an hourly wage rate of £7.20 no matter what the individual's hourly wage rate is.

The following is one week's record of production by the group:

	Hours worked	Production Units
Monday	90	24,500
Tuesday	88	20,600
Wednesday	90	24,200
Thursday	84	20,100
Friday	88	20,400
Saturday	40	10,200
	480	120,000

(a) What is the rate of the bonus per hour and what is the total bonus to be split between group members?

(b) If Jones worked for 42 hours and was paid £6.00 per hour as a basic rate what would be his total pay for this week?

Solution

(a) Actual production for the week   120,000 units

Standard production for the week

480 hours × 200 units   96,000 units

Excess production   24,000 units

Bonus percentage	=	$\dfrac{24,000}{96,000} \times 50\%$
	=	12.5%
Bonus rate	=	12.5% × £7.20
	=	£0.90 per hour

The total bonus to split between the group is therefore

480 hours × £0.90   =   £432

(b) Total pay for Jones   £

Basic pay   42 hours × £6.00   252.00

Bonus 42 hours × £0.90   37.80

                                                         289.80

13 ALLOCATION OF EMPLOYEE COSTS TO PRODUCTS

Just as the direct materials used in a product are costs of the product so are the costs of the employees that work on the product. It is, therefore, necessary not just to know that an employee has worked for the day and how many hours he has worked but also what products or jobs he has worked on.

13.1 TIME RECORDING

The clock cards discussed earlier in the chapter show the total time that an employee is at work on a particular day but further records are needed to determine which products or processes he has worked on in that day. These are explained later in this text.

13.2 ALLOCATION OF COSTS

Once it is known which products an employee has worked on and for what period of time then an appropriate proportion of that employee's wage costs can be allocated to that product as labour costs. This will be included together with the materials involved in the product in determining the total cost of the product.

13.3 TYPES OF WORK

There are various different types of work in a typical organisation and the time that employees spend on such work will be recorded in different ways.

13.4 SUPPORT WORK

Some employees never work directly on the products of the organisation but instead work in a variety of production departments. For example maintenance staff do not work on products but do work on all of the machinery necessary to produce the products. The hours that such employees work and the type of work that they have done or the department for which they have worked must be recorded in some way.

13.5 BATCH PRODUCTION

In an organisation that has continuous production on a production line then the products will tend to be produced in batches. In order to determine the cost of each batch the cost of the employees that work on that batch must be recorded.

13.6 JOB COSTING

Some employees work on a number of different large products or jobs such as a roof tiler who works on a number of different houses that an organisation is building. The jobs or houses that the tiler works on and the hours spent on each job must be recorded.

14 TIME SHEETS

Definition   A **time sheet** is a record of how a person's time at work has been spent.

The total hours that an employee has worked in a day or week are known from the employee's clock card but a breakdown of how those hours were spent will be shown on the time sheet.

14.1 FILLING OUT THE TIME SHEET

The employee fills out his or her own time sheet on a daily, weekly or monthly basis depending upon the policies of the organisation.

The employee will enter his name, clock number and department at the top of the time sheet together with details of the work he has been engaged on in the period and the hours spent on that work.

14.2 SALARIED EMPLOYEES

The purpose of a time sheet for salaried employees is simply to allocate their costs to departments or products. No calculations of the amounts payable to the employee are necessary as these are fixed by the employee's salary agreement.

Example

In the week commencing 28 March 20X4 Bernard Gill from the maintenance department spent his time as follows:

Monday 28 March	9.30 am - 12.30 pm	Machine X
	1.30 pm - 5.30 pm	Machine X
Tuesday 29 March	9.30 am - 11.00 am	Machine X
	11.00 am - 12.30 pm	Office computer
	1.30 pm - 7.30 pm	Office computer
Wednesday 30 March	Sick leave	
Thursday 31 March	9.30 am - 12.30 pm	Machine L
	1.30 pm - 5.30 pm	Machine L
Friday 1 April	Holiday	

The working day for this organisation is 7 hours per day and any overtime is paid to a salaried employee of Bernard's grade at £8.10 per hour.

Write up Bernard Gill's time sheet for the week commencing 28 March 20X4. His clock card number is 925734.

Solution

TIME SHEET						
Name: Bernard Gill				**Clock Number:** 925734		
Department: Maintenance						
Week commencing: 28 March 20X4						
Date	Job	Start	Finish	Hours	Overtime Hrs	£
28/3	Machine X	9.30	5.30	7.0		
29/3	Machine X	9.30	11.00	1.5		
	Office computer	11.00	7.30	7.5	2	
30/3	Sick leave	9.30	5.30	7.0		
31/3	Machine L	9.30	5.30	7.0		
1/4	Holiday	9.30	5.30	7.0		
Total hours				37.0	2	
Total overtime payment						16.20
Foreman's signature						

14.3 ADMINISTRATION

In the above example Bernard Gill will fill in the hours worked on each job himself. The time sheet will then be sent to an administration department where the time cost records will be updated.

The departments responsible for Machines X and L and the office computer will be charged with the cost of the hours spent by Bernard. Bernard's attendance record will be updated to show 7 hours of sick leave and 7 hours of holiday.

The administration department will calculate the overtime payment due to Bernard and this will be included in his next salary payment.

The time sheet might also include a column to record any bonus that the organisation might award.

14.4 ACCOUNTING FOR OVERTIME

When the overtime worked is essential to the task concerned, perhaps because the customer requests that the work be done at a specific time, then the extra cost of the overtime should be accounted for as a cost of that task.

Where the overtime is not essential to any particular task then the extra cost of the overtime should be shared between all of the tasks worked on in the period.

15 PAYMENT BY RESULTS

Job sheets take on an even greater importance for employees who are paid on a results or time basis. In these situations the sheet is a record of the products produced and it is also used to calculate the payment due to the employee.

15.1 EXAMPLE – PAYMENT BY RESULTS

Sheila Green is an employee in a garment factory with a clock number of 73645. She is a machinist and she is paid £3.20 for each dress she machines, £4.10 for a pair of trousers and £2.50 for a shirt.

In the week commencing 28 March 20X4 she produces 23 dresses, 14 pairs of trousers and 21 shirts. It took her 28 hours to do this work. Draft her job sheet for that week.

Solution

JOB SHEET					
Name: Sheila Green				**Clock Number:** 73645	
Department: Factory					
Week commencing: 28 March 20X4					
Product	*Units*	*Code*	*Price*	*Bonus*	*Total*
Dresses	23	DRE	3.20	-	73.60
Trousers	14	TRO	4.10	-	57.40
Shirts	21	SHI	2.50	-	52.50
Gross wages					183.50
Total hours					28
Foreman's signature:					
Date:					

A column is included in the time sheet for any bonus that the employee might earn. There is no overtime column as a payment by results employee does not earn overtime.

ACTIVITY 10

Brendan McCullough works for an organisation in the factory on an hourly pay rate of £5.40. His clock number is 59275. The standard hours for a week are 35 and any excess over these hours is paid at a rate of time and a half. Brendan works in a number of different areas of the factory and during the week commencing 28 March 20X4 his work was as follows:

Monday 28 March	8.00 am - 12.00 pm	Cutting
	12.30 pm - 5.30 pm	Cutting
Tuesday 29 March	9.00 am - 12.00 pm	Machining
	1.00 pm - 3.00 pm	Cutting
Wednesday 30 March	10.00 am - 1.00 pm	Machining
	1.30 pm - 4.30 pm	Polishing
Thursday 31 March	8.00 am - 12.00 pm	Polishing
	1.00 pm - 7.00 pm	Polishing
Friday 1 April	7.00 am - 2.00 pm	Machining

Record these details on a time sheet.

For a suggested answer, see the 'Answers' section at the end of the book.

Example continued

The time sheet shown above is that which would be submitted by Brendan. The administration department would then calculate the amount due to him.

Show the total amount due to Brendan on the 'office use' part of the time sheet (ignore the codes for each job).

Solution

TIME SHEET						
Name: Brendan McCullough				**Clock Number:** 59275		
Department: Factory						
Week commencing: 28 March 20X4						
To be completed by employee				For office use		
Date	*Start*	*Finish*	*Job*	*Code*	*Hours*	*£*
28/3	8.00	12.00	Cutting		4	21.60
	12.30	5.30	Cutting		5	27.00
29/3	9.00	12.00	Machining		3	16.20
	1.00	3.00	Cutting		2	10.80
30/3	10.00	1.00	Machining		3	16.20
	1.30	4.30	Polishing		3	16.20
31/3	8.00	12.00	Polishing		4	21.60
	1.00	7.00	Polishing		6	32.40
1/4	7.00	2.00	Machining		7	37.80
Basic pay					—	—
Overtime premium: 2 hours × (£5.40 × 50%)					37	199.80
Gross wages						5.40
						205.20
Foreman's signature:						
Date:						

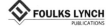

16   COST CARDS FOR BATCH PROCESSING

The production of many organisations is based upon that of the assembly line or production line. A particular product passes through a number of processes many of which have a labour cost associated with them. If an employee works on a particular process or part of production then that must be recorded.

16.1 LABOUR RECORDING

Suppose that a company manufactures lager. It is brewed in huge vats, bottled by machine and then labelled and boxed by hand. Each batch of lager comes from one original vat and it is costed on that basis.

When the lager comes out of the vat it is bottled by the machinery then the employees take over. One employee labels each bottle and then another packs the bottles into boxes of one dozen.

It is necessary to record the amount of time that the labeller and the bottler spend on each particular batch.

16.2 COST CARD

In order to record all of the work that is carried out on a particular batch of a product, it is necessary to have some sort of cost card that follows the batch through the production process.

This will record details of all employees that have worked on a particular batch of a product.

Example

Continuing with the lager example remember it is brewed in huge vats, bottled by machine and then labelled and boxed by hand. Each batch of lager comes from one original vat and it is costed on that basis.

James Bland and Sean Brown are the labeller and packager on one of the production lines of this lager.

On 28 March 20X4 1,056 bottles of lager were produced. This was packed into 88 boxes of 12 bottles each. This was batch number 2542.

James is paid by the hour at a rate of £5.20. Sean is paid by the number of boxes of lager packed at a rate of £0.55 per box.

Batch 2542 of lager required four hours of James Bland as a labeller and three hours of Sean as a packager.

Draft a cost card for this lager for 28 March 20X4 to show the cost of the labour of James and Sean.

Solution

COST CARD - LAGER BATCH 2542	
	£
Materials cost	X
Labour cost	
– production	X
– labelling (4 hours × £5.20)	20.80
– packaging (88 boxes × £0.55)	48.40

Tutorial note: this record of the work done on the batch would be completed at the time of the work rather than at the end of a day or week as is the case of completion of a time sheet. This tends to mean that such continuous production records are more accurate than time sheets.

17 COST CARDS FOR JOB COSTING

Definition   A job card is a card that records the costs involved in a particular job.

Instead of a record being kept of each employee's work a record is kept of the work performed on each job. This must of course be reconciled to the total amount of work recorded by the employee on his time sheet or clock card.

17.1 EMPLOYEE INPUT

Each employee that works on a particular job must complete the details of that work on the job card for that job.

ACTIVITY 11

A cake icer works on a number of cakes in a day and each one is costed as a separate job. The rate of pay for cake icing is £5.30 per hour. On 28 March 20X4 the icer worked on the following cakes:

28/3JN	3 hours
28/3KA	5 hours

Prepare job cards for these two jobs showing the amount of labour from the cake icer.

For a suggested answer, see the 'Answers' section at the end of the book.

18 PAYROLL

The payroll deduction working sheet is the basic document used in all aspects of accounting for wages. It is used to calculate the net pay due to employees, it provides the figures required for entry into the financial accounts and the gross pay total is required for cost accounting purposes. We do not cover here the calculation of PAYE or National Insurance or any other deductions as these are not required by this unit. However we do show the layout of a typical payroll that includes these details.

18.1 PREPARATION OF THE PAYROLL

The payroll is prepared using a number of different documents:

- the employee's personal history card which provides rates of pay and such details as pension fund contributions
- clock cards/job sheets that record the amount of attendance hours/work actually performed by the employee in the period
- tax tables necessary to calculate the deductions for PAYE and National Insurance
- other employee deduction records such as details of any Save As You Earn deductions.

18.2 PAYROLL DETAILS

The payroll lists each employee and for each one a number of figures have to be shown and calculated. A typical payroll might look like this:

			Pay				Deductions			
Name	Clock No	Hrs	Basic pay	Overtime premium	Bonus	Gross pay	Tax	NI	Other	Net pay

18.3 GROSS PAY

The first figures to be entered on the payroll are those amounts that make up the gross pay of the employee. This will be made up of the basic pay, any overtime premium and any bonus. These figures are taken from the time sheets for each employee together with information from the employee's personal history record to ascertain the basic pay rates.

Example

During the week commencing 28 March 20X4:

Bernard Gill is a salaried employee whose annual salary for 52 weeks is £10,920 per annum. Overtime for his grade is paid at £7.40 per hour. He works a standard 35 hour week plus 2 hours overtime.

Sheila Green is a payment by results employee and earns £183.50 that week.

Finally, Brendan McCullough is paid by the hour. His hourly rate of pay is £5.40 and any overtime is payable at time and a half. He works a standard 35 hour week plus 2 hours overtime.

Transfer the details of these three time sheets to the payroll for the week commencing 28 March 20X4.

Solution

			Pay				Deductions			
Name	Clock No	Hrs	Basic pay	Overtime premium	Bonus	Gross pay	Tax	NI	Other	Net pay
B Gill			222.00	2.80	-	224.80				
S Green			183.50	-	-	183.50				
B McCullough			199.80	5.40	-	205.20				

Working

Bernard Gill

Annual salary £10,920

Basic hourly rate	$\dfrac{£10,920}{52\ weeks \times 35\ hours}$	=	£6 per hour
Basic pay	37 hours × £6	=	£222.00
Overtime premium	2 hours × (£7.40 − £6)	=	£2.80

19 PAYMENT TO EMPLOYEES

Payment to employees can be made by cash or by transfer to the employee's bank account. Organisations may have both methods in operation, although it is becoming less common for wages to be paid in cash because of the security costs involved.

19.1 ERRORS AND FRAUD

As with all elements of accounting and of dealing with cash in particular, it is essential that there are the necessary checks to ensure that errors are not made in the payment of wages. With a payroll system it is also necessary to include in the system safeguards against fraud.

19.2 CHECKING OF CALCULATIONS

Whether wages are paid by cash or into a bank account it is essential that the calculations of gross pay and deductions are correct. The determination of the deductions can be quite a complex process and checks must be made on the accuracy of these calculations.

19.3 TRANSFER TO BANK ACCOUNT

In any wage payment system there must be systems in place to ensure that not only the correct amounts are paid out but that only genuine employees of the organisation are paid wages. This is particularly so when the wages are paid into a bank account as there is no physical check on who is collecting the wage.

19.4 PAYMENT OF WAGES BY CASH

If wages are to be paid by cash then this will bring with it inevitable security problems with a large amount of cash being on the organisation's premises at a particular time.

The total net pay calculated from the payroll that is to be paid by cash will have to be transported from the bank to the organisation's premises. It must then be kept safely until paid out to the employees.

19.5 PAY-PACKETS

For each employee the amount of the net pay is put into a pay-packet in cash. Checks must be made to ensure that the correct amount of cash is being put into each pay-packet.

When the pay-packets are completed there should be no cash left over. If there is cash left over then one or more pay-packets will be short and alternatively if there is not enough cash then one or more pay-packets will have had more than the net pay put into them.

19.6 DISTRIBUTION OF PAY-PACKETS

Different organisations will have different methods of organising the distribution of the pay-packets on pay day. Whatever the details of the system all systems must ensure that the correct employee receives the correct pay-packet and no one else's pay-packet.

19.7 UNCLAIMED WAGES

A particular problem in this area is unclaimed wages, for example if an employee is off sick or on holiday on pay day. It is essential that the pay-packet is not given to anyone else and there must be a system of recording any unclaimed wages and recording when they are eventually claimed. In the meantime there must be adequate security for keeping the unclaimed pay-packet on the premises.

20 DIRECT AND INDIRECT LABOUR COSTS

So far when considering the wages cost of employees we have not been particularly concerned about the type of work that they have performed. However, it is necessary at the end of this chapter to bring in this consideration in outline.

20.1 PURPOSE OF WAGES DOCUMENTATION

In this chapter there has been much discussion of the documentation that accompanies the determination and payment of wages. This documentation and the calculations made are necessary for three purposes:

- it is necessary to calculate the correct gross pay and net pay for each employee and then to pay that employee the correct amount

- for financial accounting purposes the total gross wage is the figure to be used in the profit and loss account as the labour cost for the period

- for management accounting purposes the aim is to allocate the total labour cost of the period to the products produced during the period.

20.2 MANAGEMENT ACCOUNTING AND LABOUR COSTS

Labour is a cost of producing the products of the organisation. Just as it is necessary to know the cost of the materials input into each product the organisation produces so it is also necessary to know the amount or cost of the labour time spent on each product as this is also a cost of the product.

20.3 DIRECT LABOUR COSTS

Many of the labour hours worked by employees are hours that are worked directly on producing the product. For example the employee who works on the production line each day is working directly on the products that pass along the production line. The packer of a product into boxes is working directly on that product. The roof tiler in a construction business is working directly on each house.

These are known as direct labour costs.

20.4 INDIRECT LABOUR COSTS

There will also be many other jobs in an organisation that do not require any direct work to be done on the products of the business. For example the maintenance engineer works on the machines that make the products but not on the products themselves. The canteen workers do not work on the products themselves but are necessary to feed those who do work on the products. The accountant does not work on the products directly but is a necessary part of an organisation that can properly produce its products.

These labour costs are known as indirect labour costs.

The distinction between direct and indirect labour costs and their differing accounting treatment will be considered in more detail later in the text.

21 IDLE TIME

Definition   **Idle time** or **down time** is time paid for that is non-productive.

Idle time will exist in most organisations. What is important is that the amount of idle time and the reasons for it are accurately assessed, reported to management for corrective action if necessary and treated correctly in terms of allocation of the cost to products.

21.1 EFFECT OF IDLE TIME

The simplest effect of idle time is that for a set number of hours of work, if there is idle time or non-productive time within that period, then less will be produced than expected.

Example

Suppose that a workforce of 10 employees is expected to work a 35 hour week each. In those 350 hours in total it is expected that 175 units will be produced i.e. each unit requires two hours of labour.

Now suppose that the employees only actually work for 320 of those hours although they will be paid for the full 350 hours.

How many units would be likely to be made in that week? How would the 30 hours that were paid for but not worked be described?

Solution

The anticipated number of units to be produced would be 160 rather than the expected amount of 175. However, the workforce would still be paid for the full 350 hours.

The 30 hours paid for but not worked are an example of idle time.

21.2 RECORDING IDLE TIME

The amount of hours that are paid for but are not used for production represent wasted hours for the organisation and therefore warrant close control from management.

To assist control, time booking procedures i.e. time sheets, job cards etc, should permit analysis of idle time by cause. That analysis should disclose whether the idle time was capable of being avoided by action within the business.

21.3 AVOIDABLE AND UNAVOIDABLE IDLE TIME

Idle time can be classified as avoidable (or controllable) and unavoidable (or uncontrollable). Such classification is often a matter for discretionary judgement. For example, are the idle time effects of a power cut avoidable? In most situations the answer is probably not but if a standby generator was available but unused then the idle time would be classified as avoidable.

21.4 EXAMPLES OF AVOIDABLE IDLE TIME

The main causes of avoidable idle time are:

(a)   Production disruption: this could be idle time due to machine breakdown, shortage of materials, inefficient scheduling, poor supervision of labour etc.

(b)   Policy decisions: examples of this might include run-down of stocks, changes in product specification, retraining schemes etc.

21.5 AVOIDABLE IDLE TIME COSTS

The costs of paying for the hours of avoidable idle time are costs that simply should not have been incurred. Therefore if such costs were included in the cost of products each unit of the product would be overpriced.

Avoidable costs should, therefore, be written off to the profit and loss account and monitored closely so that corrective action can be taken to prevent a recurrence.

ACTIVITY 12

On a particular day in a factory one of the machines was out of order for 2.5 hours. It was possible to reschedule the work of most of the employees but three employees had no work for two hours each. These employees were paid on an hourly basis for the hours spent at work at the rate of £6.00 per hour.

What is the cost of this machine breakdown in terms of wages and how should it be treated?

This activity covers performance criterion C in element 6.1.

For a suggested answer, see the 'Answers' section at the end of the book.

21.6 EXAMPLES OF UNAVOIDABLE IDLE TIME

Unavoidable idle time is idle time that cannot be helped, an uncontrollable or necessary cost of the business.

This might include payments for tea breaks or rest periods as well as idle time due to outside influences such as a sudden and unexpected fall in demand for a product or a strike at a supplier affecting vital supplies.

21.7 UNAVOIDABLE IDLE TIME COSTS

An unavoidable idle time cost is a realistic cost of a unit of a product. As such it should therefore be included as part of the cost of the product.

Not only that, but the future standard cost of the units of the product concerned should be modified to include such idle time costs.

ACTIVITY 13

The 30 employees that work in a factory work on a shift basis from 12.00 noon to 7.00 pm and they are paid £5.50 per hour for each of those seven hours.

However, in total the tea and rest breaks for each employee within that seven hour period total 1 hour and 15 minutes.

What is the cost of a day's work for those 30 employees to the organisation and how should this be treated?

This activity covers performance criterion C in element 6.1.

For a suggested answer, see the 'Answers' section at the end of the book.

22 OVERTIME

In an earlier chapter the calculation of overtime and overtime premiums was discussed.

Definition   **Overtime** is time that is paid for, usually at a premium, over and above the basic hours for the period.

Overtime might be incurred for two reasons - either to make up for lost time earlier in the production process or in order to produce more of the product than was originally anticipated.

22.1 EFFECT OF OVERTIME

Whatever the reason for the overtime being worked the effect will be that more units of a product are produced. However, if the overtime is being worked to make up for lost production earlier in the process then the units produced in the overtime may simply be enough to bring production back up to its anticipated level.

22.2 AVOIDABLE AND UNAVOIDABLE OVERTIME

Overtime that is being worked in order to make up for unnecessarily lost production time is avoidable and should not have occurred.

Overtime that is necessary in order to fulfil customer orders is unavoidable overtime.

22.3 TREATMENT OF OVERTIME COSTS

The rationale for the treatment of overtime costs is similar to that expressed for idle time costs. Avoidable overtime costs should be charged to the profit and loss account for the period. Unavoidable or necessary overtime costs are valid costs of the units of production and as such should be charged in full to those units.

22.4 OVERTIME PREMIUM

Where avoidable overtime is to be charged to the profit and loss account rather than to the cost of the products then it is clearly only the additional cost of the overtime premium that is charged to the profit and loss account.

If additional hours are spent making products then the cost of the labour for those hours is the basic hourly rate. Only the overtime premium is the additional unnecessary cost and only that should be written off to the profit and loss account.

Example

During a particular month the workers in a factory worked on production for 2,500 hours. Of these 200 hours were hours of overtime of which 50 hours were to cover lost production and 150 were spent on an urgent job.

The basic wage rate was £6.00 per hour and overtime was paid at the rate of time and a third.

Calculate the total wage cost for the month and show any amounts to be written off to the profit and loss account.

Solution

Total wage cost	
(2,300 hours × £6) + (200 hours × £8)	£15,400

This can be broken down as follows:

	£
Normal production costs	
2,300 hours × £6	13,800
Additional production to cover lost	
time 50 hours × £6	300
Special overtime for special order	
150 hours × £8	1,200
Overtime premium written off to the	
profit and loss account in relation	
to avoidable production losses	
50 hours × (£8 – £6)	100
	15,400

23 ABSENTEEISM

An employee can be absent from work for a variety of reasons. These might include holiday, sickness, maternity leave, training or simply unexplained absence.

23.1 HOLIDAY

In most organisations employees are given a certain number of paid days of holiday a year. The wage cost of the employee for the year is, therefore, the cost for the entire year and not just the weeks that he works.

Example

A salaried employee might be paid an annual salary of £26,000. He is only expected to work for 48 weeks each year as the remaining four weeks are paid holiday.

What is the weekly wage cost of this employee?

Solution

Weekly wage cost $\dfrac{£26,000}{52 \text{ weeks}}$ = £500

The annual salary is for 52 weeks of the year not just the 48 that are worked.

ACTIVITY 14

An hourly paid employee is paid a basic hourly rate of £6.00 per hour and expected to work for 35 hours a week at that rate. He only has to work for 48 weeks in the year as the remaining four weeks are paid holiday i.e. for those four weeks he is paid £210 per week (35 hours × £6.00) even though he is on holiday.

Give two possible methods of costing an hour of this employee's work.

For a suggested answer, see the 'Answers' section at the end of the book.

23.2 SICKNESS

When an employee is absent from work due to ill health then in most circumstances the organisation must pay him something. There are statutory levels of sick pay that the employer must pay and over and above that some employers choose to pay more.

Conclusion When an employee is off work due to sickness he is being paid at some level by the organisation although this may not be at his normal rate, but he is not producing any goods.

23.3 MATERNITY LEAVE

In a similar way to sick pay, an employer is legally bound to pay a particular amount to an employee who is on maternity leave. Again however this is not likely to equate to the normal basic pay rate of the employee.

Conclusion Employees on maternity leave are paid, although not at the full basic rate of their pay, but they are not producing any goods.

23.4 TRAINING COURSES

In almost all circumstances employees receive their full rate of pay for the periods in which they attend training courses.

Conclusion Employees on training courses are paid in full but are not producing any products.

23.5 UNEXPLAINED ABSENCE

If an employee is absent but it is not part of their holiday, they cannot produce a certificate from their doctor to indicate ill health and are not on maternity leave or a training course, then their absence will be unexplained.

Such absence from work will not only require investigation and possibly disciplinary action but it will also mean that the employee is not paid for the period of absence.

Conclusion If an employee's absence is unexplained then the employee will not be paid for the period of absence. The employee will equally not be producing any products. Therefore, the amount of production will be decreased but the hours not worked are not being paid for.

23.6 ABSENTEEISM AND IDLE TIME

Most forms of absenteeism are simply different forms of idle time. They are periods of absence when hours are being paid for but not worked.

The exception to this is unexplained absenteeism where the employee is both not producing and not being paid.

23.7 REPORTING OF ABSENTEEISM

If an employee is absent due to taking part of their annual holiday or attending a training course then this is simply recorded in that employee's record of attendance.

Equally if an employee is off work due to sickness this will also be recorded in the attendance record. Many organisations also produce reports indicating the amount of sick leave per employee and also per department or operational centre. This might indicate low levels of morale for a particular employee or for a group of employees. If the sick level in a particular department is especially high then this may need to be investigated and the departmental manager held responsible.

CONCLUSION

This chapter explained the different methods of recording labour costs in an organisation and the methods of payment used.

These records are the source documents for calculating payroll but also enable an organisation to calculate the labour cost relevant to individual products by firstly identifying whether a cost is direct or indirect. This topic is explained further in later chapters.

SELF TEST QUESTIONS

		Paragraph
1	What information is contained on a personnel record card?	1.1
2	What are clock cards?	3.1
3	What is piecework?	5
4	What types of bonus schemes are there?	11
5	What are timesheets and how are they used?	14, 14.1
6	How do cost cards for job costing operate?	17

KEY TERMS

Clock card – a document on which is recorded the starting and finishing time of an employee for ascertaining total actual attendance time.

Piecework – where a fixed amount is paid per unit of output achieved irrespective of the time spent.

Differential piece-work system – where the piece rate increases as successive targets for a period are achieved and exceeded.

Flat rate bonus – where all employees are paid the same amount of bonus each regardless of their individual salary.

Percentage bonus – where the amount paid to each employee as bonus is a set percentage of that employee's annual salary.

Individual bonus schemes – those that benefit individual workers according to their own results.

Group bonus scheme – where the bonus is based upon the output of the workforce as a whole or a particular group of the workforce. The bonus is then shared between the individual members of the group on some pre-agreed basis.

Time sheet – a record of how a person's time at work has been spent.

Job card – a card that records the costs involved in a particular job.

Idle time or down time – time paid for that is non-productive.

Overtime – time that is paid for, usually at a premium, over and above the basic hours for the period.

FOULKS LYNCH
PUBLICATIONS

Chapter 4

DIRECT AND INDIRECT EXPENSES

In this chapter we examine the third main category of expenditure - expenses. It is convenient to classify all expenditure other than materials and labour under the general heading of 'expenses'.

This chapter forms a bridge between elements 6.1 and 6.2. Element 6.1 deals exclusively with direct costs and so far in this book we have covered direct materials and direct labour. As we saw earlier, expenses are for the most part indirect and in this chapter we therefore move to element 6.2. However, not all expenses are indirect and we commence the chapter with a brief study of direct expenses, before moving on to the more usual indirect expenses.

We revisit the concepts of cost units and cost centres which we studied in the first chapter, and we analyse how expenses are allocated to cost units and cost centres. However, this is a fairly complicated issue and the full treatment is reserved for the later chapter on the apportionment of overheads

CONTENTS

KNOWLEDGE AND UNDERSTANDING

		Reference
1	Procedures and documentation relating to expenses	Item 7
2	Relationships between the accounting system and the expenses costing system	Item 21
3	The sources of information for revenue and costing data	Item 27

PERFORMANCE CRITERIA

		Reference
1	Identify direct costs in accordance with the organisation's costing procedures	A (element 6.1)
2	Calculate direct costs in accordance with the organisation's policies and procedures	C (element 6.1)
3	Identify overhead costs are established in accordance with the organisation's procedures	A (element 6.2)
4	Record and analyse information relating to overhead cost in accordance with the organisation's procedures.	D (element 6.2)

LEARNING OUTCOMES

At the end of this chapter you should have learned the following topics.

Main types of expenses: expenses directly charged to cost units (e.g. sub-contracting charges), indirect expense, depreciation charges

- Define and give examples of expenses
- Define and identify cost units
- Contrast direct and indirect expenses and give examples of each
- Contrast fixed and variable expenses and give examples of each
- Understand that certain expenses may not be allocated directly to cost units

Procedures and documentation relating to expenses

- Understand why expenses will have different procedures from material and labour costs
- Describe a typical authorisation procedure for expenses

Allocation of expenses to cost centres

- Define and be able to identify cost centres
- Understand how certain expenses may be allocated directly to cost centres
- Understand how certain expenses may not be allocated directly to cost centres
- Understand in outline that once costs have been allocated to a cost centre, they have to be allocated to cost units

Objectives of depreciation accounting

- Understand the difference between revenue and capital expenditure
- Understand that depreciation is an expense that has to be borne by cost centres and cost units
- Give examples of depreciation being allocated to cost centres

1   DIRECT AND INDIRECT EXPENSES

1.1   INTRODUCTION

To a cost accountant there are three types of business expenditure. These are materials, labour and expenses.

Definition   **Expenses** are all business costs that are not classified as materials or labour costs.

1.2   DIRECT EXPENSES

Definition   A **direct expense** is expenditure that can be identified with a specific saleable unit.

As stated earlier, the main purpose of cost accounting is to ascertain the cost of a cost unit. For some expenses (albeit very few) it will be obvious that they relate to a particular cost unit. These are known as direct expenses.

Examples – direct expenses

Direct expenses that may be attributed to a particular product or cost unit might include the following:

- running costs of a machine used only for one product
- packaging costs for a product
- royalties payable per product
- subcontractors fees attributable to a single product.

1.3   INDIRECT EXPENSES

Other expenses may relate to a number of different cost units and these are known as indirect expenses.

Definition   An **indirect expense** is expenditure which cannot be identified with a specific saleable unit.

Examples – indirect expenses

Indirect expenses that cannot be attributed to a particular product or cost unit but are expenses that relate to a number of different products or cost units might include the following:

- lighting and heating for the factory
- cleaning of the factory
- cost of running a fleet of vans or lorries for distribution
- telephone bills
- loan interest.

Conclusion   The majority of materials and labour costs will be direct costs as they can be specifically attributed to cost units. The majority of expenses, however, will tend to be indirect costs as they will be items of expenditure that relate to a number of different products or cost units.

1.4 TYPES OF EXPENSES

An organisation will incur many different types of expenses. There may be expenses associated with the manufacturing process or the factory, the selling process, general administration or the day to day running of the business and the financing of the business.

These are nearly all indirect.

1.5 EXAMPLES – MANUFACTURING EXPENSES

Examples of expenses incurred during the manufacturing process include:

- the power necessary for the machinery to be running
- the lighting and heating of the factory
- general running costs of the machinery such as oil
- insurance of the machinery
- cleaning of the factory and machines
- costs of protective clothing.

1.6 EXAMPLES – SELLING EXPENSES

During the process of selling the goods to the customer the types of expenses that might be incurred include:

- advertising costs
- packaging costs
- costs of delivering the goods to the customer
- commission paid to salesmen
- costs of after sales care
- warehouse rental for storage of goods.

1.7 EXAMPLES – ADMINISTRATION EXPENSES

The everyday running of the organisation will involve many different expenses including the following types of items:

- rent of the buildings
- business rates on the buildings
- insurance of the buildings
- telephone bills
- postage and fax costs
- computer disks
- stationery
- costs of providing a canteen for the employees
- auditor's fees.

1.8 EXAMPLES – FINANCE EXPENSES

The costs of financing an organisation might include the following:

- loan interest
- lease charges if any equipment or buildings are leased rather than purchased.

2   COST UNITS

The main aim of cost accounting is to ascertain the cost of each product or unit of output of the business. The method used to do this is firstly to identify the cost units of the business and then to ascertain which costs relate to those cost units. We have already studied this in chapter 1, but in this paragraph cost units will be considered again as the concept is particularly important in the context of expenses.

2.1   COST UNITS

Definition   A **cost unit** is a unit of product or service in relation to which costs are determined.

The physical measure of product or service for which costs can be determined is a cost unit.

In manufacturing businesses the cost unit will normally be a suitable number or measure of the product manufactured. The cost unit therefore might be one physical unit of the product manufactured but it need not be so. In some organisations where a large number of smaller items are made then the cost unit might be 100 units or 5,000 units, whatever is most meaningful for gathering costs in the context of the business.

In service industries there will also be cost units but these require perhaps a little more thought. For example, in a hotel the unit might be each room available for letting.

Conclusion   A cost unit is simply the unit chosen by an organisation for which it will gather together all of the relevant costs. It might be one individual unit of output or a batch of units of output.

3   COST CENTRES

In the last section the distinction between direct costs and indirect costs was considered. If a cost can be specifically attributed to a cost unit then it will be directly included in the cost of that cost unit as a direct cost.

However, a large number of expenses of an organisation cannot be specifically attributed to a cost unit. They can however be attributed to some slightly larger part of the organisation than a cost unit. This might be a machine or a department or even a sub-division of a department. This element of the business to which costs can be attributed is known as a cost centre.

3.1   COST CENTRE

Definition   A **cost centre** is a production or service location, function, activity or item of equipment whose costs are collected in the cost centre and then may be attributed to cost units.

The costs that will be allocated to cost centres are those that are not direct costs of a product. Therefore they are indirect costs. These indirect costs are nevertheless part of the cost of products and therefore must be attributed to products in some way (see later in this text).

Examples of cost centres

A cost centre may be any of the following:

*   a single machine

*   a group of machines supervised by the same person

*   a department, division or section within the factory such as the assembly or finishing departments

- a department, division or section that deals directly with the factory such as the stores function or the warehouse

- a service department that provides a service to the factory such as the maintenance department

- a service department that provides a service to not only factory workers but other employees as well, such as the canteen staff or the personnel department.

4 SUMMARY OF DIRECT AND INDIRECT COSTS

It is important to remember that the distinction between direct and indirect costs is a **practical** distinction rather than a purely theoretical one. The ideas behind the definitions are clear enough (can a cost/expense be attributed directly to a cost unit? - if it can it's a direct cost). However, you must remember that an important part of the definition is not just whether one could in theory attribute the cost directly to a cost unit but whether one can do it 'economically' or easily.

Some costs are easy. The steel that goes into a car - a direct cost - you can **easily** calculate the cost of steel per car. The labour on the production line that assembles the car - a direct cost - you can **easily** calculate the labour required per car.

Some costs are more difficult. Consider the electricity cost of running a machine which generally produces only one type of product. Some would say that this is indirect because you cannot allocate the cost to a specific unit. Others would say that it is direct because in exactly the same way as you treat the wages of the machine minder as direct (you take his hourly rate and pro-rate the appropriate amount to the product depending on the time taken), so you can treat the appropriate amount of the machine cost as direct.

In theory then you could treat the machine cost in either way. In practice however, most costing systems would probably not consider the electricity cost in isolation but aggregate all the machine costs together (electricity, depreciation, maintenance etc) and treat them all as indirect to be allocated to a cost centre rather than directly to a cost unit.

5 ALLOCATION OF COSTS TO COST CENTRES

The costs that are to be allocated to cost centres are indirect costs of the organisation. There are many types of indirect costs and their allocation to cost centres will depend upon their analysis by the accounts department.

Examples

Some indirect costs are obviously specific costs of a particular cost centre. Examples of these might include the following:

- the factory supervisor's salary is an indirect cost which should be allocated to the factory or production department

- the insurance of the factory machinery is an indirect cost that should also be allocated to the factory or production department

- the costs of protective clothing for factory workers are indirect costs that can be directly allocated to the factory

- the rent of the warehouse is an indirect cost that should be allocated to the warehouse or storage cost centre

- the advertising costs of a product should be allocated to the sales and marketing department

- the cost of oil and lubricants should be allocated to the maintenance department

- the cost of food should be allocated to the canteen.

Conclusion   Many indirect costs affect only one cost centre and therefore are quite evidently allocated to that cost centre.

6 COSTS NOT DIRECTLY ALLOCATED TO COST CENTRES – APPORTIONMENT

The allocation of some indirect costs to cost centres is self evident as was discussed above. However there are many costs that cannot be specifically related to a particular cost centre. The problem is that some costs relate to a number of different cost centres.

These costs are 'spread over' the various cost centres they relate to - a process called apportionment which is covered later in this text.

Examples

Examples of indirect costs that cannot be allocated to one particular cost centre include the following:

- Electricity and gas bills. These will relate to all physical areas of the business such as the factory, stores, warehouse, canteen and office buildings.

- Cleaning costs. If contract cleaners are employed then their bill will cover all areas that they clean, which probably includes the factory, warehouse, canteen and offices.

- Rent, rates and insurance on buildings will be for the entire building complex that the organisation occupies. The total building complex will be split into the factory, warehouse, canteen or offices.

Conclusion   Not all indirect costs can be allocated directly to a cost centre. Many indirect costs cover a number of different cost centres and therefore some method of splitting these costs amongst the cost centres must be devised (see later in this text).

7 COST PER COST UNIT

The final purpose of all this analysis of costs is to produce a cost per cost unit. The direct costs are allocated directly to the cost units and the indirect costs are attributed via cost centres.

Costs allocated to a specific cost centre will be attributed to the cost units on some appropriate basis. Costs that must be split between a number of different cost centres must first be apportioned between the relevant cost centres on some appropriate basis and then the cost centre totals attributed to cost units.

Conclusion   The aim of cost accounting is to provide a total cost figure for each product. The direct costs of a product can be attributed first and then any indirect costs are attributed to cost centres. The indirect costs can be allocated to a particular cost centre or may need to be split amongst a number of cost centres. In either case the costs included in the cost centres will eventually be attributed to cost units.

8 DEPRECIATION

8.1 INTRODUCTION

Definition   **Depreciation** is the measure of the wearing out, consumption or other reduction in the useful economic life of a fixed asset.

Depreciation is a way of reflecting that when an asset is owned and used in a business there will be a cost to the business of using this asset. This will not just be the cost of

running and maintaining the asset but also a cost in terms of using up some of the working life of the fixed asset.

Depreciation is a method of charging some of the initial cost of a fixed asset to the accounts in each period that the asset is used. The reason for doing this is that the asset is being used to benefit the business by making goods or earning revenues, therefore a proportion of the asset's cost should be charged to the business as an expense in order to match with these revenues.

Example

A machine is purchased at a cost of £10,000. It is expected to be used for five years in the business to make goods and will have no value at the end of that five year period. The machine will cost £60 each year to insure, £100 to maintain and service and approximately £150 of power to run it for a year.

What are the actual costs to the business associated with this machine?

Solution

	£
Annual costs	
Insurance	60
Maintenance	100
Running costs	150
Depreciation	2,000

As well as the costs of running and maintaining the machine there is also another cost to the business, depreciation. For each year that the asset is being used in the business some of its life is being used up. If it is assumed that this life is being used up in equal amounts over the five year period then the original cost of £10,000 can simply be divided by five in order to give an approximation of the amount of the value of the machine used up each year. In this case it is £2,000. This is then the annual depreciation charge for the machine.

8.2 METHODS OF DEPRECIATION

In the example above the cost of the fixed asset was simply divided by the number of years of the life of the asset. This method of calculating depreciation is known as the straight line method and is one that is commonly used in practice. In the example above the depreciation rate would have been expressed as 20% on a straight line basis indicating that 20% (£2,000) of the original cost of the asset should be charged as depreciation each year.

There are many other methods of calculating annual depreciation charges but only two others are likely to be relevant to this syllabus. These are the reducing balance method and the machine hours method.

ACTIVITY 1

Suppose that a car is purchased for £15,000 and is expected to have a resale value of £5,140 in three years time when the organisation disposes of it.

Calculate the annual depreciation charge for the car on a straight line basis.

For a suggested answer, see the 'Answers' section at the end of the book.

8.3 REDUCING BALANCE METHOD OF DEPRECIATION

The reducing balance method of depreciation is one where the percentage depreciation rate is applied to the net book value of the asset in order to calculate the annual depreciation charge.

ACTIVITY 2

Using the same information as before suppose that a car is purchased for £15,000 and is expected to have a resale value of £5,140 in three years time when the organisation will dispose of it.

Calculate the depreciation charge for each of the three years if a rate of 30% is applied using the reducing balance method.

For a suggested answer, see the 'Answers' section at the end of the book.

8.4 MACHINE HOURS METHOD OF DEPRECIATION

The machine hours method of calculating depreciation is based upon the actual usage of the asset rather than the passage of time. As such it is often more appropriate for cost accounting purposes than other methods.

ACTIVITY 3

A machine has been purchased for £10,000 and has an estimated residual value after the five years that it will be used by the organisation of zero. During those five years it is estimated that the machine will be operational for 15,000 hours. In the first year of operations the machine was used for 2,000 hours.

Using the machine hours method of calculating depreciation what is the depreciation charge for the first year?

For a suggested answer, see the 'Answers' section at the end of the book.

9 PROCEDURES FOR EXPENSES

9.1 INTRODUCTION

In earlier chapters of the text the procedures and documentation required for materials and labour costs were examined. Materials purchases and receipts are closely monitored by the use of extensive documentation and authorisation policies. Labour costs are documented in detail in attendance records, time sheets, job cards etc, and then recorded in total in the payroll.

9.2 EXPENSES

The expenses of the business are also major costs and the procedures and documentation involved are necessary to ensure adequate control over the expenses. As was discussed earlier in this chapter there are many different types of expenses and the procedures and documentation will differ. However the principle of control over the expenses remains.

9.3 EXPENSE BILLS

In most cases a large proportion of the expenses of a business will be items for which bills are received to reflect the amount that has been used or an agreed payment for a period. This will include such items as telephone, electricity and gas bills and the rent, rates and insurance payable on the premises.

Such bills will be sent directly to the accounts department, checked for accuracy or reasonableness and paid by the due date.

9.4 LABOUR EXPENSES

Some expenses might be part of the payments made to the labour force. An example would be the commission due to salesmen on the quantity of sales in the period. Such information may be recorded as part of the time recording and payroll records.

9.5 PURCHASES EXPENSES

The other category of expenses are physical items that have to be purchased rather than services that are used - for example stationery for the administration office or protective clothing for workers in the factory. Procedures are as necessary for these items as they are for purchases of raw materials for the factory.

9.6 TYPICAL PROCEDURES AND DOCUMENTATION FOR PURCHASED EXPENSES

The procedures necessary for physical items of expenses that are actually purchased will differ in some details from the procedures for items of raw materials being purchased as the items being purchased are of a different nature. However the main flow of documentation is similar.

One particular difference is in the receiving of the goods. When raw materials were purchased they would be delivered directly to a central stores department and control would be exercised there. If for example stationery is delivered it will be delivered to the user department and the invoice probably sent directly to the accounts department.

Conclusion   The payment of expense items that have been purchased requires similar controls and documentation to that of the purchases of raw materials. There are also expenses that are billed such as the telephone charge which require less detailed checking before payment.

9.7 SUMMARY

The procedures for expense purchases can be summarised in diagrammatical form as follows:

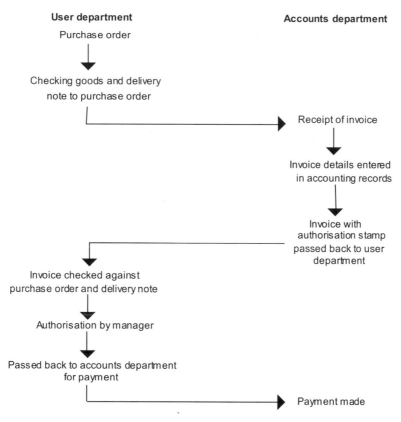

CONCLUSION

This chapter describes the main categories of direct and indirect expenses, including depreciation. Direct expenses are attributed to cost units but indirect expenses must firstly be allocated or apportioned to suitable cost centres. Finally the procedures and documentation relating to expenses has been explained.

SELF TEST QUESTIONS

		Paragraph
1	What is the definition of direct and indirect expenses?	1.2, 1.3
2	What are cost units?	2.1
3	What are cost centres?	3.1
4	What is allocation of costs?	5
5	What is apportionment?	6
6	What are the main methods of depreciation?	8.2

KEY TERMS

Expenses – all business costs that are not classified as materials or labour costs.

Direct expense – expenditure that can be identified with a specific saleable unit.

Indirect expense – expenditure which cannot be identified with a specific saleable unit.

Cost unit – a unit of product or service in relation to which costs are determined.

Cost centre – a production or service location, function, activity or item of equipment whose costs are collected in the cost centre and then may be attributed to cost units.

Depreciation – the measure of the wearing out, consumption or other reduction in the useful economic life of a fixed asset.

Chapter 5

ABSORPTION COSTING

This chapter explains how the costs of products or services are established using a system of costing known as absorption costing. In absorption costing, the main problem is how to charge a fair share of overhead costs to products or services.

CONTENTS

1   Product costs and service costs

2   Treatment of overheads in absorption costing

3   Overhead allocation

4   Apportionment of overhead costs

5   Overhead analysis sheet

6   Service centre cost apportionment

7   The arbitrary nature of overhead apportionments

8   Overhead absorption

9   Under- and over-absorption of overheads

10   Over-/Under-absorbed overhead and the profit and loss account

11   Accounting for production overheads

12   Investigating the causes of under- or over-absorbed overhead

13   Fixed, variable and semi-fixed overheads

KNOWLEDGE AND UNDERSTANDING

		Reference
1	Recording of cost and revenue data in the accounting records.	Item 4
2	Bases of allocating and apportioning indirect costs to responsibility centres: direct and step down methods	Item 8
3	The arbitrary nature of overhead apportionments	Item 10
4	Bases of absorption	Item 11
5	Calculation of product and service cost	Item 12
6	Absorption costing	Item 23

PERFORMANCE CRITERIA

		Reference
1	Identify overhead costs in accordance with the organisation's procedures	A (element 6.2)

FOULKS LYNCH
PUBLICATIONS

2	Attribute overhead costs to production and service cost centres in accordance with agreed bases of allocation and apportionment	B (element 6.2)
3	Calculate overhead absorption rates in accordance with agreed bases of absorption	C (element 6.2)
4	Record and analyse information relating to overhead costs in accordance with the organisation's procedures	D (element 6.2)
5	Make adjustments for under- and over-recovered overhead costs in accordance with established procedures	E (element 6.2)
6	Review methods of allocation, apportionment and absorption at regular intervals in discussions with senior staff and ensure agreed changes to methods are implemented	F (element 6.2)
7	Consult staff working in operational departments to resolve any queries in overhead cost data	G (element 6.2)

LEARNING OUTCOMES

At the end of this chapter you should have learned the following topics.

- Define fixed costs and variable costs (revision)

- Identify fixed and variable costs from typical cost data (revision)

- Define overhead costs which need to be attributed to cost centres - indirect material, labour and expenses (revision)

- Identify overhead costs from typical data (revision)

- Understand the meaning and purpose of apportionment

- Understand why overhead costs (fixed and variable) need to be apportioned

- Understand the meaning of a 'responsibility centre'

- Understand the relationship between indirect costs and overheads

- Understand that the basis of apportioning an overhead depends on the physical/causal relationship between the overhead and the cost centres

- Explain the basis of apportionment of typical overheads:

- Understand why the bases of apportionment are arbitrary

- Give examples of how different bases could be chosen for the same overheads

- Draw up and use a typical apportionment pro forma

- Apportion typical overheads to cost centres given bases of apportionment

- Determine overhead recovery rates for cost centres

- Absorb overhead to cost units, using appropriate recovery rates

1 PRODUCT COSTS AND SERVICE COSTS

Commercial organisations either sell products or provide services. They should want to know what their products or services cost. There are several reasons for wanting to know about product costs and service costs:

- We need to know about costs in order to decide whether the products or services are profitable.

- In some cases, products or services might be priced by adding a profit mark-up on cost.

- In the case of products, closing stocks have to be valued at their cost.

We have seen that the costs incurred by an organisation can be categorised as direct or indirect. Unlike direct costs, indirect costs cannot be associated directly with products or services.

Definition   Overheads is a **term for indirect costs.**

A key issue with product costing and service costing is deciding what to do about overhead costs.

Example

A company makes two products, X and Y. During a given period, the company makes 1,000 units of each product and the direct costs of Product X are £50,000 and the direct costs of Product Y are £80,000. Overhead costs for the period are £150,000.

If we want to establish a cost for Product X and Product Y, the direct costs of each product are easily established. But what about the overheads? Should each product be given a share of the overhead costs? If the overhead costs are to be divided between the two products, on what basis should the total cost be shared?

Definition   **Absorption costing** is a method of costing in which the costs of an item (product or service or activity) are built up as the sum of direct costs and a fair share of overhead costs, to obtain a full cost or a fully-absorbed cost.

1.1   PRODUCT COSTS AND ABSORPTION COSTING

When costs are incurred, they can be recorded as:

- direct materials

- direct labour

- (sometimes) direct expenses, or

- overheads.

Overhead costs are charged to a cost centre (or 'responsibility centre'), which might represent:

- production overheads

- administration overheads

- selling and distribution overheads

- general overheads.

Fully-absorbed product costs can therefore be built up as follows (with illustrative figures included):

	£
Direct materials	12
Direct labour	8
Direct expenses	2
Direct cost	22
Production overhead	16
Full production cost	38
Administration overhead	6
Selling and distribution overhead	10
Full cost of sale	54

Notes:

1   In the balance sheet, closing stocks are valued at their full production cost.

2   Some businesses that use absorption costing calculate a full production cost for their products, but do not add administration overhead and selling and distribution overhead to calculate a full cost of sale. The administration overheads and selling and distribution overheads in such cases are simply charged as a period cost against profits for the period in which they are incurred.

1.2   SERVICE COSTS AND ABSORPTION COSTING

Fully-absorbed service costs can be built up in the same way. A service business must first of all decide what a unit of service should be. For example:

- for a telecommunications business, a unit of service might be a cost per telephone call per minute or the cost of a communications link

- for a private hospital, a cost might be a cost per patient day

- for an electricity supply business, a unit cost might be a cost per unit of electricity supplied.

Service costs might be established as follows:

	£
Direct materials	2
Direct labour	10
Direct expenses	_4_
Direct cost	16
Operating overhead	_28_
Full operating cost	44
Administration overhead	10
Selling and distribution overhead	_16_
Full cost of sale	_70_

1.3   FIXED AND VARIABLE OVERHEADS

Overhead costs might be fixed costs or variable costs. In absorption costing, production overheads, administration overheads and selling and distribution overheads might therefore be separated into their fixed and variable cost components.

In absorption costing for products, the full production cost of a product might therefore consist of direct materials, direct labour, direct expenses, variable production overhead and fixed production overhead.

- **Fixed overheads** remain the same whatever the level of output or activity during a period. It does not vary with changes in output levels or activity, but remains constant.

- **Variable overheads** are amounts of indirect cost that vary with the level of output or activity. As the level of output or activity rises then so does any variable overhead cost.

ACTIVITY 1

An organisation has the following types of expenses or costs. Classify each as either a fixed or a variable cost.

(a)   Production workers' basic wages.

(b) Overtime premium paid to production workers.

(c) Wages paid to factory cleaners.

(d) Metal used in the manufacture of the product.

(e) Wages to repair staff working on machinery.

(f) Salaries paid to office staff.

(g) Electricity bill.

(h) Oil for machinery.

(i) Rent of warehouse.

(j) Heating cost for factory.

This activity covers performance criterion A in element 6.2.

For a suggested answer, see the 'Answers' section at the end of the book.

ACTIVITY 2

Using the list of expenses from the previous activity now identify which are direct costs are which are indirect costs or overheads.

(a) Production workers' basic wages.

(b) Overtime premium paid to production workers.

(c) Wages paid to factory cleaners.

(d) Metal used in the manufacture of the product.

(e) Wages to repair staff working on machinery.

(f) Salaries paid to office staff.

(g) Electricity bill.

(h) Oil for machinery.

(i) Rent of warehouse.

(j) Heating cost for factory.

This activity covers performance criterion A in element 6.2.

For a suggested answer, see the 'Answers' section at the end of the book.

1.4 REASONS FOR ABSORPTION COSTING

The main reasons for wanting to calculate full costs, as indicated earlier, are mainly to value stocks or manufactured goods, and possibly also to calculate a selling price based on full costs.

Stock valuation

The costs of making a product include the costs of direct materials, direct labour and direct expenses. In some organisations products are simply valued at this total figure for costing purposes. However the overheads incurred by the production departments are costs that are necessary to make those products. Production overheads, although indirect costs of the cost units, are as much a cost of the product as the direct costs.

Therefore in order to value closing stocks at the full cost of producing each product or cost unit that cost unit's share of the overheads incurred must be included in the product cost.

The full cost of producing an item of production or cost unit is therefore not only the direct costs of the product but also its share of indirect production costs.

FOULKS LYNCH
PUBLICATIONS

Pricing at a mark-up over full cost

One reason for costing products at their full cost could be for pricing purposes. If the price of a product is to cover all of the costs of the product plus some margin to give a profit then the full cost must be known in order to apply the profit margin.

Example

The cost of a unit of Product X is as follows:

	£
Direct materials	1.60
Direct labour	2.20
Direct expenses	0.40
Indirect expenses	0.80

If the organisation's policy is to cover all costs of a product and then make a profit equal to 20% of the total costs, at what price must product X be sold?

Solution

Total cost of Product X

	£
Direct materials	1.60
Direct labour	2.20
Direct expenses	0.40
Indirect expenses	0.80
	———
	5.00
Profit (20% × £5.00)	1.00
	———
Selling price	6.00
	———

2 TREATMENT OF OVERHEADS IN ABSORPTION COSTING

In absorption costing, products, services or activities are charged with a fair share of indirect costs. There is a three-stage process involved in charging overhead costs to products or services:

- overhead allocation

- overhead apportionment

- overhead absorption, also called overhead recovery.

Each of these stages is explained below. However, in order to appreciate overhead allocation and overhead apportionment, it is first of all necessary to know something about cost centres or responsibility centres.

2.1 RESPONSIBILITY CENTRES AND COST CENTRES

Definition   A **responsibility centre** is an area of the business or an item of cost that is the responsibility of a particular manager of the business. Organisations can be divided into a large number of different responsibility centres.

Responsibility centres can be investment centres, profit centres or cost centres. A feature of responsibility centres is that costs can be traced directly to them. All costs incurred within an organisation can be charged to a cost centre.

Definition   A **cost centre** is an area of the business where costs are gathered.

A business can decide what its cost centres should be. Generally-speaking, cost centres within a manufacturing organisation are likely to consist of:

- **Production departments**, in which items of product are manufactured. There could be several production departments within any organisation, and production might flow from one department to another and then another. For example, production might flow from a machining department to an assembly department and then a finishing department. Similarly, in textile production, work might flow from a carding department to a spinning department to a weaving department. Each production department might be a separate cost centre. Alternatively, a cost centre might be a single machine or a group of machines under the direction of one supervisor.

- **'Service departments'** within the production area. These are departments operating within the production function that are not involved directly in the manufacture of products. Instead, they provide service and support to production departments. These can include a stores department, a maintenance and repairs department, a production control department, and so on.

- **Administration departments** or functions, for administration overheads.

- **Selling and distribution departments** or functions, for selling and distribution costs.

- **General cost items** that cannot be attributed to a single department or work area. Examples are rental costs for a factory building, lighting and heating costs, building security and maintenance costs, and so on.

In the description of absorption costing that follows, administration overheads and selling and distribution overheads are ignored, and the focus of attention is on full production costs. Costs centres will therefore be categorised as production departments, service departments and general costs.

3   OVERHEAD ALLOCATION

Overhead allocation is the first of the three stages in establishing a full cost for a product or service.

Definition   **Overhead allocation** is the process of charging each item of cost to a cost centre.

Every overhead cost incurred by a business should be chargeable directly and in full to a cost centre. Costs can therefore be built up for each cost centre.

ACTIVITY 3

A manufacturing business operates with two production departments, P and Q and a service department S. It manufactures widgets. It incurs the following costs in a given period.

	£
Labour costs in department S	6,500
Direct labour costs in department P	4,700
Costs of supervision in Department Q	2,100
Material costs of widgets	10,300
Machine repair costs, Department Q	800
Materials consumed in department S	1,100
Depreciation of machinery in department S	700
Indirect materials consumed in department P	500
Lighting and heating	900
Costs of works canteen	1,500

Task

Allocate these costs as overhead costs to the following cost centres:

(a)   Production department P

(b)   Production department Q

(c)   Service department S

(d)   A cost centre for general costs.

Indicate with reasons why you have not allocated any of the cost items in the list.

This activity covers performance criterion B in element 6.2.

For a suggested answer, see the 'Answers' section at the end of the book.

4   APPORTIONMENT OF OVERHEAD COSTS

When overhead costs have been allocated to cost centres (or responsibility centres), all costs will be classified as:

- the overhead cost of a production centre

- the cost of a service centre

- an administration overhead cost

- a selling and distribution overhead cost, or

- a general cost.

The next stage in absorption costing is to share out all the overhead costs so that they are attributable to:

- a production department

- administration overheads or

- selling and distribution overheads.

To do this, we have to re-charge all general overhead costs between production centres, administration and selling and distribution. We must also re-charge the costs of the service departments to production departments.

General costs and service department costs are re-charged by a process called overhead apportionment.

Definition   **Overhead apportionment** is the process of sharing out overhead costs on a fair basis.

Apportionment should be on a fair basis, but there are no rules about what 'fair' means.

4.1   DIRECT METHODS AND STEP-DOWN METHODS OF OVERHEAD APPORTIONMENT

There are two broad approaches to overhead apportionment. The difference between them relates to how production overhead costs are apportioned.

- Using a **direct method** of apportionment, each item of overhead cost for general costs and service department costs is taken in turn. Each cost is then shared between the production departments (and administration overhead and selling and distribution overhead where appropriate) on a fair basis. The basis for sharing out the cost differs fore ach item of cost.

- Using a **step-down method** of apportionment, each item of overhead cost for general costs is taken in turn. The cost is then shared between the production departments and the service departments (and administration overhead and selling and distribution overhead where appropriate). Next, the costs of the service departments, which now include a share of general overhead costs, are shared between the production departments.

With the direct method, apportionment is a single stage process. With the step-down method, apportionment happens in two stages, first an apportionment of general costs to production departments and service departments and then an apportionment of service department costs to production departments.

The end-result is the same. All overhead costs are charged to production departments, or as administration or as selling and distribution overheads. However, the amount of overheads charged to each production department will be different. In other words, the direct method and the step-down method will share out the overhead costs in a different way.

4.2   APPORTIONMENT OF GENERAL COSTS

As stated above, apportionment of overhead costs should be on a fair basis. An organisation should establish, for each item of general cost, what this basis ought to be. For many costs, there are two or more different bases that could be used.

The basis of apportionment used should be based on a rationale view of what is 'fair' in relation to the item of cost. Some examples should help to illustrate the considerations involved.

Example 1

A general cost in a manufacturing company is factory rental. Annual rental costs are £80,000. How should this cost be apportioned between production departments and service departments?

Rental costs are usually apportioned between departments on the basis of the floor space taken up by each department. For example, suppose that three departments have floor space of 10,000 square metres, 15,000 square metres and 25,000 square metres, and annual rental costs are £80,000. If we apportion rental costs between the departments on the basis of their floor space, the apportionment would be as follows.

Annual rental	£80,000
Total floor space (10,000 + 15,000 + 25,000)	50,000 square metres
Apportionment rate (£80,000/50,000)	£1.60/square metre
	£
Apportion to department with 10,000 square metres	16,000
Apportion to department with 15,000 square metres	24,000
Apportion to department with 25,000 square metres	<u>40,000</u>
	<u>80,000</u>

Example 2

The costs of heating and lighting might also be apportioned on the basis of floor space. Alternatively, since heating relates to volume rather than floor space, it could be argued that the costs should be apportioned on the volume of space taken up by each department. Yet another view is that electricity costs relate more to the consumption of electrical power by machines, therefore the apportionment of these costs should be on the basis of the number and power of the machines in each department.

A reasonable argument could be made for any of these bases of apportionment.

Example 3

The costs of operating a works canteen could be apportioned on any of the following bases:

- the number of employees in each department

- the number of full-time employees in each department (on the grounds that part-time employees probably don't use the canteen)

- the hours worked by employees in each department (on the grounds that use of the canteen relates more to the number of hours in attendance at work rather than the numbers of employees.

ACTIVITY 4

A manufacturing business operates with two production departments, X and Y and three service departments. The costs of its works canteen in a given period are £22,880. These costs are to be apportioned between departments on the basis of employee numbers in each department. Employee numbers are as follows.

	Number of employees
Department X	33
Department Y	27
Stores department	8
Engineering department	14
Production control department	6

Task

Apportion the canteen costs between the production and service departments:

(a) using the direct method of apportionment

(b) using the step-down method of apportionment

This activity covers performance criterion B, element 6.2.

For a suggested answer, see the 'Answers' section at the end of the book.

ACTIVITY 5

What would be the most appropriate basis of apportionment of the following overheads:

(a)   oil used for machine lubrication

(b)   depreciation of machinery

(c)   petrol for vehicles used by the organisation.

This activity covers performance criterion B in element 6.2.

For a suggested answer, see the 'Answers' section at the end of the book.

4.3   APPORTIONMENT OF SERVICE DEPARTMENT COSTS

Service department costs should be apportioned between production departments.

- With the direct method of apportionment, the costs of each service department are the allocated overhead costs of the department.

- With the step-down method of apportionment, the costs of each service department are the allocated overhead costs of the department plus a share of general overhead costs.

Example 1

The costs of a stores department might be apportioned between production departments on the basis of:

- the number of materials requisitions made from stores by each department, or

- the value/cost of materials requisitioned from stores by each department.

Example 2

The costs of a repairs and maintenance department might be apportioned on the basis of:

- the time spent by the department on repairs and maintenance work for each production department, if time records are kept, or

- the machine hours operated in each production department.

As with the apportionment of general costs, the apportionment of service department costs should be on a fair basis. However, there are no rules about what is fair, and different organisations might choose to apportion similar costs in different ways.

5   OVERHEAD ANALYSIS SHEET

A record of the overheads allocated and apportioned can be set out on an overhead analysis sheet. In the examples below, administration overheads and selling and distribution overheads are ignored, although they can be included in the analysis if required.

5.1   OVERHEAD ANALYSIS SHEET: DIRECT METHOD OF APPORTIONMENT

If the direct method of overhead apportionment is used, there will be one row in the overhead analysis sheet for each item of general overhead cost and service department allocated costs. There should be one column in the analysis sheet for each production department.

The purpose of the analysis sheet is to show how the overhead costs are built up for each production department.

An example is shown below, with illustrative figures.

OVERHEAD ANALYSIS SHEET		PERIOD ENDING		
	Total	Production department X	Production department Y	Production department Z
	£	£	£	£
Allocated costs	87,000	34,000	32,000	21,000
Factory rent	11,000	3,100	5,200	2,700
Heating and lighting	2,100	700	1,200	200
Building repairs	5,600	1,300	1,700	2,600
Insurance	8,000	2,100	4,800	1,100
Canteen	12,000	4,100	2,300	5,600
Stores	15,600	8,300	2,900	4,400
Engineering support	25,700	6,900	12,500	6,300
Machinery depreciation	8,500	3,000	4,500	1,000
	175,500	63,500	67,100	44,900

5.2 OVERHEAD ANALYSIS SHEET: STEP-DOWN METHOD OF APPORTIONMENT

If the step-down method of apportionment is used, there are columns for the service departments as well as the production departments.

An overhead analysis sheet might be drawn up as follows:

OVERHEAD ANALYSIS SHEET		PRODUCTION		SERVICE	PERIOD ENDING....................
	TOTAL	Assembly	Finishing	Stores	Canteen
	£	£	£	£	£
Overheads allocated directly to cost centres	133,000	49,000	36,000	27,000	21,000
Overheads to be apportioned					
Rent (Apportionment basis: ....)	76,000	26,000	24,000	15,000	11,000
Equipment depreciation (Apportionment basis: ....)	15,000	8,000	1,000	5,000	1,000
Total overhead	224,000	83,000	61,000	47,000	33,000
Apportioning of stores (Apportionment basis: ....)		31,000	16,000	(47,000)	
Apportioning of canteen (Apportionment basis: ....)		14,000	19,000		(33,000)
		128,000	96,000	–	–

5.3 WORKED EXAMPLE

The example below illustrates the apportionment of overheads using an overhead analysis sheet. In this example, the step-down approach is used, and overhead costs are apportioned to service departments as well as production departments.

This example stops at the point where general overheads have been apportioned to production departments and service departments. It does not show how service departments are apportioned to the production departments.

Study the example very carefully. You might like to attempt your own solution before reading ours.

An organisation has two production departments, A and B, and two service departments, stores and the canteen.

The overhead costs for the organisation in total are as follows:

	£
Rent	32,000
Building maintenance costs	5,000
Machinery insurance	2,400
Machinery depreciation	11,000
Machinery running expenses	6,000
Power	7,000

FOULKS LYNCH
PUBLICATIONS

There are also specific costs that have already been allocated to each cost centre as follows:

	£
Department A	5,000
Department B	4,000
Stores	1,000
Canteen	2,000

The following information about the various cost centres is also available:

	Total	Dept A	Dept B	Stores	Canteen
Floor space (sq ft)	30,000	15,000	8,000	5,000	2,000
Power usage	100%	45%	40%	5%	10%
Value of machinery (£'000)	250	140	110	-	-
Machinery hours ('000)	80	50	30		
Value of equipment (£'000)	20	-	-	5	15
Number of employees	40	20	15	3	2
Value of stores requisitions (£'000)	150	100	50	-	-

Task

Allocate and apportion the costs to the four departments.

Do not reapportion the service centre costs to the production departments.

FOULKS LYNCH
PUBLICATIONS

5.4 SOLUTION

OVERHEAD ANALYSIS SHEET				PERIOD ENDING..................	
	TOTAL	PRODUCTION		SERVICE	
		Dept A	Dept B	Stores	Canteen
	£	£	£	£	£
Overheads allocated directly to cost centres	12,000	5,000	4,000	1,000	2,000
Overheads to be apportioned					
Rent Basis: floor space	32,000				
15/30 × £32,000		16,000			
8/30 × £32,000			8,534		
5/30 × £32,000				5,333	
2/30 × £32,000					2,133
Building maintenance Basis: floor space	5,000				
15/30 × £5,000		2,500			
8/30 × £5,000			1,333		
5/30 × £5,000				834	
2/30 × £5,000					333
Machinery insurance Basis: machine value	2,400				
140/250 × £2,400		1,344			
110/250 × £2,400			1,056	-	-
Machinery depreciation Basis: machine value	11,000				
140/250 × £11,000		6,160			
110/250 × £11,000			4,840	-	-
Machinery running expenses Basis: machine hours	6,000				
50/80 × £6,000		3,750			
30/80 × £6,000			2,250	-	-
Power Basis: power usage percentages	7,000				
£7,000 × 45%		3,150			
£7,000 × 40%			2,800		
£7,000 × 5%				350	
£7,000 × 10%					700
Allocated and apportioned costs	75,400	37,904	24,813	7,517	5,166

6 SERVICE CENTRE COST APPORTIONMENT

The aim of allocating and apportioning production overheads is to establish the total overhead costs for each production department (production responsibility centre).

It has already been stated that the costs of service departments should be shared between production departments on a fair basis.

- With the direct method of apportionment, these costs consist of the allocated overhead costs of the service department.

- With the step-down method of apportionment, these costs include not only the allocated costs of the service department, but also a share of general overhead costs.

With the direct method of overhead apportionment, the allocated costs of each service department are shared out between the production departments, using a fair basis. Each service department's costs are apportioned separately.

With a step-down method of apportionment, the method used to apportion service department costs can be a bit more complex.

Three different situations need to be considered.

- Where the service centres do not provide services to one another

- Where one service centre provides services to another

- Where both service centres provide services to each other.

6.1 SERVICE DEPARTMENTS DO NO WORK FOR OTHER SERVICE DEPARTMENTS

Assume that a manufacturing business has two production departments and two service departments, whose allocated and apportioned overhead costs have been analysed as follows.

OVERHEAD ANALYSIS SHEET   PERIOD ENDING.................

	TOTAL	PRODUCTION		SERVICE	
		Dept A	Dept B	Stores	Canteen
	£	£	£	£	£
Total overhead	75,400	37,904	24,813	7,517	5,166

The apportionment of the stores department costs will be on the basis of the value of requisitions by each production department. The apportionment of the canteen costs should be on the basis of the number of employees in production departments A and B.

It is assumed that the stores department does no work for the canteen and the canteen does no work for the stores department.

Consequently, none of the stores costs should be apportioned to the Canteen and none of the canteen costs should be apportioned to Stores.

The following data is available.

	Total	Dept A	Dept B	Stores	Canteen
Number of employees	40	20	15	3	2
Value of stores requisitions (£000)	150	100	50	-	-

Task

Show how the service department costs should be apportioned, and the resulting total overhead costs of each production department.

Solution

OVERHEAD ANALYSIS SHEET		PERIOD ENDING..................			
	TOTAL	PRODUCTION		SERVICE	
		Dept A	Dept B	Stores	Canteen
	£	£	£	£	£
Allocated/apportioned overhead	75,400	37,904	24,813	7,517	5,166
Apportion stores Basis: requisitions 100/150 × £7,517 50/150 × £7,517		5,011	2,506	(7,517)	
Apportion canteen Basis: number of employees 20/35 × £5,166 15/35 × £5,166		2,952	2,214		(5,166)
Total overhead		45,867	29,533		

Conclusion This is the simplest situation, where the service cost centres are isolated from each other. The assumption is implicit that the stores personnel do not use the canteen and that the canteen does not use the stores function. This is a situation where service centres do not service each other.

6.2 ONE SERVICE DEPARTMENT DOES WORK FOR ANOTHER

Another assumption that might be used for apportioning service department costs is that one service department does some work for another.

For example, suppose there are two production departments P1 and P2, and two service departments S1 and S2, and that it is assumed that:

- S1 does 30% of its work for department P1, 40% of its work for P2 and 30% of its work for S2.

- S2 does 75% of its work for P1, 25% for P2 but none for S1.

We can apportion service department overheads by a **step-down method**. We can start with the service department that does some work for the other service department and apportion its costs between all the departments that it does work for. In the example above, we would start with service department S1, and apportion its costs 30:40:30 between P1, P2 and S2 respectively.

Next, we can take the service department that does not do any work for the other service department, and apportion its costs between the production departments. In the example above, we would apportion the costs of S2, which now include a share of S1 costs, between P1 and P2 in the ratio 75:25.

All the overhead costs will now be allocated and apportioned to the production departments.

The key to this step-down method of apportionment is to start by apportioning the overhead costs of the service department that does work for the other service department.

Example

The ABC Washing Machine Co produces a standard washing machine in three production departments (Machining, Assembling and Finishing) and two service departments (Materials handling and Production control).

Costs for last year, when 2,000 machines were produced, were as follows:

Materials:

Machine shop	£240,000
Assembly	£160,000
Finishing	£40,000
Materials handling	£4,000

Wages:

Machining	10,000	hours at £3.72
Assembly	5,000	hours at £2.88
Finishing	3,000	hours at £3.60
Materials handling	£8,000	
Production control	£11,200	

Other costs:

Machine shop	£41,920
Assembly	£12,960
Finishing	£7,920
Materials handling	£8,000
Production control	£2,400

It is estimated that the benefit derived from the service departments is as follows:

Materials handling:

Machine shop	60%
Assembly	30%
Finishing	10%

Production control:

Machine shop	40%
Assembly	30%
Finishing	20%
Materials handling	10%

Task

Prepare a statement showing the overhead apportioned to each of the production departments.

Solution

Materials and wages incurred by the production departments are assumed to be direct costs and are therefore excluded from the overhead distribution.

	Total	Machining	Assembly	Finishing	Production control	Materials handling
	£	£	£	£	£	£
Indirect materials	4,000	-	-	-	-	4,000
Indirect wages	19,200	-	-	-	11,200	8,000
Other	73,200	41,920	12,960	7,920	2,400	8,000
	96,400	41,920	12,960	7,920	13,600	20,000
Production control	-	5,440	4,080	2,720	(13,600)	1,360
Materials handling	-	12,816	6,408	2,136	-	(21,360)
	96,400	60,176	23,448	12,776	-	-

Service department costs are apportioned to production departments using the percentage benefit obtained. As 10% of the production control overhead is to be charged to materials handling, the costs of this department must be apportioned first.

ACTIVITY 6

A manufacturing business has two production departments and two service departments. The allocated overhead costs and apportioned general overhead costs for each department are as follows.

	£
Production department P1	140,000
Production department P2	200,000
Service department S1	90,000
Service department S2	120,000

Tasks

1   Show how the overheads would be charged to each production department if it is assumed that neither service department does any work for the other. Department S1 does 60% of its work for P1 and 40% of its work for P2. Department S2 does one-third of its work for P1 and two-thirds of its work for P2.

2   Show how the overheads would be charged to each production department if it is assumed that service department S2 does work for department S1 as well as the two production departments, as indicated in the table below.

	Apportionment ratio			
	Dept P1	Dept P2	Dept S1	Dept S2
Department S1	60%	40%	-	-
Department S2	25%	50%	25%	-

This activity covers performance criterion B in element 6.2.

For a suggested answer, see the 'Answers' section at the end of the book.

More than two service departments

This same approach can be taken when there are more than two service departments, provided that no two service departments do work for each other. For example, suppose that there are two production departments P1 and P2 and three service departments S1, S2 and S3.

An estimate of the work done by each service department is as follows.

	Dept P1	Dept P2	Dept S1	Dept S2	Dept S3
Department S1	55%	45%	-	-	-
Department S2	30%	20%	50%	-	-
Department S3	25%	25%	10%	40%	-

A step-down method of apportionment can be used as follows.

(a) Start with S3 costs, because S3 does work for both S1 and S2. Apportion its costs in the ratio 25:25:10:40 between departments P1, P2, S1 and S2.

(b) Next, apportion S2 costs, because S2 does some work for S1. S2 costs consist of its allocated costs, a share of general overhead costs and a share of S3 costs. Apportion its costs in the ratio 30:25:50 between departments P1, P2 and S1.

(c) Next, apportion S1 costs between P1 and P2 in the ratio 55:45. S1 costs consist of its allocated costs, a share of general overhead costs and a share of S3 and S2 costs.

6.3 SERVICE CENTRE COST APPORTIONMENT – RECIPROCAL APPORTIONMENT

When service departments do work for each other, it might be decided that this should be provided for in the way that service department overheads are apportioned. For example, the maintenance department and factory payroll section might do some work for each other.

The costs of these two departments can be apportioned in a way that allows for the work they do for each other.

Overhead costs should be apportioned from each service department in turn, to both the production departments and the other service department. The process of apportionment should be repeated several times over, taking each service department in turn, until all the overheads have been apportioned to the production departments only.

An example should illustrate how this process of apportionment works.

Example

A factory has two production departments and three service departments. The costs of each department, and the amount of work done by each department for the others, is set out in the table below.

	Production			Service	
Department	A	B	C	P	Q
Costs	£3,000	£4,000	£2,000	£2,500	£2,700
Percentage of P's cost used by other departments	20	30	25	–	25
Percentage of Q's cost used by other departments	25	25	30	20	–

Here, each service department does some work for the other service department, so a simple step-down apportionment of service department overheads is not possible.

Task

Apportion the costs of service department P and service department Q to the production departments A, B and C.

Solution

Reciprocal reallocations

You can start by apportioning the costs of either P or Q. It doesn't matter which service department you begin with.

	Production			Service	
Department	A	B	C	P	Q
	£	£	£	£	£
Costs	3,000	4,000	2,000	2,500	2,700
Reallocate P's costs	500 (20%)	750 (30%)	625 (25%)	(2,500)	625 (25%)
				Nil	3,325
Reallocate Q's costs	831 (25%)	831 (25%)	997 (30%)	665 (20%)	(3,325)
				665	Nil
Reallocate P's costs	133 (20%)	199 (30%)	166 (25%)	(665)	166 (25%)
				Nil	166
Reallocate Q's costs	41 (25%)	41 (25%)	50 (30%)	33 (20%)	(166)
	10	10	13	(33)*	–
	4,515	5,831	3,851	Nil	Nil

Tutorial note: P's cost could be reallocated to Q once more but the allocation is now small enough to share between the three production cost centres, rounding the allocations in a suitable manner

7 THE ARBITRARY NATURE OF OVERHEAD APPORTIONMENTS

At the end of the process of allocation and apportionment of overheads, all overhead costs have been charged to production cost centres, or as administration or selling and distribution overheads.

The process of apportionment attempts to be fair, but the selection of the bases for apportionment is based on judgement and assumption.

- General cost items can often be apportioned on any of two or more different bases, and depending on the basis chosen, the amount of cost charged to each responsibility centre/cost centre will differ.

- Similarly, the basis for apportioning service department costs to production departments can differ, depending on the assumptions made or point of view taken.

- The decision about whether to allow for the work done by service departments for other service departments is also significant. The assumption chosen will affect the amount of overheads charged from the service departments to each production departments.

Methods of apportioning overheads should be kept under review, to make sure that they remain valid and sensible.

If a basis of apportionment no longer appears valid, a change in the apportionment basis should be proposed to management, giving the reasons for the proposed change.

8 OVERHEAD ABSORPTION

Allocation and apportionment are the first two stages in the process of charging overhead costs to products or services.

The third stage in the absorption costing process is overhead absorption, also called overhead recovery.

Definition   **Overhead absorption** is the process of adding overhead costs to the cost of a product or service, in order to build up a fully-absorbed product cost or service cost.

As a result of overhead absorption, in theory at least, the total amount of overheads incurred should be absorbed into the costs of the products manufactured (or services provided) by the business.

8.1 BASIS OF ABSORPTION

Production overhead costs are absorbed into product costs on a basis selected by the organisation. The absorption basis should be appropriate for the particular products or services. The most common bases of absorption are:

- an absorption rate per unit, but only if the organisation produces a single product or several standard products

- an absorption rate per direct labour hour worked

- an absorption rate per machine hour worked

- an absorption rate based on a percentage of direct labour costs

- an absorption rate based on a percentage of prime cost (a percentage of direct materials, direct labour and direct expense costs).

The most common bases for absorption are direct labour hours and machine hours.

8.2 ABSORPTION RATES

An absorption rate is the rate at which overheads are added to costs.

- If the absorption basis is units produced, the absorption rate will be £X per unit.

- If the absorption basis is direct labour hours worked, the absorption rate will be £Y per direct labour hour. For example, if the absorption rate for production

overhead is £5 per direct labour hour, a job taking 4 direct labour hours will be charged with £20 of overhead.

- If the absorption basis is machine hours worked, the absorption rate will be £Z per machine hour. For example, if the absorption rate for production overhead is £15 per machine hour, a job taking 2 machine hours will be charged with £30 of overhead.

The absorption rate is calculated as:

$$\frac{\text{Overhead costs}}{\text{Volume of activity (direct labour hours, machine hours etc)}}$$

Overhead costs for any production departments are the allocated and apportioned overheads, assembled by the methods described above.

An organisation might have just one absorption rate for its entire production operations. However, an organisation with more than one production department is likely to have a different absorption rate for each department, so that separately-calculated production overheads are added to product costs for the work done in each department.

The basis of absorption can differ between production departments and the absorption rate can differ between departments.

Example

Job 1234 goes through three production departments. The direct materials cost of the job are £200 and the direct labour costs are:

Department 1	(3 direct labour hours)	£18
Department 2	(1.5 direct labour hours)	£12
Department 3	(6 direct labour hours)	£48

The job takes 3 machine hours in department 2.

The production overhead absorption rates are:

Department 1	£5 per direct labour hour
Department 2	£10 per machine hour
Department 3	£12 per direct labour hour

Task

Calculate the full production cost of job 1234.

Solution

		£	£
Direct materials			200
Direct labour:			
Department 1		18	
Department 2		12	
Department 3		48	
			78
Production overhead:			
Department 1	(3 direct labour hours at £5 per hour)	15	
Department 2	(3 machine hours at £10 per hour)	30	
Department 3	(6 direct labour hours at £12 per hour)	72	
			117
Full cost of the job			395

ACTIVITY 7

Cuecraft Ltd manufacture pool and snooker cues. It has three producing cost centres:

- Machining
- Finishing
- Packing

The planned overhead for the next budget period has been allocated and apportioned to the cost centres as:

Machining	£65,525
Finishing	£36,667
Packing	£24,367

Budgeted cost centre volume for the same period shows:

Machining	7,300 machine hours
Finishing	6,250 direct labour hours
Packing	5,200 direct labour hours

Task

Determine separate overhead absorption (recovery) rates for each cost centre on the following bases.

- Machining – machine hours
- Finishing – direct labour hours
- Packing – direct labour hours.

This activity covers performance criterion C in element 6.2.

For a suggested answer, see the 'Answers' section at the end of the book.

ACTIVITY 8

Assume that Cuecraft produce a pool cue 'pot 3' and it takes 4 hours to complete.

The activity takes place in the following cost centres:

Machining	3 hrs
Finishing	0.9 hr
Packing	0.1 hr

Show the overhead recovered in the unit of pot 3.

This activity covers performance criterion C in element 6.2.

For a suggested answer, see the 'Answers' section at the end of the book.

8.3 ABSORPTION RATES BASED ON THE BUDGET

It might seem logical that overhead absorption rates should be based on the actual overhead costs in a period and the actual volume of activity (direct labour hours or machine hours worked, or units produced).

In practice, this is not the case. Overhead absorption rates are based on budgeted overhead costs and the budgeted volume of activity

FOULKS LYNCH
PUBLICATIONS

$$\text{Absorption rate} = \frac{\text{Budgeted overhead costs}}{\text{Budgeted volume of activity}}$$

The reason we use the budget to obtain absorption rates is that if we used actual costs we would have to wait until after the end of the period to calculate product costs. This is because actual overhead costs cannot be known until the period has ended and information about actual costs has been gathered and analysed.

By using absorption rates based on budgeted overhead spending and budgeted activity volume, we can establish absorption rates in advance, and charge overhead costs to products as soon as they are made (and to services as soon as they are performed).

9 UNDER- AND OVER-ABSORPTION OF OVERHEADS

Overhead absorption rates are based on budgeted overhead costs and the budgeted volume of activity.

In practice, we should expect that:

- actual overhead expenditure will differ from budgeted overhead expenditure, and

- the actual volume of activity will differ from the budgeted volume of activity.

As a consequence, the amount of overheads charged to product costs will differ from the actual overhead expenditure.

We might charge more overhead costs to production than the amount of overheads expenditure actually incurred. If so, there is over-absorbed or over-recovered overheads.

We might charge less in overhead costs to production than the amount of overheads expenditure actually incurred. If so, there is under-absorbed or under-recovered overheads.

Example

A company has a single production department. Its budgeted production overheads for 20X4 were £200,000 and its budgeted volume of production was 50,000 direct labour hours. It has decided to absorb production overheads into product costs on a direct labour hour basis.

During 20X4, actual production overhead expenditure was £195,000 and 54,000 direct labour hours were worked.

The absorption rate is £4 per direct labour hour (£200,000/50,000 hours, based on the budget).

The overheads absorbed into product costs are £4 for each direct labour hour actually worked.

	£
Total production overheads absorbed (54,000 hours x £4)	216,000
Overheads actually incurred	195,000
Over-absorbed overheads	21,000

Here, overheads are over-absorbed because £216,000 in production overhead costs has been charged to the cost of items produced, but actual overhead spending was only £195,000. Production has been charged with too much overhead.

Over-absorbed overhead is taken to the profit and loss account as an addition to profit in the period, to compensate for the fact that the recorded costs of production are in excess of actual expenditure.

Example

For the year ended 31 December 20X4 the planned overhead for the Machining Cost Centre at Cuecraft Ltd was:

Overhead   £132,000

Volume of activity   15,000 machine hours

In January 20X4 the cost centre incurred £12,000 of overhead and 1,350 machine hours were worked.

Task

Calculate the pre-determined overhead rate per machine hour and the overhead under or over-recovered in the month.

Solution

Absorption rate, based on the budget:

$$\frac{\text{Planned overhead}}{\text{Machine hours}} = \frac{£132,000}{15,000 \text{ machine hours}} = £8.80 \text{ per machine hour}$$

	£
Overhead absorbed	
1,350 machine hours at £8.80	11,880
Overhead incurred	12,000
Under-absorption	120

Here, the amount of overheads actually charged to production are £11,880, which is less than actual expenditure. We therefore have under-absorption of overhead.

Under-recovery of overheads is shown as a separate item in the costing profit and loss account. Since production has been charged with less overheads than the amount of overheads incurred, an adjustment to profit for under-absorption is downwards. In other words, under-absorption is a 'loss' item.

ACTIVITY 9

A manufacturing business has two production departments, X and Y, for which the following annual budgeted figures have been prepared.

	Department X	Department Y
Budgeted overhead expenditure	£840,000	£720,000
Overhead absorption basis	Machine hours	Direct labour hours
Budgeted activity	40,000 machine hours	60,000 direct labour hours

Actual overhead expenditure and actual activity levels for the year were:

	Department X	Department Y
Actual overhead expenditure	£895,000	£735,000
Actual activity	41,500 machine hours	62,400 direct labour hours

Task

1   Establish the overhead absorption rates for each department for the year.

2   Calculate the under- or over-absorbed overhead in each department for the year.

This activity covers performance criteria C and E in element 6.2.

For a suggested answer, see the 'Answers' section at the end of the book.

10 OVER-/UNDER-ABSORBED OVERHEAD AND THE PROFIT AND LOSS ACCOUNT

Over-absorbed overhead during a period is treated as an addition to profit, because it is an adjustment to allow for the fact that too much overhead cost has been charged to the items produced in the period. Similarly, under-absorbed overhead during a period is treated as a reduction in profit, because it is an adjustment to allow for the fact that the overhead cost charged to the items produced in the period is less than the actual overhead costs incurred.

It is usual to present the adjustment for over- or under-absorbed overheads in the following way.

Example

A manufacturing business that uses absorption costing has a single production overhead department, and the budgeted data for 20X4 is as follows.

Budgeted overhead expenditure	£450,000
Absorption basis	Direct labour hours
Budgeted activity	50,000 direct labour hours

Actual results for the year were as follows.

	£
Sales	2,000,000
Value of opening stock, 1 January	18,000
Value of closing stock, 31 December	26,000
Direct materials costs of production	317,000
Direct labour costs of production	528,000
Production overhead expenditure incurred	447,000
Administration overheads	115,000
Selling and distribution overheads	271,000

Actual number of direct labour hours worked	48,000 hours

Task

Prepare a profit and loss account for the year, in absorption costing format.

Solution

Workings

The overhead absorption rate is £9 per direct labour hour (£450,000/50,000 hours).

	£
Overheads absorbed into production costs (48,000 hours × £9)	432,000
Actual overheads incurred	447,000
Under-absorbed overhead	(15,000)

Profit and loss account for the year ended 31 December 20X4

	£	£	£
Sales			2,000,000
Opening stock		18,000	
Production costs			
Direct materials	317,000		
Direct labour	528,000		
Production overhead (absorbed)	432,000		
		1,277,000	
		1,295,000	
Less: Closing stock		(26,000)	
Production cost of sales			1,269,000
			731,000
Under-absorbed overhead			(15,000)
			716,000
Administration overhead		115,000	
Selling and distribution overhead		271,000	
			386,000
Profit			330,000

ACTIVITY 10

Factory Ltd uses absorption costing. It has a single production overhead department, and the budgeted data for 20X3 is as follows.

Budgeted overhead expenditure	£960,000
Absorption basis	Direct labour hours
Budgeted activity	80,000 direct labour hours

Actual results for the year were as follows.

	£
Sales	4,090,000
Value of opening stock, 1 January	201,000
Value of closing stock, 31 December	172,000
Direct materials costs of production	1,642,000
Direct labour costs of production	1,200,000
Production overhead expenditure incurred	955,000

Administration overheads	420,000
Selling and distribution overheads	719,000

Actual number of direct labour hours worked	81,000 hours

Task

Prepare a profit and loss account for the year, in absorption costing format.

This activity covers performance criteria C, D and E in element 6.2.

For a suggested answer, see the 'Answers' section at the end of the book.

11 ACCOUNTING FOR PRODUCTION OVERHEADS

(**Note**: You might prefer to return to this section of the chapter after you have read the chapter on coding and accounting for costs.)

If a manufacturing business maintains cost accounts in a cost ledger, overheads are accounted for within the double entry book-keeping system of the cost ledger.

Three accounts are particularly relevant to accounting for production overheads:

- the production overhead account
- the work -in-progress account
- the under- or over-absorbed overhead account.

The entries in these accounts are as follows.

Production overheads account

Debit side (overheads incurred)	£	Credit side (overheads absorbed)	£
Stores account (indirect materials)	X	Work in Progress account (overheads absorbed)	X
Wages control account (indirect labour)	X		
Various accounts (indirect expenses)	X		
[Under-absorbed overhead]	X	[Over-absorbed overhead]	X
	X		X

Work-in-progress account

Debit side (elements of production cost)	£	Credit side (completed production)	£
Opening stock, work in progress			
Stores account (direct materials)	X	Finished goods account (completed production)	X
Wages control account (direct labour)	X		
Production overhead account (production overhead absorbed)	X	Closing stock, work in progress	X
	X		X

If under-absorbed

Under-/over-absorbed overhead account

Debit side	£	Credit side	£
Production overhead account	X̲	Profit and loss account	X̲
	X̲		X̲

If over-absorbed

Under-/over-absorbed overhead account

Debit side	£	Credit side	£
Profit and loss account	X̲	Production overhead account	X̲
	X̲		X̲

Example

A manufacturing business has a single production department. It uses absorption costing and absorbs production overhead into costs on a direct labour hour basis.

The production overhead budget for the year to 30 June 20X4 was £800,000, and budgeted direct labour hours were 100,000.

During the year to 30 June 20X4, the following costs were incurred.

	£
Direct materials	420,000
Indirect materials	40,000
Direct labour	750,000
Indirect labour	315,000
Indirect expenses	505,000

Opening stock of work-in-progress was £90,000 and closing work-in-progress was £70,000.

The number of labour hours actually worked was 110,000 hours.

Task

Prepare the following accounts in the cost ledger of the business:

- production overhead account
- work-in-progress account
- under-/over-absorbed overhead account.

Solution

Workings

The overhead absorption rate is £8 per direct labour hour (£800,000/100,000 hours).

Production overheads absorbed were £880,000 (110,000 hours × £8 per hour).

Production overheads account

	£		£
Stores account	40,000	Work in Progress	880,000
Wages control account	315,000		
Indirect expenses	505,000		
Over-absorbed overhead	20,000		
	880,000		880,000

Work-in-progress account

	£		£
Opening stock	90,000	Finished goods	2,070,000
Stores	420,000	(balancing figure)	
Wages control	750,000		
Production overhead	880,000	Closing stock	70,000
	2,140,000		2,140,000

Under-/over-absorbed overhead account

	£		£
Profit and loss account	20,000	Production overhead account	20,000
	20,000		20,000

ACTIVITY 11

ZXC Limited is a manufacturing company. It uses absorption costing and has just one production department. The following budgeted data was prepared for the year to 30 September 20X4:

Budgeted production overhead	£600,000
Absorption basis	machine hours
Budgeted activity	40,000 machine hours

The following actual data was obtained for the year to 30 September 20X4:

	£
Direct materials	416,000
Indirect materials	25,000
Direct labour	272,000
Indirect labour	375,000
Indirect expenses	220,000
Opening stock, work-in-progress	64,000
Cost of finished goods produced	1,255,000

During the year, 39,000 machine hours were actually worked.

Task

Prepare the following accounts in the cost ledger of the business:

- production overhead account

- work-in-progress account

- under-/over-absorbed overhead account.

This activity covers performance criteria C, D and E in element 6.2.

For a suggested answer, see the 'Answers' section at the end of the book.

12 INVESTIGATING THE CAUSES OF UNDER- OR OVER-ABSORBED OVERHEAD

The intention of absorbing production overhead is to share the costs of the overheads among the various products manufactured or jobs worked on. Ideally, the amount of overhead absorbed should equal the amount of overhead expenditure incurred. In practice, this rarely happens, and there are some under- or over-absorbed overheads. This is because the absorption rate is decided in advance, based on the budgeted overhead expenditure and budgeted volume of activity.

Even so, the amount of under- or over-absorbed overhead should not usually be large, provided the budgeting is realistic and provided that actual results meet budgeted expectations.

If the amount of under- or over-absorbed overhead is large, something could have gone wrong, which should be a matter of some concern to management. Certainly, management should expect to be informed of the reasons why there has been a large amount of under- or over-absorption.

The accountant will be expected to investigate the reasons for the under- or over-absorption, and report his or her findings to management.

There are several reasons why a large amount of under- or over-absorption of overhead might occur.

- Actual overhead expenditure was much higher than budgeted, possibly due to poor control over overhead spending.

- Actual overhead expenditure was much less than budgeted, possibly due to good control over overhead spending.

- Actual overhead expenditure was much higher or lower than budgeted, due to poor budgeting of overhead expenditure.

- The actual volume of activity was higher or lower than budgeted, for operational reasons that the production manager should be able to explain.

- The actual volume of activity was higher or lower than budgeted, due to poor budgeting of the volume of activity.

13 FIXED, VARIABLE AND SEMI-FIXED OVERHEADS

(*Note*: You might prefer to return to this part of the chapter after you have read the chapters on marginal costing and CVP analysis.)

In the examples above, overheads have been treated as a total cost. An organisation might, however, distinguish between its fixed overheads and variable overheads, and apply a different overhead absorption rate for each.

To do this, it might be necessary in the budget to separate semi-fixed and semi-variable overhead costs into their fixed and variable elements.

This can be done using the high-low method, as follows.

- Obtain budgeted estimates for total production overhead costs at two different levels of activity.

- At each level of activity, the total overhead costs represent fixed costs plus variable costs.

- Fixed costs are the same at all levels of activity, so the difference between the total overhead costs at the two levels of activity must be the difference in their variable overhead costs.

- The difference in the total costs at the two activity levels (= difference in variable overhead costs)is the variable overhead cost for the difference in activity levels. We can therefore calculate a variable cost per unit of activity.

- Having calculated the variable overhead cost per unit of activity, we can take the total costs at either of the two levels of activity and deduct the variable costs to calculate the fixed costs.

Example

It has been estimated that total production overhead costs are as follows.

	£
At 16,000 direct labour hours of work	86,000
At 19,000 direct labour hours of work	89,750

Task 1

These estimates should be used to obtain a fixed overhead absorption rate and a variable overhead absorption rate for the budget period, in which the budgeted level of activity is 18,000 direct labour hours. Both the fixed overhead and variable overhead absorption rate should be on a direct labour hour basis.

Task 2

Suppose that actual results during the period were as follows:

Total overheads incurred	£90,600
Direct labour hours worked	17,400

Calculate the amount of under- or over-absorbed overhead.

Solution

Task 1

		£
Total overhead cost of:	19,000 hours	89,750
Total overhead cost of:	16,000 hours	86,000
Variable overhead cost for:	3,000 hours	3,750

Variable overhead cost per hour (£3,750/3,000)	£1.25

This should be the absorption rate for variable overheads.

	£
Total overhead cost of 19,000 hours	89,750
Variable overhead cost of 19,000 hours (× £1.25)	23,750
Therefore fixed costs	66,000

The absorption rate for fixed overhead, given a budget of 18,000 direct labour hours, should therefore be £3.667 per direct labour hour.

Task 2

	£
Absorbed overheads:	
Fixed (17,400 hours × £3.67)	63,858
Variable (17,400 × £1.25)	21,750
Total absorbed overheads	85,608
Overheads incurred	90,600
Under-absorbed overhead	4,992

ACTIVITY 12

A manufacturing business uses absorption costing, and establishes separate absorption rates for fixed production overhead and variable production overhead. The absorption rates for next year will be based on 40,000 direct labour hours. Expenditure budgets for fixed and variable costs should be derived from the following estimates of cost:

	£
At 37,000 direct labour hours of work	145,500
At 42,000 direct labour hours of work	153,000

Actual results for the period were:

Direct labour hours worked	41,500 hours
Variable overhead costs incurred	£67,500
Fixed overhead costs incurred	£91,000

Task 1

Establish a fixed overhead absorption rate and a variable overhead absorption rate for the year.

Task 2

Calculate the amount of under- or over-absorbed overhead for both fixed and variable overhead

Task 3

Prepare the following accounts for the cost ledger:

- Production overhead account

- Under-/ over-absorbed overhead account

This activity covers performance criteria C, D and E in element 6.2.

For a suggested solution, see the 'Answers' section at the end of the book.

ACTIVITY 13

For the year ended 31 December 20X4 the planned overhead for finishing and packing cost centres at Cuecraft Ltd was £74,000 and £49,000 and cost centre volume was planned as 12,750 and 10,500 direct labour hours.

During January 20X4 the following information was available:

	Finishing	Packing
Overhead incurred	£6,900	£4,000
Activity		
Direct labour hours	1,100	900

Calculate the pre-determined overhead recovery rates and the overhead under or over-recovered for each cost centre for the month, showing clearly the entries in the overhead control account.

This activity covers performance criteria C, D and E in element 6.2.

For a suggested answer, see the 'Answers' section at the end of the book.

SELF TEST QUESTIONS

		Paragraph
1	What are responsibility centres?	2.1
2	What bases of apportionment are used for overheads?	4.2
3	What are service cost centres?	6
4	What are the particular problems of dealing with service cost centres?	6
5	What are the common methods of absorbing overhead?	8.1
6	What is over- and under-recovery of overhead?	9

KEY TERMS

Overheads – a term for indirect costs.

Absorption costing – a method of costing in which the costs of an item (product or service or activity) are built up as the sum of direct costs and a fair share of overhead costs, to obtain a full cost or a fully-absorbed cost.

Responsibility centre – an area of the business or an item of cost that is the responsibility of a particular manager of the business. Organisations can be divided into a large number of different responsibility centres.

Cost centre – an area of the business where costs are gathered.

Overhead allocation – the process of charging each item of cost to a cost centre.

Overhead apportionment – the process of sharing out overhead costs on a fair basis.

Overhead absorption – the process of adding overhead costs to the cost of a product or service, in order to build up a fully-absorbed product cost or service cost.

FOULKS LYNCH
PUBLICATIONS

Chapter 6

CODING AND ACCOUNTING FOR COSTS

In earlier chapters of this text the classification of costs has been discussed. It is possible to classify costs according to their function e.g. materials or wages, their behaviour e.g. fixed or variable or their relationship to the product being produced e.g. direct or indirect.

Each type of classification is useful for different purposes. The main aim of the cost accountant however is to determine the cost of each of the organisation's products. In order to do this, expenses must be capable of being handled in some manageable form. In practice this is often done by classifying each expense according to its cost centre and the type of expense. A cost code is then allocated to the expense to represent this classification.

We then examine how direct and indirect costs are recorded in the ledgers (the 'T' accounts). The previous chapter showed how overheads are accounted for, but this chapter explains the overall system for recording costs in the cost ledger accounts.

CONTENTS

1 Classification and coding of costs

2 Accounting for materials

3 Work in progress account

4 Materials issued

5 Accounting for wages

6 Classification of wages cost

7 Accounting for expenses

8 Absorption of production overhead

9 Accounting for finished goods

10 WIP and finished goods balances

11 Complete cost bookkeeping system

KNOWLEDGE AND UNDERSTANDING

		Reference
1	Recording of cost and revenue data in the accounting records	Item 4
2	Relationship between the labour costing system and the payroll accounting system	Item 20
3	The sources of information for revenue and costing data	Item 27

LEARNING OUTCOMES

At the end of this chapter you should have learned the following topics.

Accounting for materials

- Understand the role of the materials cost ledger control account in controlling the material stock ledger accounts.

- Post amounts for materials purchased to the materials control account and the stock ledger accounts

- Understand the role of the Work in Progress account

- Transfer amounts for material issued to production to the materials control account, the stock ledger accounts and the Work in Progress account

Accounting for wages

- Post amounts for wages and salaries to the wages control account

- Transfer amounts from the wages control account to the WIP account and the production overhead account

Accounting for expenses

- Post amounts for overhead expenses to the individual expense accounts

- Transfer the expenses to the production overhead account

- Transfer the production overhead to the WIP account in accordance with agreed rates of absorption

Accounting for finished goods

- Transfer amounts from the WIP account to the finished goods account

- Reconcile the balance on the WIP account to the jobs and job cards in progress

- Reconcile the balance on the finished goods account to completed jobs

Overall system

- Post all the entries required to produce a complete system of non-integrated cost and financial accounts

---

1 CLASSIFICATION AND CODING OF COSTS

1.1 INTRODUCTION

Definition   A **code** is a system of symbols designed to be applied to a classified set of items, to give a brief accurate reference, facilitating entry to the records, collation and analysis.

A cost code is a code used in a costing system.

1.2 COST CENTRE CODE

The first step will be to determine the cost centre to which the cost relates and then to allocate the correct cost centre code.

Example

If a cost relates to Machine Group 7 the cost centre code might be 07. If the cost relates to the canteen the cost centre code might be 16.

1.3 GENERIC OR FUNCTIONAL CODE

Once a cost has been allocated its correct cost centre code then it may also be useful to know the particular type of expense involved. Therefore possibly another two digits might be added to the cost centre code to represent the precise type of cost.

Example

If an expense for Machine Group 7 is for oil then its code might be 07 (for its cost centre) followed by 23 to represent indirect materials.

If an expense of the canteen is identified as frozen peas then its cost code might be 16 (its cost centre) followed by 02 to represent food purchases.

1.4 SPECIFIC CODE

Finally it may be necessary for cost allocation, decision making or accounting purposes to allocate a code which specifically identifies the item of cost.

Example

The oil for Machine Group 7 might eventually be coded as:

072304

This represents Machine Group 7 (07) indirect material use (23) of oil (04).

The frozen peas for the canteen might be coded as:

160219

This represents canteen (16) food purchases (02) of frozen peas (19).

Conclusion   A **cost code** is designed to analyse and classify the costs of an organisation in the most appropriate manner for that organisation. Therefore there are no set methods of designing a cost code and the cost code of a particular organisation will be that which best suits the operations and costs of that business.

ACTIVITY 1

Suppose that a cost coding system is such that the first two letters of the code represent the cost centre, the third letter the type of expense and the fourth letter the detail of the expense.

Codes are as follows:

S	Salesman's expenses
ED	Eastern Division
P	Petrol

Code an Eastern Division's salesman's petrol expenses.

For a suggested answer, see the 'Answers' section at the end of the book.

1.5 PURPOSE OF COST CODES

The main purposes of cost codes are to:

(a)   assist precise information: costs incurred can be associated with pre-established codes, so reducing variations in classification

(b)   facilitate electronic data processing: computer analysis, summarisation and presentation of data can be performed more easily through the medium of codes

(c)   facilitate a logical and systematic arrangement of costing records: accounts can be arranged in blocks of codes permitting additional codes to be inserted in logical order

(d)   simplify comparison of totals of similar expenses rather than all of the individual items

(e)   incorporate check codes within the main code to check the accuracy of the postings.

Example

The following is a short extract from an organisation's code structure.

Cost centres

		Code
Factory		
	Machine shop A	301
	Machine shop B	302
	Boiler house	303
	etc	
Administration		
	Accounts department	401
	Secretary	402
	Security officers	403
	etc	
Selling		
	South area	501
	North area	502
	East area	503
	etc	

Type of expense

Materials		
	Machine lubricants	001
	Cleaning supplies	002
	Stationery	003
	etc	
Wages		
	Supervisor's salary	051
	Cleaning wages	052
	etc	
Expenses		
	Depreciation of machinery	071
	Insurance of machinery	072
	etc	

How would the following items be likely to be coded?

(a)   A stores requisition for an issue of machine lubricant to machine shop B.

(b)   The salary of an East area sales supervisor.

(c)   The depreciation expense for the machine shop A machinery.

Solution

(a)   302001

(b)   503051

(c)   301071

2 ACCOUNTING FOR MATERIALS

In earlier chapters of this text a number of aspects of materials usage have been considered. The procedures necessary for the purchasing of materials, the recording of purchases and issues in the stock ledger accounts and the pricing of materials issues are separate topics that have been dealt with in various chapters. The accounting procedures for materials overall will now be brought together.

2.1 MATERIALS STOCK LEDGER ACCOUNTS

As was discussed in earlier chapters of the text a stock ledger account is set up for each type of material purchased by an organisation. This stock ledger account records details of all receipts of the material as well as all issues of the material to production.

Stock ledger accounts can either be in a columnar format or in the format of a ledger account. In the earlier chapters a columnar format was used. An illustration of the format would be as follows:

Receipts			Issues			Stock
Date	Ref	Quantity	Date	Ref	Quantity	level

Alternatively similar information could be shown in a T account format as illustrated below:

Stock ledger account - X

	£		£
Receipts	X	Issues	X
	—	Bal c/d	X
	X		—
	—		X
Bal b/d	X		—

In the examples below that are illustrating the accounting aspects of cost recording the T account format will be used.

2.2 MATERIALS COST LEDGER ACCOUNT

The materials cost ledger account is the summary account for all of the individual stock ledger accounts. The materials cost ledger account shows in total all of the entries that have taken place in the individual stock ledger accounts. The materials cost ledger account therefore records the total materials purchases for the organisation.

2.3 PURCHASE OF MATERIALS

When materials are purchased the credit side of the entry will either be to cash or creditors, if a period of credit has been allowed. The debit entry records the purchase of the actual materials.

Example

Ogden Ltd is a small company that was set up at the beginning of May 20X4 by the issue of £20,000 of shares for cash. Ogden Ltd purchases three types of material, A, B and C. During the month of May 20X4 the purchases of each type of material were as follows:

Material A

3 May	£2,000
24 May	£9,000

Material B

6 May	£5,000
10 May	£3,000
21 May	£7,000

Material C

1 May	£4,000
7 May	£4,000
28 May	£4,000

Purchases of materials A and B are for cash and material C is on credit of 45 days.

Record these transactions in the stock ledger accounts as well as the cash and creditor accounts.

Solution

Stock ledger account A

	£		£
3 May	2,000		
24 May	9,000		

Stock ledger account B

	£		£
6 May	5,000		
10 May	3,000		
21 May	7,000		

Stock ledger account C

	£		£
1 May	4,000		
7 May	4,000		
28 May	4,000		

Cash account

		£		£
1 May	Share capital a/c	20,000	3 May Material A	2,000
			6 May Material B	5,000
			10 May Material B	3,000
			21 May Material B	7,000
			24 May Material A	9,000

Creditors account

	£		£
		1 May Material C	4,000
		7 May Material C	4,000
		28 May Material C	4,000

3 WORK IN PROGRESS ACCOUNT

The work in progress account records the details of all of the materials, labour and expenses incurred on the current units being produced. In practice there will be a work in progress account for each individual product and a total or control work in progress account to record the total figures. In the examples that follow an organisation with a single product and therefore only one work in progress account will be assumed.

3.1 PURPOSE OF WORK IN PROGRESS ACCOUNT

The work in progress account records details of all of the inputs, materials, labour and expenses, into the products started in the period. Any balance on the account represents the value of the inputs into any units that are still incomplete at the end of the period.

Example of a work in progress account

A typical work in progress account would have the following type of entries:

Work in progress

	£		£
Direct materials	X	Transfer to finished goods	X
Direct labour	X	Bal c/d	X
Direct expenses	X		
	—		—
	X		X
	—		—

4 MATERIALS ISSUED

When materials are issued, this is reflected in the materials cost ledger account, the individual stock ledger accounts and the work in progress account.

The value of the issue of each type of material is credited to the individual material's stock ledger account, credited to the material cost ledger account and debited to the work in progress account.

4.1 VALUE OF ISSUES

In an earlier chapter of the text the value that is to be placed on each issue of materials was discussed. This value, however determined, is the amount to be credited to the stock ledger account and materials cost ledger account and debited to the work in progress account.

ACTIVITY 2

Continuing the example from the previous paragraph now suppose that Ogden Ltd made the following issues of materials to production:

Material A	7 May	£1,000
	27 May	£7,000
Material B	8 May	£3,000
	10 May	£4,000
Material C	2 May	£3,000
	8 May	£3,000
	29 May	£3,000

The materials purchased in May had been recorded as follows (assuming no opening stock of materials). Record these issues of materials in the ledger accounts:

Stock ledger account A

	£		£
3 May	2,000		
24 May	9,000		

Stock ledger account B

	£		£
6 May	5,000		
10 May	3,000		
21 May	7,000		

Stock ledger account C

	£		£
1 May	4,000		
7 May	4,000		
28 May	4,000		

Work in progress

	£		£

For a suggested answer, see the 'Answers' section at the end of the book.

5 ACCOUNTING FOR WAGES

You should remember from you earlier studies that the wages cost of an organisation is the gross wage paid to its employees plus the employer's National Insurance contribution.

5.1 WAGES CONTROL ACCOUNT

The wages control account is the account where the total wages are recorded. The amount posted will consist of the gross wage to the employees in total and the employer's total National Insurance contribution for the period.

The full double entry is as follows:

		£
DR	Wages control account	Gross wages
CR	Cash	Net wage paid
	PAYE creditor	PAYE
	National Insurance creditor	Employee's NI due to IR
and		
DR	Wages control account	Employer's NI
CR	National Insurance creditor	Employer's NI

The National Insurance creditor and PAYE creditor accounts are normally merged into a single creditor account because the payment is made on a single cheque to the Inland Revenue.

ACTIVITY 3

The gross wages cost for Ogden Ltd for May was £43,000 and the net wage paid in cash £37,000. The employer's National Insurance due for the same period was £3,700.

Write up these items in the relevant accounts.

For a suggested answer, see the 'Answers' section at the end of the book.

6 CLASSIFICATION OF WAGES COST

The wages of an organisation can be classified as either direct or indirect wages. Each type will be treated differently for accounting purposes.

6.1 DIRECT WAGES

Direct wages are a direct cost of producing a product and as such should be included as part of the cost or valuation of work in progress. Therefore gross direct wages should be debited to the work in progress account. This is done by crediting the wages control account with the relevant amount.

6.2 INDIRECT WAGES

Indirect wages are a part of the production overhead together with any indirect materials there might be and all of the indirect expenses of the organisation.

The gross indirect wages cost is therefore not debited to work in progress but instead debited to a production overhead account. The credit entry is again to the wages control account.

6.3 EMPLOYER'S NATIONAL INSURANCE CONTRIBUTIONS

The employer's National Insurance contributions are normally treated as part of the production overhead for the period. Therefore the wages control account is credited with the employer's National Insurance contribution for the period and the production overhead account is debited.

Example

Ogden Ltd's gross wage cost of £43,000 is made up, upon investigation, of £35,000 of direct wages costs and £8,000 of indirect wages costs.

Post the entries from the wages control account to work in progress and production overhead accounts. The work in progress account as it stands after the materials entries is reproduced below.

Work in progress

	£		£
2 May Material C	3,000		
7 May Material A	1,000		
8 May Material B	3,000		
8 May Material C	3,000		
10 May Material B	4,000		
27 May Material A	7,000		
29 May Material C	3,000		

Solution

Wages control account

	£		£
Cash/PAYE/NI	43,000	Work in progress	35,000
NI	3,700	Production overhead	
		(£8,000 + £3,700)	11,700
	46,700		46,700

Work in progress

	£		£
2 May Material C	3,000		
7 May Material A	1,000		
8 May Material B	3,000		
8 May Material C	3,000		
10 May Material B	4,000		
27 May Material A	7,000		
29 May Material C	3,000		
31 May Direct wages	35,000		

Production overhead account

	£		£
Indirect wages	11,700		

7 ACCOUNTING FOR EXPENSES

When an expense is incurred by an organisation the double entry is:

Dr   Expense account

Cr   Cash/creditor account

The majority of expenses of an organisation will be classified as indirect expenses or overheads and therefore will be transferred from the individual expense account to the production overhead account.

Example

Ogden Ltd incurs the following cash expenses in the month of May:

	£
Rent	2,000
Rates	600
Power	800
Insurance	500

Post these amounts to the relevant expense accounts and the cash account and then show the transfer to the production overhead account reproduced below.

Solution

Rent account

	£		£
Cash	2,000	Production overhead account	2,000

Rates account

	£		£
Cash	600	Production overhead account	600

Power account

	£		£
Cash	800	Production overhead account	800

Insurance account

	£		£
Cash	500	Production overhead account	500

Cash account

	£		£
		31 May Rent	2,000
		31 May Rates	600
		31 May Power	800
		31 May Insurance	500

Production overhead account

	£		£
Indirect wages	11,700		
Rent	2,000		
Rates	600		
Power	800		
Insurance	500		

8 ABSORPTION OF PRODUCTION OVERHEAD

In the previous chapter the absorption of overheads into the cost of products was discussed. The overheads are a part of the cost of a product but are absorbed on the basis of a predetermined overhead absorption rate.

8.1 ACCOUNTING ENTRIES

As the overheads are part of the cost of the products produced they should be included in the work in progress account. There will therefore be a transfer from production overhead to work in progress as follows:

Dr   Work in progress

Cr   Production overhead

8.2 AMOUNT OF TRANSFER OF OVERHEAD

The amount of overhead transferred from the production overhead account to the work in progress account is based upon the actual number of units of production and the predetermined overhead absorption rate. This is the amount of overhead absorbed into the costs of the products.

Example

If the overhead absorption rate for overheads is set at £10 per product and 100 products are produced then the transfer from the production overhead account to the work in progress account would be as follows:

Dr	Work in progress (£10 × 100 units)	£1,000
Cr	Production overhead	£1,000

8.3 UNDER AND OVER ABSORPTION

If the amount of overhead absorbed into the cost of products i.e. transferred from production overhead to work in progress, is different to the actual amount of production overhead incurred then there will be an under or over absorption of overhead.

This was discussed in the previous chapter. You should remember that any amount that is under absorbed is debited to the costing profit and loss account as an expense. Any amount that is over absorbed is credited back to the costing profit and loss account.

ACTIVITY 4

Continuing the example of Ogden Ltd the production overhead account and work in progress account are currently showing the following amounts:

Production overhead account

	£		£
Indirect wages	11,700		
Rent	2,000		
Rates	600		
Power	800		
Insurance	500		

Work in progress

	£		£
2 May Material C	3,000		
7 May Material A	1,000		
8 May Material B	3,000		
8 May Material C	3,000		
10 May Material B	4,000		
27 May Material A	7,000		
29 May Material C	3,000		
31 May Direct wages	35,000		

During the period under review Ogden produced 1,600 units of its product. The overhead absorption rate is set at £10.00 per unit.

Enter the amounts for absorption of overheads into the relevant accounts showing any under or over absorption clearly.

For a suggested answer, see the 'Answers' section at the end of the book.

9 ACCOUNTING FOR FINISHED GOODS

In the previous paragraphs the transfers have taken place to the work in progress account of all of the costs involved in producing the products. When the goods are finally completed then these costs are transferred from the work in progress account to the finished goods account.

9.1 DOUBLE ENTRY

The double entry for transferring the cost of the completed products from the work in progress account to the finished goods account is:

Dr   Finished goods

Cr   Work in progress

9.2 WORK IN PROGRESS ACCOUNT

The value of the finished goods to be transferred out of the work in progress account is the cost of the goods that have actually been completed. Any balance remaining on the work in progress account is the cost to date of any items that are still incomplete.

Example

Returning to the example of Ogden Ltd the work in progress account to date is as follows:

Work in progress

	£		£
2 May Material C	3,000		
7 May Material A	1,000		
8 May Material B	3,000		
8 May Material C	3,000		
10 May Material B	4,000		
27 May Material A	7,000		
29 May Material C	3,000		
31 May Direct wages	35,000		
31 May Production overhead absorbed	16,000		

At the end of May the value of the goods that are completed and ready for sale is £70,000.

Show how this amount will be accounted for including the calculation of any balance remaining on the work in progress account.

Solution

Work in progress

	£		£
2 May Material C	3,000	31 May Finished goods	70,000
7 May Material A	1,000	31 May Bal c/d	5,000
8 May Material B	3,000		
8 May Material C	3,000		_____
10 May Material B	4,000		75,000
27 May Material A	7,000		
29 May Material C	3,000		_____
31 May Direct wages	35,000		
31 May Production overhead absorbed	16,000		
	_____		
	75,000		
	_____		

Finished goods

	£		£
Work in progress	70,000		

10 WIP AND FINISHED GOODS BALANCES

The previous section illustrated that when amounts are transferred from work in progress to the finished goods account this will usually result in a balance remaining on the work in progress account as well as a balance on the finished goods account.

10.1 WORK IN PROGRESS BALANCE

The balance on the work in progress account represents the costs incurred to date on goods that are not yet completed. This balance on the work in progress account should be verifiable from the production records.

The job cards or batch cards for products will show the amount of production that has not been completed at the end of the period. This can be reconciled to the balance on the work in progress account.

ACTIVITY 5

The balance on the work in progress account for Ogden Ltd for May is as follows:

Work in progress

	£		£
2 May Material C	3,000	31 May Finished goods	70,000
7 May Material A	1,000	31 May Bal c/d	5,000
8 May Material B	3,000		
8 May Material C	3,000		———
10 May Material B	4,000		75,000
27 May Material A	7,000		
29 May Material C	3,000		———
31 May Direct wages	35,000		
31 May Production overhead			
absorbed	16,000		
	———		
	75,000		
	———		
1 Jun Bal b/d	5,000		

The job cards are examined and it is discovered that the following products are incomplete at the end of May:

200 units valued to date at £16.27 per unit

100 units valued to date at £17.46 per unit

Reconcile the total balance on the work in progress account with the amount of work outstanding.

For a suggested answer, see the 'Answers' section at the end of the book.

10.2 FINISHED GOODS BALANCE

The balance on the finished goods account at this stage represents the total cost of the goods that have been made ready for sale during the period. The value of the finished goods balance should reconcile with the value of completed goods not yet sold.

Example

The finished goods account for Ogden Ltd currently stand as follows:

Finished goods

	£		£
Work in progress	70,000		

If the production records or job sheets are checked then the total of the cost of completed jobs during the period per those records should also equal £70,000.

11 COMPLETE COST BOOKKEEPING SYSTEM

11.1 OUTLINE OF A COST LEDGER ACCOUNTING SYSTEM

In the last few paragraphs most of the cost bookkeeping entries have been completed. What is left is simply to complete the accounting entries in order to determine a profit for the period and to list any remaining balances in a balance sheet.

A cost ledger is a set of cost accounts. Cost accounts can be kept separate from normal financial accounts in the main (nominal) ledger, or the 'financial accounts' and the 'cost accounts' can be integrated into a single set of accounts. In the summary below, an integrated set of accounts is assumed.

The outline below does not include all the accounts you might find in a cost accounting system. For example, in a process costing system, there can be more than one work in progress account (one for each production process) and there can be accounts for losses. However, the outline shows all the accounts that should appear in an absorption costing system for a manufacturing business. These are:

- One or more accounts for sales. There can be separate sales accounts for different products, if required.

- Accounts to show the movement of stocks through the production and selling cycle, from raw materials, to work in progress to finished goods and then to cost of sales. The cost of raw materials and components are recorded in the stores account.

- Accounts for other costs: a wages and salaries control account and sundry expenses accounts.

- Accounts for overhead costs: production overhead, administration overhead, selling and distribution overhead and under- or over-absorbed overhead.

- A cost of sales account and a profit and loss account.

These accounts and their contents are summarised in the outline below.

Stores account (Stock ledger account)

Debit	£	Credit	£
Opening stock of materials	X	**Work in progress**: direct materials issued to production	X
Creditors/cash: Cost of materials purchased	X	**Production overhead**: indirect materials issued to production	X
		Administration overhead: indirect materials issued to administration cost centres	X
		Selling and distribution overhead: indirect materials issued to selling and distribution cost centres	X
		Closing stock of materials	X
	X		X

Work in progress account

Debit	£	Credit	£
Opening stock of unfinished production	X	**Finished goods account**: cost of completed production	X
Stores account: cost of direct materials issued to production	X		
Wages and salaries control account: cost of direct labour	X		
Production overhead account: production overhead absorbed	X	**Closing stock** of unfinished production	X
	X		X

Finished goods account

Debit	£	Credit	£
Opening stock of unsold finished goods stocks	X	**Cost of sales account**: cost of finished goods sold	X
		Closing stock of unsold finished goods	X
	X		X

Cost of sales account

Debit	£	Credit	£
Finished goods: cost of finished goods sold	X	**Profit and loss account**	X
	X		X

Sales account

Debit	£	Credit	£
Profit and loss account	X	**Debtors/cash**: sales in the period	X
	X		X

Wages and salaries control account

Debit	£	Credit	£
Bank/PAYE creditor/NIC creditor: wages and salaries costs in the period	X	**Work in progress**: direct production labour costs	X
		Production overhead: indirect production labour costs	X
		Administration overhead: indirect administration labour costs	X
		Selling and distribution overhead: indirect selling and distribution labour costs	X
	X		X

Sundry expenses accounts

Debit	£	Credit	£
Creditors/cash: expenses incurred in the period	X	**Work in progress**: direct production expenses (if any)	X
		Production overhead: indirect production expenses	X
		Administration overhead: administration expenses	X
		Selling and distribution overhead: selling and distribution expenses	X
	X		X

Production overheads account

Debit	£	Credit	£
Stores account: cost of indirect materials issued to production	X	**Work in progress account**: production overhead absorbed into production costs	X
Wages and salaries control account: cost of indirect production labour	X		
Sundry expenses accounts: indirect production expenses			
Under-/over-absorbed overhead account: production overhead over-absorbed	X	**Under-/over-absorbed overhead account**: production overhead under-absorbed	X
	X		X

Under-/over absorbed overheads account

Debit	£	Credit	£
Production overheads account: production overhead under-absorbed	X	**Production overheads account**: production overhead over-absorbed	X
Profit and loss account: the balance on this account, which can be either debit or credit, is transferred to the profit and loss account	X	**Profit and loss account**: the balance on this account, which can be either debit or credit, is transferred to the profit and loss account	X
	X		X

Administration overheads account

Debit	£	Credit	£
Stores account: cost of materials issued to administration departments	X	**Profit and loss account**: total administration costs for the period	X
Wages and salaries control account: cost of labour in administration departments	X		
Sundry expenses accounts: expenses incurred by administration departments	X		
	X		X

Selling and distribution overheads account

Debit	£	Credit	£
Stores account: cost of materials issued to selling and distribution departments	X	**Profit and loss account**: total selling and distribution costs for the period	X
Wages and salaries control account: cost of labour in selling and distribution departments	X		
Sundry expenses accounts: expenses incurred by selling and distribution departments	X		
	X		X

Profit and loss account

Debit	£	Credit	£
Cost of sales account	X	**Sales**	X
Under-absorbed overheads	X	**Over-absorbed overheads**	X
Administration overheads	X		
Selling and distribution overheads			
Profit (transfer to capital account)	X	**Loss** (transfer to capital account)	
	X		X

There will be either a profit or loss for the period. The corresponding double entry is recorded in the capital account.

Example

The recording of cost data in the costing records will be illustrated using the example of Ogden Ltd that has been used throughout the chapter.

The ledger accounts that have been written up for Ogden Ltd so far are as follows:

Creditors account

	£		£
Bal c/d	12,000	1 May Material C	4,000
		7 May Material C	4,000
	12,000	28 May Material C	4,000
			12,000

Stock ledger account A

	£		£
3 May	2,000	7 May	1,000
24 May	9,000	27 May	7,000
		Bal c/d	3,000
	11,000		11,000

Stock ledger account B

	£		£
6 May	5,000	8 May	3,000
10 May	3,000	10 May	4,000
21 May	7,000	Bal c/d	8,000
	15,000		15,000

Stock ledger account C

	£		£
1 May	4,000	2 May	3,000
7 May	4,000	8 May	3,000
28 May	4,000	29 May	3,000
		Bal c/d	3,000
	12,000		12,000

NI and PAYE creditor account

	£		£
Bal c/d	9,700	31 May Employee's NI and PAYE (£43,000 – (£37,000)	6,000
	9,700	Employer's NI	3,700
			9,700

Wages control account

	£		£
Cash/PAYE/NI	43,000	Work in progress	35,000
NI	3,700	Production overhead (£8,000 + £3,700)	11,700
	46,700		46,700

◆ **FOULKS LYNCH** PUBLICATIONS

Rent account

	£		£
Cash	2,000	Production overhead account	2,000

Rates account

	£		£
Cash	600	Production overhead account	600

Power account

	£		£
Cash	800	Production overhead account	800

Insurance account

	£		£
Cash	500	Production overhead account	500

Cash account

	£		£
1 May Share capital a/c	20,000	3 May Material A	2,000
		6 May Material B	5,000
		10 May Material B	3,000
		21 May Material B	7,000
		24 May Material A	9,000
		31 May Net wages	37,000
		31 May Rent	2,000
		31 May Rates	600
		31 May Power	800
		31 May Insurance	500

Production overhead account

	£		£
Indirect wages	11,700	Work in progress overhead	
Rent	2,000	absorbed	16,000
Rates	600		———
Power	800		16,000
Insurance	500		
Over absorption - P & L	400		———
	———		
	16,000		
	———		

Work in progress

	£		£
2 May Material C	3,000	Finished goods	70,000
7 May Material A	1,000	Bal c/d	5,000
8 May Material B	3,000		
8 May Material C	3,000		75,000
10 May Material B	4,000		
27 May Material A	7,000		
29 May Material C	3,000		
31 May Direct wages	35,000		
31 May Production overhead			
absorbed	16,000		
	75,000		

Finished goods

	£		£
Work in progress	70,000		

There are still some further entries however that need to be made as Ogden Ltd had the following additional transactions for the month of May 20X4:

	£
Sales (all for cash)	100,000
Administration expenses (cash)	6,000
Selling and distribution expenses (cash)	4,000

At the end of May there were finished goods with a total cost of £10,000 that were still unsold.

In order to complete the bookkeeping the following stages remain:

Step 1   Write up the ledger accounts for these final transactions.

Step 2   Write up the cost of sales account and profit and loss account.

Step 3   List any remaining balances on the balance sheet for the end of May 20X4.

Solution

Step 1

Sales: Dr Cash

     Cr Sales

Administration and selling and distribution expenses:

     Dr Expense account

     Cr Cash

Cash account

	£		£
1 May Share capital a/c	20,000	3 May Material A	2,000
31 May Sales	100,000	6 May Material B	5,000
		10 May Material B	3,000
		21 May Material B	7,000
		24 May Material A	9,000
		31 May Net wages	37,000
		31 May Rent	2,000
		31 May Rates	600
		31 May Power	800
		31 May Insurance	500
		31 May Administration	6,000
		31 May Selling and distribution	4,000

Sales account

	£		£
31 May P & L	100,000	31 May Cash	100,000

Administration

	£		£
31 May Cash	6,000	31 May P&L	6,000

Selling and distribution

	£		£
31 May Cash	4,000	31 May P&L	4,000

Step 2

The cost of the goods that are actually sold by Ogden Ltd are transferred from the finished goods account to the cost of sales account. The closing stock of finished goods is £10,000 therefore £60,000 is transferred to cost of sales as follows:

Finished goods

	£		£
Work in progress	70,000	31 May Cost of sales	60,000
		31 May Bal c/d	10,000
	70,000		
			70,000

Cost of sales account

	£		£
31 May Finished goods	60,000	31 May P&L	60,000

The profit and loss account can now be produced (also in T account format). This will include transfers from sales, cost of sales, administration overhead, selling and distribution overhead and also any under or over absorption from the production overhead. All of the

other expenses, materials, labour and overheads are of course already included in the value of cost of sales having come from the finished goods account via the work in progress account.

Profit and loss account

	£		£
31 May Cost of sales	60,000	31 May Sales	100,000
31 May Gross profit c/d	40,000		
			100,000
	100,000		
		31 May Gross profit b/d	40,000
31 May Administration		31 May Production overhead	
overhead	6,000	- over absorption	400
31 May Selling and			
distribution overhead	4,000		40,400
31 May Net profit c/d	30,400		
	40,400		

Step 3

The final stage is to enter any remaining balances in the balance sheet.

Remember that there will be a share capital account with a credit balance of £20,000 representing the initial capital paid into the business on 1 May 20X4.

Ogden Ltd Balance sheet as at 31 May 20X4

	£	£
Stocks:		
Raw materials	14,000	
Work in progress	5,000	
Finished goods	10,000	
	29,000	
Cash at bank	43,100	
		72,100
Trade creditors	12,000	
PAYE and NI creditor	9,700	
		21,700
		50,400
Share capital		20,000
Profit and loss		30,400
		50,400

CONCLUSION

This chapter explains how direct and indirect costs are coded and recorded in the costing ledger. In a standard costing system all stocks of raw materials, WIP and finished goods are held at standard cost so standard cost variances must be recorded in variance accounts and written off to P&L.

SELF TEST QUESTIONS

		Paragraph
1	What is a coding system?	1
2	What are the purposes of cost codes?	1.5
3	How do you account for materials issued?	4
4	How do you account for wages?	5
5	How do you account for under/over absorption?	8.3

KEY TERMS

Code – a system of symbols designed to be applied to a classified set of items, to give a brief accurate reference, facilitating entry to the records, collation and analysis.

Chapter 7

JOB AND BATCH COSTING

We saw at the start of this book that costing methods could be analysed into specific order costing and process costing.

CONTENTS

1   Specific order costing

2   Job costing

3   Batch costing

KNOWLEDGE AND UNDERSTANDING

		Reference
1	Costing system appropriate to the organisation: job, batch, unit and process costing systems.	Item 26

LEARNING OUTCOMES

At the end of this chapter you should have learned the following topics.

•   Describing a job costing system

•   Describing a batch costing system

1   SPECIFIC ORDER COSTING

The purpose of costing is to calculate the cost of each cost unit of an organisation's products. In order to do this the costs of each unit should be gathered together and recorded in the costing system. This is the overall aim but the methods and system used will differ from organisation to organisation as the type of products and production methods differ between organisations.

1.1   COST UNITS

The cost units of different organisations will be of different types and this will tend to necessitate different costing systems. The main types of cost units are as follows:

(a)   Individual products designed and produced for individual customers. Each individual product is a cost unit.

(b)   Groups of different products possibly in different styles, sizes or colours produced to be held in stock until sold. Each of the batches of whatever style, size or colour is a cost unit.

FOULKS LYNCH
PUBLICATIONS

(c)   Many units of identical products produced from a single production process. These units will be held in stock until sold. Each batch from the process is a cost unit.

2   JOB COSTING

2.1   JOBS

Definition   A **job** is an individual contract or product produced as a single order or product.

A job will normally be requested by a customer and that customer's individual requirements and specifications considered. The organisation will then estimate the costs of such a job, add on their required profit margin and quote their price to the customer. If the customer then accepts that quote then the job will proceed according to the timetable agreed between customer and supplier.

2.2   JOB PRICING

As was mentioned above each job will tend to be an individual order or contract and as such will normally differ in some respects from other jobs and contracts that the organisation performs. Therefore there will be no set price for each job.

Instead the estimated costs for each job must be determined.

This will include direct material, direct labour, direct expenses and any associated overheads. The organisation will then add to this their own required or expected profit margin in order to arrive at the cost of the job.

2.3   JOB COST CARD

All of the actual costs incurred in a job are eventually recorded on a job cost card. A job cost card can take many forms but is likely at least to include the following information.

JOB COST CARD	
Job number Estimate ref: Start date: Invoice number:	Customer name: Quoted estimate: Delivery date: Invoice amount:
COSTS: **Materials** Date Code Qty Price £	**Labour** Date Grade Hours Rate £
Expenses Date Code Description £	**Production overheads** Hours OAR £
Cost summary: Direct materials Direct labour Direct expenses Production overheads Administrative overheads Selling and distribution overheads Total cost Invoice price Profit/loss	

The job cost card may travel with the particular job as it moves around the factory. However it is more likely in practice that the job cost cards will be held centrally by the accounts department and all relevant cost information for that job forwarded to the accounts department.

2.4 DIRECT MATERIALS

When materials are requisitioned for a job then the issue of the materials will be recorded in the stock ledger account. They will also be recorded, at their issue price, in the job cost card as they are used as input into that particular job. Materials may be issued at different dates to a particular job but each issue must be recorded on the job cost card.

Example

The materials requisitions and issues for job number 3867 for customer OT Ltd at their issue prices are as follows:

1 June	40 kg Material code T73 @ £60 per kg
5 June	60 kg Material code R80 @ £5 per kg
9 June	280 metres Material code B45 @ £8 per metre

Record these on a job cost card for this job which is due to be delivered on 17 June.

Solution

JOB COST CARD									
Job number: 3867					**Customer name: OT Ltd**				
Estimate ref:					Quoted estimate:				
Start date: 1 June					Delivery date: 17 June				
Invoice number:					Invoice amount:				
COSTS:									
Materials					**Labour**				
Date	Code	Qty	Price	£	Date	Grade	Hours	Rate	£
1 June	T73	40 kg	£60	2,400					
5 June	R80	60 kg	£5	300					
9 June	B45	280m	£8	2,240					
				――					
				4,940					
				――					
Expenses					**Production overheads**				
Date	Code	Description		£	Hours		OAR		£
				――					――
				――					――
Cost summary:									
									£
Direct materials									
Direct labour									
Direct expenses									
Production overheads									
Administration overheads									
Selling and distribution overheads									
									――
Total cost									
Invoice price									
									――
Profit/loss									
									――

2.5 DIRECT LABOUR COST

In an earlier chapter dealing with labour costs the system of recording hours worked in a job costing system was considered.

In summary a job card travels with each individual job and the hours worked by each grade of labour are logged onto this card. The card is then sent to the accounts department and the hours are transferred to the job cost card. The relevant hourly labour rate is then applied to each grade of labour to give a cost for each grade and a total cost for the job.

ACTIVITY 1

The labour records show that the hours worked on job 3867 were as follows:

1 June	Grade II	43 hours
2 June	Grade II	12 hours
	Grade IV	15 hours
5 June	Grade I	25 hours
	Grade IV	13 hours
9 June	Grade I	15 hours

The hourly rates for each grade of labour are as follows:

	£
Grade I	4.70
Grade II	5.80
Grade III	6.40
Grade IV	7.50

Record the labour worked on job 3867 on the job cost card.

For a suggested answer, see the 'Answers' section at the end of the book.

2.6 DIRECT EXPENSES

The third category of direct costs are any expenses that can be directly attributed to that particular job. Such expenses will be recorded by the cost accountant when incurred and coded in such a way that it is clear to which job or jobs they relate.

ACTIVITY 2

A specialised piece of machinery has been hired at a cost of £1,200. It is used on job numbers 3859, 3867 and 3874 and has spent approximately the same amount of time being used on each of those jobs. The accounts code for machine hire is 85.

Record any cost relevant to job 3867 on the job cost card.

For a suggested answer, see the 'Answers' section at the end of the book.

2.7 PRODUCTION OVERHEADS

In an earlier chapter the apportionment of overheads to cost units was considered and it was determined that the most common method of allocating overheads to specific cost units was on the basis of either the labour hours worked or machine hours worked on that particular cost unit.

This is exactly the same for jobs and so the production overhead will be absorbed into jobs on the basis of the pre-determined overhead absorption rate.

2.8 OTHER OVERHEADS

In order to arrive at the total cost for a particular job any administration, selling and distribution overheads must also be included in the job's cost. Therefore when the job is completed an appropriate proportion of the total administration, selling and distribution overheads will also be included on the job cost card.

ACTIVITY 3

The production overhead absorption rate for this period is £4 per labour hour. The administration overhead to be charged to job 3867 totals £156 and the selling and distribution overhead for the job is £78.

The job was completed by the due date and the customer was invoiced the agreed price of £7,800 on 17 June (invoice number 26457).

Using this information complete the job cost card for job 3867.

For a suggested answer, see the 'Answers' section at the end of the book.

2.9 ACCOUNTING FOR JOB COSTS

As well as recording the job costs on the job cost card they must also be recorded in the cost ledger accounts. Each job will have its own job ledger account to which the costs incurred are all debited.

In order to keep track of all of the individual job ledger accounts there will also be a job in progress control account. Again all of the costs incurred on a job must also be debited to this control account. The job in progress control account fulfils the same role as the work in progress control account studied in the previous chapter.

The balance on the job in progress control account at the end of each accounting period should be equal to the total of all of the balances on the individual job ledger accounts.

3 BATCH COSTING

The second type of costing system that must be examined is a batch costing system. A batch costing system is likely to be very similar to a job costing system and indeed a batch is in all respects a job.

3.1 BATCH

Definition   A **batch** is a group of identical but separately identifiable products that are all made together.

A batch is for example a group of 100 identical products made in a particular production run.

3.2 BATCH COSTING

Each batch is very similar to a job and in exactly the same way as in job costing the costs of that batch are gathered together on some sort of a batch cost card. These costs will be the materials input into the batch, the labour worked on the batch, any direct expenses of the batch and the batch's share of overheads.

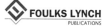

The layout of the batch cost card will be similar to that of a job cost card. This will show the total cost of that particular batch of production.

3.3 COST OF A COST UNIT

Remember that a batch does however differ from a job in that a batch is made up of a number of identical products or cost units. In order to find the cost of each product or cost unit the total cost of the batch must be divided by the number of products in that batch.

Example

Batch number 0692 has the following inputs:

15 June   Material X   20 kg @ £30 per kg

40 hours of grade II labour @ £6.00 per hour

16 June   Material Y   15 kg @ £10 per kg

60 hours of grade III labour at £5.00 per hour

Production overhead is to be absorbed into the cost of each batch on the basis of labour hours at a rate of £0.50 per labour hour.

The number of products produced from batch 0692 was 100.

Calculate the cost of each product from batch 0692.

Solution

Materials cost

	£
Material X 20 kg × £30	600
Material Y 15 kg × £10	150
Labour cost	
Grade II 40 hours × £6	240
Grade III 60 hours × £5	300
Production overhead	
100 hours × £0.50	50
	——
	1,340
	——

Cost per cost unit or product

$$\frac{£1,340}{100 \text{ units}} = £13.40$$

SELF TEST QUESTIONS

		Paragraph
1	What is job costing?	2.1
2	What does a job cost card look like?	2.3
3	How is labour cost included in a job cost card?	2.5
4	How are production overheads dealt with in job costing?	2.7
5	What is batch costing?	3

KEY TERMS

Job – an individual contract or product produced as a single order or product.

Batch – a group of identical but separately identifiable products that are all made together.

Chapter 8

PROCESS COSTING

In Chapter 1 of this textbook we highlighted the various costing methods, one of which was process costing. This chapter explains process costing in much more detail.

CONTENTS

KNOWLEDGE AND UNDERSTANDING

		Reference
1	Costing system appropriate to the organisation: job, batch, unit and process costing systems.	Item 26

LEARNING OUTCOMES

At the end of this chapter you should have learned the following concepts related to process costing:

- The nature and purpose of process costing

- The treatment of normal losses

- The treatment of abnormal losses and abnormal gains

- The equivalent unit

- The variation of work-in-progress using average cost method

- The valuation of finished stock

---

1   FEATURES OF PROCESS COSTING

1.1   INTRODUCTION

Process costing is a method of costing used in so-called process industries including brewing, food processing, quarrying, paints, chemicals and textiles.

The cost per unit of finished output is calculated by dividing the process costs by the number of units. Process costs consist of direct materials, direct labour and production overheads. When processing goes through several successive processes, the output from

---

one process becomes an input direct material cost to the next process. Total costs therefore build up as the output goes through each successive processing stage.

Example

Input to a process is 100 kg of materials. The cost of the direct materials is £200, and the costs of converting these materials into finished output consists of £100 of direct labour and £250 of production overheads. Output from the process was 100 kg of finished product.

The total costs of processing are £550 and the cost per kilogram of output is £5.50 (£550/100 kg).

1.2 PROCESS INDUSTRY MANUFACTURING

Process production has certain features that make it different from other types of manufacturing.

- In some process industries, output is manufactured in batches. In continuous processing, however, manufacturing operations never stop. Materials are continually being added to the process and output is continually produced.

- It is usual to make a distinction in process costing between the cost of the direct materials and the costs of converting these materials into finished output. These 'conversion costs' are the costs of direct labour and absorbed production overhead.

- There could be just one process, and output from the process is ready for external sale to customers. Alternatively, there could be two or more consecutive processes, with output from one process being input to the next process, and finished output only being produced from the final process. For example, suppose there are three consecutive processes, A, B and C. Raw materials might be added to Process A to produce output that is then input to Process B. Further raw materials might be added in Process B, and mixed in with the output from Process A. The output from Process B might then be input to Process C. Output from Process C is the finished product that is sold to customers.

- When processing is continuous, there will be opening stock in process at the start of any period and closing stock in process at the end of the period. A problem is to decide what value to put to part-finished stock in process. Usually, it is necessary to make an estimate of the degree of completion of the closing stock (which is then part-finished opening stock at the start of the next period). For example, it might be estimated or measured that closing stock in a process consists of 100 units of product, which is 100% complete for direct materials but only 50% complete for conversion costs. A value (cost) will then be calculated for the stock.

- There could be losses in process. By this we mean that if 100 kg of direct materials are input to a process, the output quantity could be less than 100 kg. Loss could be a natural part of the production process, occurring because of evaporation or chemical change or natural wastage.

The main problems with process costing are therefore:

- how to treat losses

- how to value stock and finished output when there are opening and closing stocks of work in process.

2 LOSSES

In many processes, some losses in processing are inevitable. When losses occur, the problem arises as to how they should be accounted for.

Suppose that 100 units of materials are input to a process and the processing costs are £720. Losses in the process are 10 units, and so 90 units are output. What is the cost of the output and how should the loss be accounted for?

- One approach would be to say that the cost for each unit is £7.20 (£720/100 units). The cost of the finished goods would therefore be £648 (90 × £7.20) and the cost of the loss would be £72 (10 × £7.20). The loss would be written off as an expense in the profit and loss account.

- Another approach is to say that if losses are a regular and expected aspect of the processing, it is unsatisfactory to make a charge to the profit and loss account for losses every time, knowing that the losses are unavoidable. A more sensible approach is therefore to calculate a cost per unit based on the expected output from the process. In this example, if the expected loss from the process is 90 units, the cost of the finished units would be £8 (£720/90 units). The cost of production would therefore be £720 (90 × £8) and the expected loss, or 'normal loss', has no cost.

This second approach is taken in process costing. The cost per unit of output is calculated after allowing for 'normal loss'. However, a distinction is made between normal loss and unexpected loss or 'abnormal loss'. Abnormal loss is given a cost, which is charged as an expense to the profit and loss account.

Definition	**Normal loss** is the expected amount of loss in a process. It is the level of loss or waste that management would expect to incur under normal operating conditions.
Definition	**Abnormal loss** is the amount by which actual loss exceeds the expected or normal loss in a process. It can also be defined as the amount by which actual production is less than normal production. Normal production is calculated as the quantity of input units of materials less normal loss.

2.1 NORMAL LOSS

Normal loss is not given a cost.

- If units of normal loss have no scrap value, their value or cost is nil.

- If units of normal loss have a scrap value, the value of this loss is its scrap value, which is set off against the cost of the process. In other words, the cost of finished output is reduced by the scrap value of the normal loss.

Example: Normal loss with no scrap value

Input to a process in June consisted of 1,000 units of direct materials costing £4,300. Direct labour costs were £500 and absorbed production overheads were £1,500. Normal loss is 10% of input. Output from the process in the month was 900 units.

Task

Calculate the cost per unit of output, and show how this would be shown in the work in process account in the cost ledger.

Solution

Actual loss = 1,000 – 900 units = 100 units.

Normal loss = 10% of 1,000 = 100 units.

All loss is therefore normal loss.

 **FOULKS LYNCH**
PUBLICATIONS

Total production costs were £6,300 (£4,300 + £500 + £1,500).

$$\text{Cost per unit of expected output} = \frac{£6,300}{900\,\text{units}} = £7\,\text{per unit}$$

Transactions recorded in the process account will be as follows.

Process account

	£		£
Direct materials	4,300	Normal loss	-
Direct labour	500	Finished goods	6,300
Production overhead absorbed	1,500	(900 units x £7)	
	6,300		6,300

Normal loss with a scrap value

When normal loss has a scrap value, the value of this loss is set against the costs of production. In the cost accounts, this is done by means of:

Debit   Normal loss account

Credit   Process account

with the scrap value of the normal loss.

Then:

Debit   Bank (or Debtors)

Credit   Normal loss account

Example

Input to a process in June consisted of 1,000 units of direct materials costing £4,300. Direct labour costs were £500 and absorbed production overheads were £1,500. Normal loss is 10% of input. Loss has a scrap value of £0.90 per unit. Output from the process in the month was 900 units.

Task

Calculate the cost per unit of output, and show how this would be shown in the process account in the cost ledger.

Solution

Actual loss = 1,000 – 900 units = 100 units. Normal loss = 10% of 1,000 = 100 units. All loss is therefore normal loss. The normal loss has a value of £90, and will be sold for this amount.

Production costs are £6,300 (£4,300 + £500 + £1,500) less the scrap value of normal loss, £90. Production costs are therefore £6,210.

$$\text{Cost per unit of expected output} = \frac{£6,210}{900\,\text{units}} = £6.90\,\text{per unit}$$

Transactions recorded in the process account will be as follows.

Process account

	£		£
Direct materials	4,300	Normal loss	90
Direct labour	500	Finished goods	6,210
Production overhead absorbed	1,500	(900 units x £6.90)	
	6,300		6,300

Normal loss account

	£		£
Process account	90	Bank	90

2.2 ABNORMAL LOSS

Unlike normal loss, abnormal loss is given a cost. The cost of a unit of abnormal loss is the same as a cost of one unit of good output from the process. The cost of abnormal loss is treated as a charge against profit in the period it occurs.

The cost per unit of good output and abnormal loss is the cost of production divided by the expected quantity of output.

In the cost accounts, abnormal loss is accounted for in an abnormal loss account. The double entry transactions are:

Debit   Abnormal loss account

Credit   Process account

with the cost of the abnormal loss

Then:

Debit   Profit and loss account

Credit   Abnormal loss account

Example

Input to a process in November was 2,000 units. Normal loss is 5% of input. Costs of production were:

Direct materials	£3,700
Direct labour	£1,300
Production overhead	£2,600

Actual output during November was 1,780 units.

Tasks

Calculate the cost per unit of output.

Record these transactions in the cost accounts.

Solution

Expected output = 2,000 units less normal loss of 5% = 2,000 – 100 = 1,900 units.

Actual output = 1,780 units.

Abnormal loss = 1,900 – 1,780 = 120 units.

Total costs of production = £7,600 (£3,700 + £1,300 + £2,600).

$$\text{Cost per unit of expected output} = \frac{£7,600}{1,900\,\text{units}} = £4\,\text{per unit}$$

Both good output and abnormal loss are valued at this amount

These transactions should be recorded in the cost accounts as follows.

Process account

	£		£
Direct materials	3,700	Normal loss	-
Direct labour	1,300	Abnormal loss (120 x £4)	480
Production overhead	2,600	Finished goods (1,780 x £4)	7,120
	7,600		7,600

Abnormal loss account

	£		£
Process account	480	Profit and loss account	480

ACTIVITY 1

Dunmex produces a product in process A.

The following information relates to the product for week ended 7 January 20X4.

Input 1,900 tonnes, cost £28,804.

Direct labour	£1,050
Process overhead	£1,800

Normal loss is 2% of input.

Output to finished stock was 1,842 tonnes.

Task

Prepare the process A account together with any other relevant accounts.

For a suggested answer, see the 'Answers' section at the end of the book.

Abnormal loss with a scrap value

When loss has a scrap value, normal loss is accounted for in the way already described.

With abnormal loss, the cost per unit of loss is calculated and recorded in the way also described above. The scrap value of the loss, however, is set off against the amount to be written off to the profit and loss account.

This is done by means of:

Credit   Abnormal loss account

Debit   Bank

with the scrap value of the abnormal loss units.

The balance on the abnormal loss account is then written off to the profit and loss account.

3   ABNORMAL GAIN

When actual losses are higher than expected losses, there is abnormal gain. Sometimes, actual losses are less than expected losses.

Definition   **Abnormal gain** is the amount by which actual output from a process exceeds the expected output. It is the amount by which actual loss is lower than expected loss.

Abnormal gain can therefore be thought of as the opposite of abnormal loss.

- Abnormal gain is given a value. The value per unit of abnormal gain is calculated in the same way as a cost per unit of abnormal loss would be calculated. It is the cost of production divided by the expected units of output.

- Abnormal gain is recorded in an abnormal gain account.

- The gain is then taken to the profit and loss account as an item of profit for the period.

- If loss has any scrap value, the profit should be reduced by the amount of income that would have been earned from the sales of scrap had the loss been normal.

In the cost accounts, abnormal gain is recorded as:

Debit   Process account

Credit   Abnormal gain account

with the value of the abnormal gain

If loss has a scrap value

Debit   Normal loss account

Credit   Abnormal gain account

with the scrap value of the abnormal gain. This is income that has not been earned because loss was less than normal.

Then:

Debit   Abnormal gain account

Credit   Profit and loss account

with the balance on the abnormal gain account.

Example

Scarborough Chemical manufacture a range of industrial and agricultural chemicals. One such product is 'Scarchem 3X' which passes through a single process.

The following information relates to the process for week ended 30 January 20X5.

Input 5,000 litres of material at £12 per litre.

Normal losses are agreed as 4% of input.

Direct labour £950, process overhead £1,450.

Output is 4,820 litres. Waste units have a scrap value of £1 per litre.

Task

Prepare the process account for the period together with other relevant accounts.

Solution

Expected output = 5,000 litres less normal loss of 4% = 5,000 – 200 = 4,800 litres.

Actual output = 4,820 litres.

Abnormal gain = 4,820 – 4,800 = 20 units.

	£
Direct materials	60,000
Direct labour	710
Production overhead	2,130
	62,840
Less: scrap value of normal loss (200 x £1)	(200)
Production costs	62,640

$$\text{Cost per unit of expected output} = \frac{£62,640}{4,800 \text{ units}} = £13.05 \text{ per unit}$$

Both good output and abnormal loss are valued at this amount.

Process a/c

	Units	£		Units	£
Direct material	5,000	60,000	Output	4,820	62,901
Direct labour		710	Normal loss	200	200
Process overhead		2,130			
Abnormal gain	20	261			
	5,020	63,101		5,020	63,101

		£
Valuation of output	4,820 litres × £13.05	62,901
Valuation of abnormal gain	20 litres × £13.05	261

Abnormal gain a/c

	Units	£		Units	£
Normal loss (scrap value lost)	20	20	Process a/c	20	261
P/L a/c (balance)		259			
	20	261		20	261

Normal loss a/c

	Units	£		Units	£
Process a/c	200	200	Bank	180	780
			Abnormal gain	20	20
		200			200

Finished stock

	Units	£		Units	£
Process a/c	4,820	62,901			

Because actual loss was only 180 litres, not the normal loss (expected loss) of 200 litres, the amount of cash obtained from selling the scrap was £180. This is provided for by the adjustment between the abnormal gain account and the normal loss account.

4 WORK-IN-PROGRESS

At the end of a period, there could be unfinished production in process. Unfinished work-in-progress needs to be valued so that interim and periodic profit and loss accounts can be prepared.

Unfinished production is valued using the concept of 'equivalent units'. Closing stocks of work in progress are converted to 'equivalent units'. An equivalent unit, as the name might

suggest, means the equivalent of one finished unit of output. If closing stock of 100 units is 50% complete, they will be valued as 50 equivalent units.

In many processes, the direct materials are all input at the start of the process. If so, closing work in progress has all its direct materials, and the units are unfinished only because the processing work has not yet been completed. In these situations, the valuation of output, abnormal losses (or gain) and closing stock is separated into a valuation per unit for direct materials and a valuation per unit of conversion costs (direct labour and production overhead), each based on a different calculation of equivalent units.

Units of finished output and abnormal loss count as one equivalent unit each. Normal loss does not have a cost, and so units of normal loss are nil equivalent units each.

Example 1

The input to Process A was 4,000 litres of material. Output was 3,800 litres and at the end of the period 200 litres were still in progress. There is no loss in process.

Costs are £16,000 for direct materials, £7,920 for direct labour and £11,880 for absorbed production overhead.

An estimate has been made of the degree of completion of the closing stock.

Estimate of degree of completion:

Materials	100%	complete
Labour	80%	complete
Overhead	80%	complete

Task

Calculate the cost per equivalent unit, and write up the process account for the period.

Solution

We start by calculating the equivalent units of production. This is simply the expected units of output, allowing for the unfinished closing stock.

	Total units	Equivalent units	
		Materials	*Labour and overhead*
Finished output	3,800	3,800	3,800
Closing stock in progress	200	200	160
	4,000	4,000	3,960

We can now calculate a cost per equivalent unit, and use these costs to work out the value of finished output and closing work in process.

	Materials	*Labour and overhead*
Cost	£16,000	£19,800
Equivalent units	4,000	3,960
Cost per equivalent unit	£4	£5

		Materials		*Labour and overhead*	*Total*
		£		£	£
Finished output	(3,800 × £4)	15,200	(3,800 × £5)	19,000	34,200
Closing WIP	(200 × £4)	800	(160 × £5)	800	1,600
		16,000		19,800	35,800

The process account would be drawn up as follows:

Process a/c

	Units	£		Units	£
Direct material	4,000	16,000	Output	3,800	34,200
Direct labour		7,920	W-I-P	200	1,600
Process overhead		11,880			
	4,000	35,800		4,000	35,800

Example 2

Bay Paints Ltd manufacture a number of products, one of which is 'Paintthin 3'.

It is produced in a single process.

For week ended 31 January 20X3, the following information was available:

Input	10,000 litres of material
Cost	£7.60 per litre
Direct labour and production overhead	£14,025
Output	8,800
Normal loss	5% of input
Work-in-progress	500 units
Work-in-progress – degree of completion	
Materials	100%
Labour	70%
Overhead	70%

Task

Determine the equivalent units of work-in-progress for each element of cost.

Draw up the process account and any other relevant account

Solution

Expected output = 10,000 units less normal loss of 5% = 10,000 – 500 = 9,500 units.

Actual output = 8,800 units plus 500 units of closing stock = 9,300 units.

Abnormal loss = 9,500 – 9,300 = 200 units.

We now calculate the equivalent units pf production. This is simply the expected units of output, allowing for the unfinished closing stock.

	Total units	Equivalent units	
		Materials	Labour and overhead
Finished output	8,800	8,800	8,800
Normal loss	500	-	-
Abnormal loss	200	200	200
Closing stock in progress	500	500	350
	10,000	9,500	9,350

We can now calculate a cost per equivalent unit, and use these costs to work out the value of finished output and closing work in process.

	Materials	Labour and overhead
Cost	£76,000	£14,025
Equivalent units	9,500	9,350
Cost per equivalent unit	£8	£1.5

		Materials		Labour and overhead	Total
		£		£	£
Finished output	(8,800 x £8)	70,400	(8,800 x £1.5)	13,200	83,600
Normal loss		-		-	0
Abnormal loss	(200 x £8)	1,600	(200 x £1.5)	300	1,900
Closing WIP	(500 x £8)	4,000	(350 x £1.5)	525	4,525
		76,000		14,025	90,025

The process account would be drawn up as follows:

Process a/c

	Units	£		Units	£
Direct material	10,000	76,000	Output	8,800	83,600
Direct labour/			Abnormal loss	200	1,900
Process overhead		14,025	Closing WIP	500	4,525
	10,000	90,025		10,000	90,025

Abnormal loss a/c

	Units	£		Units	£
Process a/c	200	1,900	Profit and loss a/c	200	1,900

ACTIVITY 2

Input to Process Y in June was 5,000 units of direct materials from Process X, costing £27,500 and added materials costing £2,080. Direct labour costs in process Y were £4,000 and production overhead was £8,000. Output from the process was 4,000 units. There were 1,000 units of closing stock, 100% complete for materials from process X and 40% complete for added materials conversion costs (labour and overhead). There is no loss in process.

Added materials are of insignificant volume and are not measured in units.

Task

Calculate a cost per equivalent unit for the month and draw up the Process Y account.

For a suggested answer, see the 'Answers' section at the end of the book.

SELF TEST QUESTIONS

		Paragraph
1	Name four industries where process costing would be used.	1.1
2	Define the term normal loss.	2.1
3	Define the term abnormal loss.	2.2
4	Define the term abnormal gain.	3
5	Work-in-progress valuation is based on which concept?	4

KEY TERMS

Normal loss – expected amounts of loss in a process. It is the level of loss or waste that management would expect to incur under normal operating conditions.

Abnormal loss – the amount by which actual loss exceeds the expected or normal loss in a process. It can also be defined as the amount by which actual production is less than normal production. Normal production is calculated as the quantity of input units of materials less normal loss.

Abnormal gain – the amount by which actual output from a process exceeds the expected output. It is the amount by which actual loss is lower than expected loss.

Chapter 9

MARGINAL COSTING

This chapter compares marginal costing and absorption costing.

CONTENTS

1   Marginal costing and absorption costing

2   The two costing methods: costing and reporting

KNOWLEDGE AND UNDERSTANDING

		Reference
1	Maintaining an appropriate cost accounting system	Item 3
2	Marginal –v– absorption costing for costing and reporting purposes	Item 9
3	Marginal costing	Item 22

LEARNING OUTCOMES

At the end of this chapter you will have learned the following concepts related to marginal costing

- The concept of contribution

- Use of marginal cost as the basis of a product cost

- Use of marginal costing as a basis of reporting

- The comparison of marginal costing with absorption costing

---

1 MARGINAL COSTING AND ABSORPTION COSTING

1.1 AN ALTERNATIVE TO ABSORPTION COSTING

In **absorption costing**, the cost of production is recorded as the direct costs (direct materials, direct labour and, if there are any, direct expenses) plus absorbed production overheads.

- Gross profit, before deducting administration costs and selling and distribution costs, is measured as total sales revenue less the fully-absorbed production cost of sales, adjusted for any under- or over-absorbed overhead in the period.

- Closing stocks of work in progress and finished goods are valued at full production cost, including an amount of production overhead cost.

Marginal costing is an alternative costing system, that could be used instead of absorption costing. Marginal costing is based on the following concepts.

- Fixed cost expenditure should be the same during a period, regardless of the volume of production and sales. Variable costs are the only expenditures that change with the volume of output and sales.

- It would therefore be more informative to monitor profits by looking first at sales and variable costs, because these are the values that rise or fall with the volume of activity.

- Profitability should be measured by first taking the difference between sales revenue and the variable cost of sales. Sales minus variable costs is called contribution. (Contribution means contribution towards covering fixed costs and making a profit.)

- Fixed costs should be treated as a period charge, and charged against profits in the period they are incurred. Contribution minus fixed costs incurred equals profit for the period.

- Closing stocks of work in progress and finished goods should be valued at their variable production cost, not at full production cost.

Marginal costing is not in widespread use as a costing system for the cost accounts. However, marginal costing is a very important costing method because it can be used to assess profitability. For example, it is commonly used for forecasting profits and for providing information to management to help with decision-making.

Definition	**Marginal costing** is an accounting system in which fixed costs are not absorbed into product costs. Stocks are valued at marginal production cost. Fixed costs are treated as a period charge and written off against profit in the period in which they are incurred.
Definition	**Contribution** is the difference between sales revenue and the variable cost of sales. In marginal costing, contribution minus fixed costs equals profit for the period.

The concept of contribution is crucially important in marginal costing. It can be expressed as total contribution for the business as a whole or as a contribution for a single unit of product or service.

1.2 ABSORPTION COSTING AND MARGINAL COSTING COMPARED: NO STOCK LEVEL CHANGES

When a business has no opening stocks or closing stocks of work-in-progress and finished goods, the profit measured by absorption costing and marginal costing will be the same. However, the measurement of profit is presented differently.

Example

In March 20X4, a business had no opening or closing stocks. It manufactured and sold 5,000 units of product.

Sales price per unit	£15
Direct materials costs (£4 per unit)	£20,000
Direct labour costs (£3 per unit)	£15,000
Variable production costs (£1 per unit)	£5,000
Fixed production costs incurred	£12,000
Administration and selling costs	£8,000

Budgeted production was 4,800 units. Budgeted variable production overheads were £1 per unit and budgeted fixed overheads were £14,400.

Task

Prepare operating statements for the period under absorption costing and marginal costing principles.

Solution

The fixed production overhead absorption rate is £14,400/4,800 units = £3 per unit. Since budgeted and actual variable overheads per unit are the same, there is no under- or over-absorbed variable overhead.

Absorption costing

	£	£
Sales (5,000 units)		75,000
Less Production cost of sales:		
Direct material	20,000	
Direct labour	15,000	
Variable overhead	5,000	
Fixed overhead absorbed (at £3)	15,000	
		55,000
		20,000
Fixed overhead absorbed	15,000	
Fixed overhead incurred	12,000	
Over-absorbed overhead		3,000
		23,000
Administration and selling costs		8,000
Profit for the period		£15,000

Marginal costing

	£	£
Sales (5,000 units)		75,000
Less variable costs:		
Direct materials	20,000	
Direct labour	15,000	
Variable overhead	5,000	
		40,000
Contribution		35,000
Fixed costs		
Fixed production costs	12,000	
Administration and selling costs	8,000	
		20,000
Profit for the period		£15,000

ACTIVITY 1

A company makes two products, A and B. Cost data for September are as follows.

	Product A	Product B
Sales (units)	3,000	5,000
Selling price per unit	£40	£30
Variable costs per unit		
Direct materials	£6	£4
Direct labour	£8	£6
Variable production overhead	£2	£1.50
Variable selling costs	£3	£2.50

Fixed production costs are £50,000 for the month, administration costs (all fixed) are £18,000 and fixed selling costs are £35,000.

There is no opening stock and no closing stock of either product.

Task

Use marginal costing to establish the profit or loss in September.

For a suggested answer, see the 'Answers' section at the end of the book.

1.3 ABSORPTION COSTING AND MARGINAL COSTING COMPARED: STOCK LEVEL CHANGES

When a business has opening and closing stocks, and there is an increase or decrease in stock levels during a period, the profit reported by marginal costing will be different from the profit reported by absorption costing.

This is because in absorption costing:

- Some of the fixed production costs incurred in a period are carried forward in the closing stock value to the next period, and are not charged against profits in the current period.

- Opening stocks brought forward include an amount for fixed overheads that were incurred in the previous period.

In contrast, with marginal costing fixed overheads are charged in full against profits in the period they are incurred, and there are no fixed costs in opening or closing stock values.

Reported profits differ between absorption costing and marginal costing because the cost of sales equals opening stocks plus costs incurred minus closing stocks. If stock values differ, the cost of sales will differ and so too will profit.

This difference between marginal costing and absorption costing is simply one of timing. In the long run, reported profits will be the same. In the short-term, however, reported profits depend on which period the fixed overheads are charged as a cost of sale.

Example

Company XY produces a single product 'XY1'

	£
Selling price per unit	15
Direct materials per unit	4
Direct labour per unit	3
Variable overhead per unit	2
Fixed overhead incurred	£12,000 per month

Budgeted production and sales were 5,000 units.

Actual production was 4,800 units, but sales were just 4,700 units.

Task

Assuming that the sales price and variable costs per unit were as budgeted, and that fixed overhead expenditure was the same as budgeted, show the amount of profit that would be reported using:

- absorption costing and

- marginal costing.

Solution

Absorption costing

In an absorption costing system, the absorption rate per unit for fixed overhead is £12,000/5,000 units = £2.40 per unit.

Actual variable overhead costs were the same as budget. The only under- or over-absorbed overhead therefore relates to fixed overheads.

	£	£
Sales (4,700 units at £15)		70,500
Production costs (4,800 units)		
Direct material (£4)	19,200	
Direct labour (£3)	14,400	
Variable overhead (£2)	9,600	
Fixed overhead absorbed (at £2.40)	11,520	
	54,720	
Closing stock: 100 units at £11.40	(1,140)	
Production cost of sales		53,580
		16,920
Fixed production overhead absorbed	11,520	
Fixed production overhead incurred	12,000	
Under-absorbed fixed overhead		(480)
Profit for the period		£16,440

Marginal costing

	£
Sales (4,700 units at £15))	70,500
Variable costs of production (4,800 units)	
Direct materials (£4)	19,200
Direct labour (£3)	14,400
Variable production overhead (£2)	9,600
	43,200

Closing stock: 100 units at £9	(900)
Variable production cost of sales	42,300
Contribution	28,200
Fixed production costs incurred	12,000
Profit for the period	£16,200

The difference in profit between the two costing methods is £240 (£16,440 - £16,200). There was no opening stock, so the difference in profit is attributable to the different valuations of closing stocks. In absorption costing, the closing stock of 100 units includes £240 of fixed overheads, which are therefore carried forward as a cost of sale in the next period.

The only difference in the two statements is the treatment of fixed costs, in the marginal costing approach the fixed costs are written off against the contribution for the period, whereas in absorption costing they are part of total cost of sales.

ACTIVITY 2

Loftus Ltd produces a single produce 'L123'.

Its planned production is 20,000 per quarter.

Selling price per unit	£20
Direct materials per unit	£4
Direct labour per unit	£3
Variable overhead per unit	£2

Its output for the quarter ended 31 March was 22,000 and sales were 19,800 units.

Budgeted and actual fixed production costs were £30,000 and other unit costs were as planned.

Budgeted and actual administration and selling costs, all fixed, were £100,000.

Task

Prepare operating statements for the quarter under:

- absorption costing
- marginal costing.

Explain the difference between the two reported profit figures.

For a suggested answer, see the 'Answers' section at the end of the book.

2 THE TWO COSTING METHODS: COSTING AND REPORTING

Absorption costing and marginal costing are alternative methods of costing. We have seen that the reported profit is different between the two methods, whenever there are opening and closing stocks and changes in stock levels during a period.

So which costing method is better?

The answer is that the more appropriate costing method to use depends on what the figures are used for.

- When we want to report the profits that have been made in a period that has ended, it might be appropriate to value stocks in the same way that they are valued for the purpose of financial reporting and financial accounting. In financial reporting, stocks are valued at the lower of cost and net realisable value. This is usually at cost. 'Cost' should include an amount of production overhead, including fixed overhead. Absorption costing might therefore be more suitable for the purpose of reporting historic profits.

- When we want to make estimates for the future, and predict what profits the business should make, it is much better to use marginal costing. If fixed costs are treated as a period cost, estimates of profit can be made by working out the expected contribution and then deducting fixed costs.

The concept of contribution is extremely important for forecasting and estimating, and as a technique for providing information to management, marginal costing is much superior to absorption costing.

Applications of marginal costing will be explained in the next chapter.

SELF TEST QUESTIONS

		Paragraph
1	Define marginal costing.	1.1
2	Define contribution.	1.1
3	When reporting in marginal costing format, stocks are valued on what basis?	1.1
4	When using marginal costing, fixed costs are treated as what type of cost?	1.1
5	When reporting profits with both marginal and absorption costing, what is the cause of the differences in reported in profits between the two methods?	1.3

KEY TERMS

Marginal costing – an accounting system in which fixed costs are not absorbed into product costs. Stocks are valued at marginal production cost. Fixed costs are treated as a period charge and written off against profit in the period in which they are incurred.

Contribution – the difference between sales revenue and the variable cost of sales. In marginal costing, contribution minus fixed costs equals profit for the period.

 **FOULKS LYNCH**
PUBLICATIONS

Chapter 10

CVP ANALYSIS, BREAK-EVEN ANALYSIS AND LIMITING FACTORS

This chapter focuses on techniques used in short-term decision-making.

CONTENTS

1   CVP analysis

2   Uses of CVP analysis

3   Contribution/sales ratio (C/S ratio)

4   Break-even charts

5   CVP analysis and cost behaviour analysis

6   Limiting factors

KNOWLEDGE AND UNDERSTANDING

		Reference
1	The nature and purpose of internal reporting	Item 1
2	Management information requirements	Item 2
3	The identification of fixed, variable and semi-variable costs and their use in … cost reporting and cost analysis	Item 15
4	Cost-volume-profit analysis	Item 16
5	The identification of limiting factors	Item 17
6	Marginal costing	Item 22
7	Cost behaviour	Item 24

PERFORMANCE CRITERIA

		Reference
1	Identify information relevant to estimating current and future revenues and costs	A (element 6.3)
2	Prepare estimates of future income and costs	B (element 6.3)
3	Calculate the effects of variations in capacity on product costs	C (element 6.3)
4	Analyse critical factors affecting costs and revenues using appropriate accounting techniques and draw clear conclusions from the analysis	D (element 6.3)

5	State any assumptions used when evaluating future costs and revenues	E (element 6.3)
6	Identify and evaluate options and solutions for their contribution to organisational goals	F (element 6.3)
7	Present recommendations to appropriate people in a clear and concise way and supported by clear rationale	G (element 6.3)

LEARNING OUTCOMES

At the end of this chapter you will have learned the following:

- Cost-volume-profit analysis and its uses, including break-even analysis and target profit analysis

- Measuring the margin of safety and explaining its significance

- Measuring the contribution/sales or profit-volume ratio, and its uses

- Using marginal costing as a basis for reporting to management

- The meaning of limiting factors, how to identify them and how to establish a profit-maximising plan of action when a limiting factor exists

1   CVP ANALYSIS

1.1   COSTS, VOLUMES AND PROFIT

Cost-volume-profit (CVP) analysis is a technique for analysing how costs and profits change with the volume of production and sales. It s also called breakeven analysis.

CVP analysis assumes that selling prices and variable costs are constant per unit at all volumes of sales, and that fixed costs remain fixed at all levels of activity.

1.2   UNIT COSTS AND VOLUME

As a business produces and sells more output during a period, its profits will increase. This is partly because sales revenue rises as sales volume goes up. It is also partly because unit costs fall. As the volume of production and sales go up, the fixed cost per unit falls since the same amount of fixed costs are shared between a larger number of units.

Example

A business makes and sells a single product. Its variable cost is £6 and it sells for £11 per unit. Fixed costs are £40,000 each month.

We can measure the unit cost and the unit profit at different volumes of output and sales. The table below shows total costs, revenue and profit, and unit costs, revenue and profit, at several levels of sales.

	10,000 units	15,000 units	20,000 units
	£	£	£
Variable costs	60,000	90,000	120,000
Fixed costs	40,000	40,000	40,000
Total costs	100,000	130,000	160,000
Sales revenue	110,000	165,000	220,000
Profit	10,000	35,000	60,000
	10,000 units	15,000 units	20,000 units

	£ per unit	£ per unit	£ per unit
Variable costs	6.0	6.00	6.0
Fixed costs	4.0	2.67	2.0
Total costs	10.0	8.67	8.0
Sales revenue	11.0	11.00	11.0
Profit	1.0	2.33	3.0

As the sales volume goes up, the cost per unit falls and the profit per unit rises. This is because the fixed cost per unit falls as volume increases. In contrast to unit variable costs and the selling price per unit are constant at all volumes of sales.

To analyse how profits and costs will change as the volume of sales changes, we can adopt a marginal costing approach. This is to calculate the total contribution at each volume of sales, then deduct fixed costs to obtain the profit figure.

	10,000 units		15,000 units		20,000 units	
	£	£ per unit	£	£ per unit	£	£ per unit
Sales revenue	110,000	11.0	165,000	11.0	220,000	11.0
Variable costs	60,000	6.0	90,000	6.0	120,000	6.0
Contribution	50,000	5.0	75,000	5.0	100,000	5.0
Fixed costs	40,000		40,000		40,000	
Profit	10,000		35,000		60,000	

1.3 THE IMPORTANCE OF CONTRIBUTION IN CVP ANALYSIS

Contribution is a key factor in CVP analysis, because if we assume a constant variable cost per unit and the same selling price at all volumes of output, the contribution per unit is a constant value (and the contribution per £1 of sales is also a constant value).

Definition	**Unit contribution** = Selling price per unit – variable costs per unit.

Definition	**Total contribution**
	= Volume of sales in units × (Unit contribution), or
	= Total sales revenue × Contribution/Sales ratio

Definition	**Contribution/Sales ratio or C/S ratio**
	= Contribution per unit/Sales price per unit, or
	= Total contribution/Total sales revenue

2 USES OF CVP ANALYSIS

CVP analysis is used widely in preparing financial reports for management. It is a simple technique that can be used to estimate profits and make decisions about the best course of action to take. Applications of CVP analysis include:

- Estimating future profits

- Calculating the break-even point for sales

- Analysing the margin of safety in the budget

- Calculating the volume of sales required to achieve a target profit

- Deciding on a selling price for a product.

2.1 ESTIMATING FUTURE PROFITS

CVP analysis can be used to estimate future profits.

Example

ZC Limited makes and sells a single product. Its budgeted sales for the next year are 40,000 units

The product sells for £18.

Variable costs of production and sales are:

	£
	£
Direct materials	2.40
Direct labour	5.00
Variable production overhead	0.50
Variable selling overhead	1.25

Fixed expenses are estimated for the year as:

	£
Fixed production overhead	80,000
Administration costs	60,000
Fixed selling costs	90,000
	230,000

Task

Calculate the expected profit for the year.

Solution

Variable cost per unit = £(2.40 + 5.00 + 0.50 + 1.25) = £9.15

Unit contribution = Sales price – Unit variable cost = £18 - £9.15 = £8.85.

	£
Budgeted contribution (40,000 units x £8.85)	354,000
Budgeted fixed costs	230,000
Expected profit	124,000

2.2 BREAK-EVEN ANALYSIS

Break-even is the volume of sales at which the business just 'breaks even', so that it makes neither a loss nor a profit. At break-even point, total costs equal total revenue. Calculating the break-even point can be useful for management because it shows what the minimum volume of sales must be to avoid making a loss in the period.

At break-even point, total contribution is just about large enough to cover fixed costs. In other words, at breakeven point:

Total contribution = Fixed costs

The breakeven point in units of sale can therefore be calculated as:

$$\text{Break-even point in units of sale} = \frac{\text{Fixed costs}}{\text{Contribution per unit}}$$

Example

A business makes and sells a single product, which sells for £15 per unit and which has a unit variable cost of £7. Fixed costs are expected to be £500,000 for the next year.

Tasks

1   What is the breakeven point in sales?

2   What would be the breakeven point if fixed costs went up to £540,000?

3   What would be the breakeven point if fixed costs were £500,000 but unit variable costs went up to £9?

Solution

Task 1 : Unit variable cost = £15 - £7 = £8. Fixed costs = £500,000.

Break-even point = $\dfrac{£500,000}{£8 \text{ per unit}}$ = 62,500 units

Task 2 : Unit variable cost = £8. Fixed costs = £540,000.

Break-even point = $\dfrac{£540,000}{£8 \text{ per unit}}$ = 67,500 units

Task 3: Unit variable cost = £15 - £9 = £6. Fixed costs = £500,000.

Break-even point = $\dfrac{£500,000}{£6 \text{ per unit}}$ = 83,333 units

ACTIVITY 1

Fylindales Fabrication produce hinges. The selling price per unit is £30, raw materials and other direct costs are £10 per unit and period fixed costs are £5,000.

Task

Calculate how many hinges must be sold to break-even in a budget period.

This activity covers performance criteria A and B in element 6.3.

For a suggested answer, see the 'Answers' section at the end of the book.

2.3   MARGIN OF SAFETY

Actual sales volume will not be the same as budgeted sales volume. Actual sales will probably either fall short of budget or exceed budget. A useful analysis of business risk is to look at what might happen to profit if actual sales volume is less than budgeted.

The difference between the budgeted sales volume and the break-even sales volume is known as the **margin of safety**. It is simply a measurement of how far sales can fall short of budget before the business makes a loss. A large margin of safety indicates a low risk of making a loss, whereas a small margin of safety might indicate a fairly high risk of a loss. It therefore indicates the vulnerability of a business to a fall in demand.

It is usually expressed as a percentage of budgeted sales.

Example

Budgeted sales	:	80,000 units
Selling price	:	£8
Variable costs	:	£4 per unit
Fixed costs	:	£200,000 pa

$$\text{Break even volume} = \frac{200,000}{8 - 4}$$

$$= 50,000 \text{ units}$$

Margin of safety $= (80,000 - 50,000)$ units

$= 30,000$ units or 37½% of budget.

The margin of safety may also be expressed as a percentage of actual sales or of maximum capacity.

In this example, the margin of safety seems quite large, because actual sales would have to be almost 40% less than budget before the business made a loss.

ACTIVITY 2

Your company makes and sells a single product, which has a selling price of £24 per unit. The unit variable cost of sales is £18. Budgeted sales for the year are 140,000 units. Budgeted fixed costs for the year are £800,000.

Tasks

1 Calculate the breakeven point.

2 Calculate the margin of safety, as a percentage of budgeted sales

3 Prepare a memo for your manager, explaining the margin of safety. In your memo, suggests what this indicates about business risk and give a suggestion about how the margin of safety might be improved.

This activity covers performance criteria A – G in element 6.3.

For a suggested answer, see the 'Answers' section at the end of the book.

2.4 TARGET PROFIT

CVP analysis can also be used to calculate the volume of sales that would be required to achieve a target level of profit. To achieve a target profit, the business will have to earn enough contribution to cover all its fixed costs and then make the required amount of profit.

Target contribution = Fixed costs + Target profit

Example

Northcliffe Engineering Ltd has capital employed of £1million. Its target return on capital employed is 20% per annum.

Northcliffe manufactures a standard product 'N1'

Selling price of 'N1' = £60 unit

Variable costs per unit = £20

Annual fixed costs = £100,000

Task

What volume of sales is required to achieve the target profit?

Solution

The target profit is 20% of £1 million = £200,000.

	£
Target profit	200,000
Fixed costs	100,000
	———
Target contribution	300,000
	———

Target sales volume

$$= \frac{\text{Target contribution}}{\text{Contribution per unit}}$$

$$= \frac{£300,000}{£40}$$

$$= \textbf{7,500 units}$$

Proof:

Sales volume	7,500 units
	£
Sales	450,000
Less: Variable costs	150,000
	———
Contribution	300,000
Fixed costs	100,000
	———
Profit	200,000
	———

ACTIVITY 3

Druid Limited makes and sells a single product, product W, which has a variable production cost of £10 per unit and a variable selling cost of £4. It sells for £25. Annual fixed production costs are £350,000, annual administration costs are £110,000 and annual fixed selling costs are £240,000.

Task

Calculate the volume of sales required to achieve an annual profit of £400,000.

This activity covers performance criteria A, B and F in element 6.3.

For a suggested answer, see the 'Answers' section at the end of the book.

2.5 DECIDING ON A SELLING PRICE

CVP analysis can be useful in helping management to compare different courses of action and select the option that will earn the biggest profit. For example, management might be considering two or more different selling prices for a product, and want to select the profit-maximising price.

The profit-maximising price is the contribution-maximising price.

Example

A company has developed a new product which has a variable cost of £12. Fixed costs relating to this product are £48,000 each month. Management are trying to decide what the selling price for the product should be. A market research report has suggested that monthly sales demand for the product will depend on the selling price chosen, as follows.

Sales price	£16	£17	£18
Expected monthly sales demand	17,000 units	14,500 units	11,500 units

Task

Identify the selling price at which the expected profit will be maximised.

Solution

	£	£	£
Sales price	16	17	18
Variable cost	12	12	12
Unit contribution	4	5	6
Expected monthly sales demand	17,000	14,500	11,500
	£	£	£
Monthly contribution	68,000	72,500	69,000
Monthly fixed costs	48,000	48,000	48,000
Monthly profit	20,000	24,500	21,000

ACTIVITY 4

Your company is about to launch a new product, ZG, which has a unit variable cost of £8. Management are trying to decide whether to sell the product at £11 per unit or at £12 per unit. At a price of £11, annual sales demand is expected to be 200,000 units. At a price of £12, annual sales demand is expected to be 160,000 units.

Annual fixed costs relating to the product will be £550,000.

Task

Write a memo to your manager indicating which of the two prices will maximise expected profit and commenting on the business risk associated with actual sales turning out less than budgeted.

This activity covers performance criteria A, B, F and G in element 6.3.

For a suggested solution, see the 'Answers' section at the end of the book.

FOULKS LYNCH
PUBLICATIONS

3 CONTRIBUTION TO SALES RATIO (C/S RATIO)

In all the examples shown so far to illustrate CVP analysis, the business has sold just one product. In reality, businesses usually make and sell a range of products. CVP is still a powerful tool for forecasting and analysis, even when a business makes and sells a range of products.

This is because CVP analysis can be carried out using the contribution/sales ratio as well as a contribution per unit. However, an important assumption is that regardless of how many products a business makes and sells, the ratio of its contribution to sales will be constant.

The contribution/sales ratio or C/S ratio is:

$$\text{Contribution to sales ratio (C/S ratio)} = \frac{\text{Contribution in £}}{\text{Sales in £}}$$

The C/S ratio is usually stated as a percentage.

Note: You may encounter the term profit to volume (or P/V) ratio, which is synonymous with the contribution to sales ratio. Profit to volume is an inaccurate description, however, and should not be used.

3.1 ESTIMATING THE BUDGETED PROFIT

The C/S ratio can be used to estimate the budgeted profit for a period, given estimates for sales revenue and fixed costs.

Example

A business sells a range of products, and has estimated that the average C/S ratio on its sales is 40%. Annual fixed costs are expected to be £350,000. Budgeted sales are £1,050,000.

The budgeted profit is:

	£
Budgeted contribution (40% x £1,050,000)	420,000
Budgeted fixed costs	350,000
Budgeted profit	70,000

3.2 CALCULATING THE BREAKEVEN POINT AND MARGIN OF SAFETY

The C/S ratio can be used to calculate the breakeven point, *expressed in terms of sales revenue*.

At the breakeven point, total contribution = fixed costs, and the breakeven point in sales revenue is:

$$\frac{\text{Fixed costs}}{\text{C/S ratio}}$$

Example

A retail store incurs fixed costs of £60,000 each month. It sells its goods at a gross profit of 50% of purchase cost. The purchase cost of goods are its only variable costs.

Tasks

1　Calculate the break-even volume of sales each month

 **FOULKS LYNCH**
PUBLICATIONS

2   If budgeted monthly sales are £, calculate the margin of safety.

Solution

	%
Purchase cost (variable costs)	100
Gross profit	<u>50</u>
Sales price	<u>150</u>
C/S ratio = 50/150	33.33%

$$\text{Breakeven point} = \frac{£60,000}{0.3333}$$

$$= £180,000 \text{ per month}$$

If budgeted sales are £200,000 per month, the margin of safety is (£200,000 - £180,000) = £20,000. This is 10% of budgeted sales.

3.3   CALCULATING THE SALES REQUIRED TO ACHIEVE A TARGET PROFIT

The C/S ratio can also be used to calculate the volume of sales required to reach a target amount of profit.

Target contribution = Fixed costs + Target profit

$$\text{Sales required to achieve the target profit (in £ sales revenue)} = \frac{\text{Target contribution}}{\text{C/S ratio}}$$

Example

A company makes and sells two products, X and Y. Its budget for next year is as follows.

	Product X	Product Y	Total
Sales (units)	4,000	8,000	
	£	£	£
Sales revenue	45,000	96,000	141,000
Variable costs	<u>15,000</u>	<u>41,000</u>	<u>56,000</u>
	<u>30,000</u>	<u>55,000</u>	85,000
Fixed costs			<u>60,000</u>
Budgeted profit			<u>25,000</u>

Management are dissatisfied with this budget, and want to know what amount of sales would be required to achieve a minimum annual profit of £40,000, assuming that there is no change in selling prices and that the two products are sold in the budgeted proportions.

Solution

C/S ratio = 85,000/141,000 = 0.602837 or 60.2837%.

Target contribution = fixed costs + target profit = £60,000 + £40,000 = £100,000.

$$\text{Sales required to achieve target profit} = \frac{£100,000}{0.602837}$$

$$= £165,882 \text{ or nearly } £166,000$$

ACTIVITY 5

Fylindales Fabrication has the following budget for period 1.

	Hinges	Shutter handles	Door handles	Total
Sales units	1,000	400	600	2,000
	£	£	£	£
Sales value	30,000	2,400	3,000	35,400
Variable costs	20,000	1,300	1,700	23,000
Contribution	10,000	1,100	1,300	12,400
Fixed costs				5,000
Profit				7,400

Tasks

1   Calculate the breakeven point in sales revenue. State the assumptions on which your estimates are based.

2   Calculate the volume of sales that would be required to achieve a profit of £10,000 in period 1.

This activity covers performance criteria B, D and E in element 6.3.

For a suggested answer, see the 'Answers' section at the end of the book.

3.4   MARGIN OF SAFETY, THE C/S RATIO AND THE PROFIT/SALES RATIO

It is useful note the relationship between the margin of safety when expressed as a percentage of actual sales and the C/S ratio and the profit to sales (P/S) ratio.

P/S ratio = Margin of safety × C/S ratio.

Example

	£
Sales	10,000
Variable costs	6,000
	4,000
Fixed costs	2,500
	1,500

(a)   Profit/sales ratio $= \dfrac{1,500}{10,000}$

    = 15%

(b)   C/S ratio $= \dfrac{4,000}{10,000}$

                            $=$ 40%

(c)   Break-even sales $= \dfrac{2,500}{0.4}$

                            $=$ £6,250

     Excess sales $=$ 3,750

     Margin of safety $= \dfrac{3,750}{10,000}$

                            $=$ 37.5%

     ∴ Profit/sales ratio $=$ 37.5% × 40%

                            $=$ 15%

4   BREAK-EVEN CHARTS

4.1   THE CONVENTIONAL BREAK-EVEN CHART

CVP analysis can be presented in the form of a diagram or graph, as well as in figures. A graphical presentation of CVP analysis can be made in either:

- a conventional break-even chart, or

- a profit-volume chart.

The conventional break-even chart plots total costs and total revenues at different output levels:

1   The y axis represents revenue, costs and profit or loss.

2   The x axis represents the volume of sales, either in units of sale or in sales revenue.

3   A line is drawn on the graph for sales revenue. This is £0 when sales volume is zero. It rises in a straight line. To draw the revenue line, you therefore need to plot one more point on the graph and join this to the origin of the graph (x = 0, y = 0). For example, if a product has a sales price of £5, you might plot the point x = 100 units, y = £500 on the graph and join this to the origin.

4   A line is drawn for fixed costs. This runs parallel to the x axis and cuts the y axis at the amount of fixed costs.

5   A line is then drawn for total costs. To do this, we must add variable costs to fixed costs. When sales volume is zero, variable costs are £0, so total costs = fixed costs. To draw the total cost line, you therefore need to plot one more point on the graph and join this to the fixed costs at zero sales volume (x = 0, y = fixed costs). For example, if a product has a variable cost of £2, and fixed costs are £250 you might plot the point x = 100 units, y = £450 on the graph (variable costs of £200 plus fixed costs of £250) and join this to the fixed costs at zero sales volume (x = 0, y = fixed costs).

You should learn how to draw a conventional breakeven chart. Look at the chart below and see whether you could draw one yourself. You might like to use hypothetical figures. For example, suppose fixed costs were £40,000, the unit selling price is £10 and the unit variable cost is £6: can you draw a breakeven chart from this data?

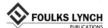

Conventional break-even chart

Cost and revenue in £

Sales revenue

Total costs

Variable costs

Fixed costs

Margin of safety

Break-even point

Budgeted or actual sales

Output (units)

The chart is normally drawn up to the budgeted sales volume.

Breakeven point is where total revenues and total costs are the same. At sales volumes below this point there will be a loss. At sales volumes above break-even there will be a profit. The amount of profit or loss at any given output can be read off the chart, as the difference between the total revenue and total cost lines.

The margin of safety can also be shown on the chart, as the difference between the budgeted sales volume and break-even sales volume.

4.2 USEFULNESS OF BREAK-EVEN CHARTS

There are variations of the conventional breakeven chart, but all breakeven charts illustrate the main relationships of costs, volume and profit. Unclear or complex charts should, however, be avoided.

Generally, break-even charts are most useful to:

- Compare the profitability of products

- Compare profitability in different time periods

- Compare actual revenues, cost and profit with the budgeted revenues costs and profits

- Show the effect of changes in circumstances or to plans

- Give a broad picture of events

Often, the same breakeven chart will show revenues, costs and profit for different products, or different time periods or for actual and budget. These charts should be kept clear, perhaps by using different colours for lines on the chart.

Example

A company has prepared the following budget.

	£
Total sales	35,400
Variable costs	23,000
Contribution	12400
Fixed costs	5,000
Profit	7,400

Task

Construct a breakeven chart from this data and identify the breakeven point on the chart.

Solution

1   As we are not given sales in units, the x axis should represent sales revenue in £.

2   To draw the revenue line, join the points x = 0, y = 0 to x = 35,400, y = 35,400.

3   To show fixed costs, draw a line parallel to the x axis at y = £5,000.

4   To show total costs, join the points x = 0, y = 5,000 to x = 35,400, y = 28,000 (variable costs of 23,000 plus fixed costs of 5,000).

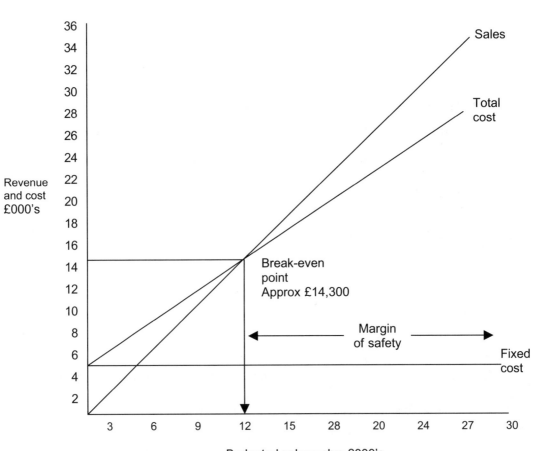

Budgeted sales value £000's

Or units of output (if one product only)

The break-even point is at a level of sales of about £14,300.

The margin of safety is:

$$\frac{(35,400 - 14,300)}{35,400} \times 100\% = 59.6\%$$

4.3   PROFIT-VOLUME CHART

Break-even charts usually show both costs and revenues over a given range of activity but it is not easy to identify exactly what the loss or profit is at each volume of

sales. A chart that simply shows the net profit and loss at any given level of activity is called a **profit-volume graph**.

Given the assumptions of constant selling prices and variable unit costs at all volumes of output, the profit-volume chart shows the line for profit or loss as a straight line.

Profit volume graph

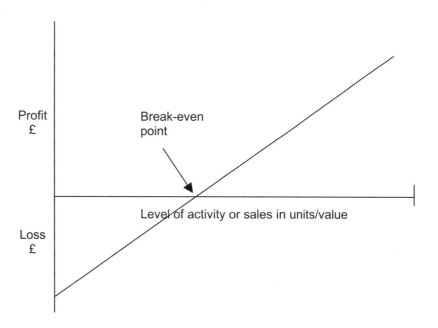

The x axis represents sales volume, in units or £.

The y axis represents loss or profit. The x axis cuts the y axis at breakeven point (profit = 0). Losses are plotted below the line and profits above the line.

To draw the chart, only two points need to be plotted on the graph. These can be:

- profit at planned or budgeted sales volume and

- loss at zero sales volume, which is equal to total fixed costs.

Example

Shireoaks Feeds Ltd manufacture a single product 'Shirefeed', an animal food stuff.

The budget for the quarter ended 31 March 20X5 showed:

Production and sales in tonnes	10,000 tonnes
Selling price per tonne	£75
Variable costs per tonne	£40
Fixed costs for the period	£150,000.

The break-even point in units for the quarter is:

$$\frac{\text{Fixed costs}}{\text{Contribution per unit}}$$

$$\frac{£150,000}{£75 - £40}$$

= 4,286 tonnes or 42.86%

Margin of safety is 57.14%.

This information can be plotted on a profit-volume graph, as follows.

Profit volume graph

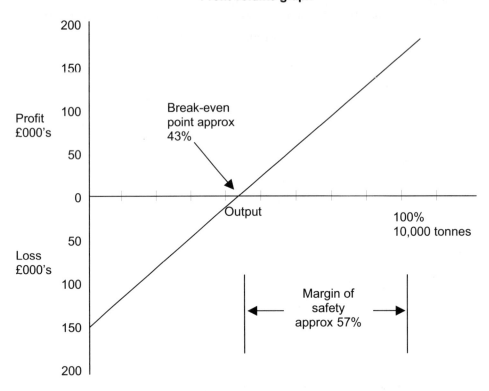

Shireoaks Feeds Ltd
Operating statement for quarter ended 31 March

Units	10,000
Sales	750,000
Less variable costs	400,000
Contribution	350,000
Fixed costs	150,000
Profit	£200,000

From the above chart the amount of net profit or loss can be read off for any given level of sales activity.

The points to note in the construction of a profit-volume chart are:

(a)   The horizontal axis represents sales (in units or sales value, as appropriate). This is the same as for a break-even chart.

(b)   The vertical axis shows net profit above the horizontal sales axis and net loss below.

(c)   When sales are zero, the net loss equals the fixed costs and one extreme of the 'profit volume' line is determined - therefore this is one point on the graph or chart.

 **FOULKS LYNCH**
PUBLICATIONS

(d)   If variable cost **per unit** and fixed costs **in total** are both constant throughout the relevant range of activity under consideration, the profit-volume chart is depicted by a straight line (as illustrated above). Therefore, to draw that line it is only necessary to know the profit (or loss) at one level of sales. The 'profit-volume' line is then drawn between this point and that determined in (c) and extended as necessary.

(e)   If there are changes in the variable cost per unit or total fixed costs at various activities, it would be necessary to calculate the profit (or loss) at each point where the cost structure changes and to plot these on the chart. The 'profit-volume' line will then be a series of straight lines joining these points together, as simply illustrated as follows:

ACTIVITY 6

The budget for the year for Shireoaks Feeds Ltd was:

Output and sales	50,000 tonnes
Selling price per tonne	£75
Variable cost per tonne	£40
Fixed costs	£650,000

Required:

(a)   Calculate the break-even point in units

(b)   Calculate the break-even point in sales value

(c)   Draft a statement to show profit for the year

(d)   Draw a break-even chart

(e)   Draw a profit volume graph (show clearly on the chart and the graph – the margin of safety).

This activity covers performance criteria A, B and C in element 6.3.

For a suggested answer, see the 'Answers' section at the end of the book.

5   CVP ANALYSIS AND COST BEHAVIOUR ANALYSIS

CVP analysis is based on marginal costing principles. Its greatest value as a technique is for estimating and providing information for decision-making. The value of CVP analysis depends on making reliable estimates of variable costs and fixed costs. Where some costs are semi-fixed and semi-variable, these should be divided into a variable cost element and a fixed cost element.

One technique for separating semi-fixed and semi-variable costs into their fixed and variable components is the high-low method.

The high-low method is based on the following assumptions.

●   Where total costs are a mixture of fixed costs and variable costs, the fixed cost and variable costs can be separated by taking total costs at a high volume of output/sales and total costs at a low volume of output/sales.

●   These total costs at the high volume and the low volume of activity are assumed to be fully representative of fixed costs and variable costs at all volumes of activity in between.

●   Total costs at any volume of activity = fixed costs plus variable costs for that level of activity.

- It follows that the difference between the total costs at the high volume of activity and the low volume of activity must consist entirely of variable costs. In fact they difference represents the variable costs of the difference in activity levels.

- We can therefore calculate a variable cost per unit of activity.

- Having calculated a variable cost per unit of activity, we can then calculate fixed costs.

Example

A company sells a single product at a price of £15 per unit. It has not worked out what its variable costs and fixed costs are, but the following reliable estimates of total cost have been produced.

At sales volume of 24,000 units, total costs = £320,000

At sales volume of 36,000 units, total costs = £380,000.

Tasks

1   Calculate the breakeven point in sales.

2   Calculate the margin of safety if budgeted sales are 27,000 units.

3   Calculate the volume of sales required to achieve a target profit of £100,000.

Solution

The first step is to calculate a variable cost per unit using the high-low method.

	£
Total costs of 36,000 units	380,000
Total costs of 24,000 units	320,000
Therefore variable costs of 12,000 units	60,000

Variable cost per unit = £60,000/12,000 = £5 per unit.

We can now calculate fixed costs, in either of the ways shown below.

	36,000 units	24,000 units
	£	£
Total costs	380,000	320,000
Variable costs at £5 per unit	180,000	120,000
Therefore fixed costs	200,000	200,000

Contribution per unit = Sales price – Variable cost = £15 - £5 = £10.

Breakeven point = £200,000/£10 per unit = 20,000 units.

Margin of safety = 27,000 – 20,000 = 7,000 units. As a percentage of budgeted sales, this is 25.9%.

To achieve a **target profit** of £100,000, total contribution must be £300,000 (£200,000 fixed costs + £100,000 profit). Required sales =

£300,000/£10 contribution per unit = 30,000 units.

ACTIVITY 7

A company makes and sells widgets. The sales price is £10 per unit. The company does not know what its variable costs and fixed costs are, but the following estimates of total cost have been produced.

At sales volume of 55,000 units, total costs = £607,500

At sales volume of 70,000 units, total costs = £675,000.

Tasks

1   Calculate the breakeven point in sales.

2   Calculate the margin of safety if budgeted sales are 68,000 units.

3   Calculate the volume of sales required to achieve a target profit of £40,000. Comment on whether you think this target profit is achievable.

This activity covers performance criteria A, B, C and D in element 6.2.

For a suggested answer, see the Answers section at the end of the book.

6   LIMITING FACTORS

CVP analysis generally assumes that the only factor stopping a business from increasing its sales volumes and profits is sales demand at the current sales price. In practice, this is often the case.

However, situations sometimes arise when a key resource is in short supply, and a business cannot make enough units to meet sales demand.

A resource in short supply is called a limiting factor, because it sets a limit on what can be achieved.

Definition   A **scarce resource** is an item in short supply. In the context of decision-making in business, it is a resource in short supply, as a consequence of which the organisation is limited in its ability to provide and sell more of products or services. Such scarce resources are called **limiting factors**.

Typically, a scarce resource could be:

*   a limit to the availability of a key item of raw materials or a key component

*   a limit to the availability of a key type of labour, such as skilled or qualified labour

*   a limit to the available time on key items of equipment or machinery. For example, if a business has just two machines for producing a range of products, the available machine time will be limited to the number of hours in which the two machines can be operated each week or month.

When a business has a limiting factor, a decision must be taken about how the available resources should be used. If the business makes and sells more than one product, and all the products make use of the scarce resource, the decision involves allocating the available resources to the production of one or more of the products, up to the point where all the scarce resources are used up.

An assumption can be made that the aim of the business should be to maximise its profits. If this assumption is accepted, marginal costing and CVP analysis can be used to identify how a scarce resource should be used to maximise profits.

However, in order to do this, a business must first of all recognise that there is a limiting factor.

6.1   IDENTIFYING A SCARCE RESOURCE

To identify a scarce resource, it is necessary to:

*   Obtain estimates of sales demand for each of the products (or services) sold by the business.

- Obtain estimates of the quantities of resources needed to make the units to meet the sales demand.

- From these estimates, calculate how many units of each resource will be needed.

- For each resource, compare the amount needed with the amount available.

- If the amount needed exceeds the amount available, the resource is in short supply and so a limiting factor.

Example

X Ltd makes two products, X and Y. One unit of Product X requires 5 kg of materials and 2 hours labour. One unit of Product Y requires 4 kg of the same material and 3 hours of the same labour. There are only 2,000 hours labour available each week and the maximum amount of material available each week is 3,000 kg. Potential sales demand each week is for units of Product X and units of Product Y.

Task

Identify whether either materials or labour is a limiting factor.

Solution

	Materials	Labour
	kg	hours
Required for 300 units of Product X	1,500	600
Required for 450 units of Product Y	1,800	1,350
Total required	3,300	1,950
Amount available	3,000	2,000
Surplus/(shortfall)	(300)	50

6.2 IDENTIFYING THE MOST PROFITABLE USE OF A SCARCE RESOURCE

When a business has a limiting factor, its total sales volume is restricted by its availability.

- If the business makes and sells just one product, all it can do is to make and sell as many units of the product that it can with the scarce resource available. This will maximise total contribution

- If the business makes and sells two or more products that each makes use of the scarce resource, profits will be maximised by using the resources in such a way as to maximise total contribution.

- For each product, we should therefore calculate the contribution earned by the product from each unit of the scarce resource that it uses.

- The products can be ranked in order of priority, according to the contribution earned per unit of limiting factor consumed. The product with the highest contribution per unit of limiting factor has the highest priority for production and sale.

A product earning the highest contribution per unit of limiting factor is not necessarily the product earning the highest profit per unit. For example, Product P might take 4 hours to make and earn a contribution of £10 per unit, and Product Q might take 2 hours to make and earn a contribution of £7 per unit. If labour is in short supply, Product Q should be given priority over Product P, because although it earns a lower unit contribution, it earns a higher contribution per labour hour (£3.50 for Product Q compared with just £2.50 for Product P).

Example

Z Ltd makes two products which both use the same type of materials and grades of
labour, but in different quantities as shown by the table below:

	Product A	Product B
Labour hours/unit	3	4
Material/unit	£20	£15

During each week the maximum number of labour hours available is limited to 600; and
the value of material available is limited to £6,000.

Each unit of product A produced and sold contributes £5 and product B £6 per unit. The
demand for each of these products is unlimited at their current sales prices.

Task

Advise Z Ltd which product it should make.

Solution

Step 1   Determine the scarce resource.

Step 2   Calculate each product's contribution per unit of the scarce resource
             consumed by its manufacture.

Each resource restricts production as follows:

Labour hours	600/3	=	200 units of A; or
	600/4	=	150 units of B
Materials	£6,000/£20	=	300 units of A; or
	£6,000/£15	=	400 units of B

It can be seen that whichever product is chosen the production is limited by the shortage
of labour hours. Labour is the limiting factor or scarce resource.

Contribution per hour

Product A contribution per labour hour

    =   £5/3 hours   =   £1.66 per hour

Product B contribution per labour hour

    =   £6/4 hours   =   £1.50 per hour

Therefore Z Ltd maximises its contribution by making and selling product A.

ACTIVITY 8

A Ltd makes two products, X and Y. Both products use the same machine and a common
raw material, supplies of which are limited to 200 machine hours and £500 per week
respectively. Individual product details are as follows:

	Product X	Product Y
Machine hours/unit	5	2.5
Cost of materials/unit	£10	£5
Contribution/unit	£20	£15

Tasks

1   Identify the limiting factor.

2   Using the data of the activity above recommend which product A Ltd should make and sell (assuming that demand is unlimited).

This activity covers performance criteria C, D and F in element 6.3.

For a suggested answer, see the 'Answers' section at the end of the book.

6.3 LIMITING FACTORS AND SALES DEMAND CONSTRAINTS

Maximum sales demand

In the above examples and activities, the sales demand for the products was unlimited. Once the contribution per unit of the limiting factor has been determined, the product earning the highest contribution per unit of limiting factor should be made until the scarce resource is fully utilised. The other products will not be made and sold at all, if the aim is to maximise total contribution and total profit.

In some situations, however, there is a maximum level of sales demand for each product. In these situations, there is no point in making more units of a product than it can sell. The problem is then to decide which products to make and sell, given the limiting factor and the limitations of sales demand. To solve such problems, a ranking approach is used. The products (or services) of the business are ranked in order of their contribution per unit of limiting factor.

Example

R Ltd makes three products which use the same type of materials but in different quantities, as shown by the table below:

Product	P	Q	R
Material/unit	3 kg	4 kg	5 kg
Contribution/unit	£10	£12	£20
Maximum demand per month (units)	100	150	300

The available materials are limited to 1,680 kg per month.

Task

Advise R Ltd as to the quantities of each product that it should make.

Solution

Step 1	To meet sales demand in full, R Ltd would need 2,400 kg of materials (300 for P plus 600 kg for Q plus 1,500 kg for R). There are insufficient materials to meet sales demand in full. Materials are therefore a limiting factor. Calculate the contribution per kilogram of materials consumed for each product.
Step 2	Rank the three products in order of their contribution per unit of limiting highest first
Step 3	Calculate the quantity of each product to be produced and sold.

Product	P	Q	R
Contribution per kg of material	$\dfrac{£10}{3kg} = £3.33$	$\dfrac{£12}{4kg} = £3.00$	$\dfrac{£20}{5kg} = £4.00$
Ranking	2nd	3rd	1st

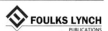

The resources are then allocated according to these rankings subject to the maximum demand constant.

Product R has the highest benefit from the use of the materials; its demand is limited to 300 units per month.

300 units of product R require 5 kg of material per unit or 1,500 kg in total (300 × 5 kg). There is no benefit from making more units of product R because they cannot be sold.

Since there is a total of 1,680 kg of material available and only 1,500 kg are used to produce product R there are 180 kg of material still available.

The next best product is product P which has a maximum demand of 100 units, each of which requires 3 kg of material. The maximum quantity of product P would require 300 kg (100 × 3 kg) but we only have 180 kg available so we can only produce

$$\frac{180kg}{3kg/unit} = 60 \text{ units of product P.}$$

All of the available materials have now been allocated. The production plan which maximises profit is:

Total contribution

				£
300 units of R	using	1,500 kgs of material		3,000
60 units of P	using	180 kgs of material		1,200
		1,680 kgs		£4,200

There is insufficient material to make any units of product Q.

ACTIVITY 9

C Ltd makes three products: A, B and C. All three products use the same type of labour which is limited to 1,500 hours per month. Individual product details are as follows:

Product	A	B	C
Contribution/unit	£25	£40	£35
Labour hours/unit	5	6	8
Maximum demand	100	200	400

Task

Advise C Ltd as to the quantities of each product it should make.

For a suggested answer, see the 'Answers' section at the end of the book.

Minimum sales demand

In some situations there may be a minimum sales demand for a product as well as a maximum sales demand. This may occur where a contract has already been signed with a customer to supply some units of a product.

Example

M plc makes three products from the same type of labour. Individual product details are as follows:

Product	L	M	N
Contribution/unit	£20	£18	£15
Labour hours/unit	5	3	3
Maximum demand	100	200	400
Minimum demand	50	50	100

Labour hours are limited to 1,300 hours.

Task

Advise M plc as to the most profitable use of the labour hours subject to these demand constraints.

Solution

Step 1	Labour is a scarce resource, since it would require 2,300 hours to make enough of all three products to meet the maximum sales demand. Calculate for each product the contribution per unit of the scarce resource.
Step 2	Rank the three products in order of their contribution per labour hour, highest first.
Step 3	Calculate the quantity of the scarce resource consumed by manufacturing the minimum sales demand quantities.
Step 4	Calculate the additional quantities of each product to be made with the remaining quantity of the limiting factor available. Production of any product should not exceed its maximum sales demand.
Step 5	Add the minimum and additional quantities of each product to state the optimal production plan.

Product	L	M	N
Contribution per labour hour:	$\dfrac{£20}{5} = £4.00$	$\dfrac{£18}{3} = £6.00$	$\dfrac{£15}{3} = £5.00$
Ranking	3rd	1st	2nd

The number of labour hours required to meet the minimum sales demand is:

Product L:	50 units	×	5 hours/unit	=	250 hours
Product M:	50 units	×	3 hours/unit	=	150 hours
Product N:	100 units	×	3 hours/unit	=	300 hours
					700 hours
Total hours available					1,300 hours
Hours available after meeting minimum demand					600 hours

This leaves a balance of 600 hours to be allocated, using the ranking order of the three products (1,300 hours available – minimum usage of 700 hours).

- The product which makes the most profitable use of the labour is product M which has a maximum demand of 200 units. This includes the minimum demand of 50 units for which the resources are already allocated, therefore the maximum number of additional units of product M is:

200 units – 50 units = 150 units

150 additional units of M require 3 labour hours per unit, a total of 450 labour hours.

This leaves a balance of 150 hours (600 hours – 450 hours)

- The next most profitable product is product N which has a maximum demand of 400 units and a minimum demand of 100 units. The maximum number of additional units is therefore 300 units but as each one requires 3 labour hours (900 hours in total) this is not possible.

  The balance of 150 hours is used to produce 50 additional units of product N (150 hours/3 hours per unit).

Therefore the final production plan is found by adding together the minimum and additional units of each product:

Product	Units	Hours	Contribution £
M (maximum demand)	200	600	3,600
N (minimum demand + 50 additional).	150	450	2,250
L (minimum demand only)	50	250	1,000
Total		1,300	6,850

ACTIVITY 10

Z Ltd makes three products using the same machine. The number of machine hours available is limited to 1,700 hours. Individual product details are as follows:

Product	X	Y	Z
Contribution/unit	£15	£9	£12
Machine hours/unit	3	2	4
Minimum demand	100	50	150
Maximum demand	300	200	500

Task

Advise Z Ltd as to the quantity of each product to be produced in order to maximise profit subject to the demand constraints.

This activity covers performance criteria A – G in element 6.3.

For a suggested answer, see the 'Answers' section at the end of the book.

KEY TERMS

A **scarce resource** – an item in short supply. In the context of decision-making in business, it is a resource in short supply, as a consequence of which the organisation is limited in its ability to provide and sell more of products or services. Such scarce resources are called **limiting factors**.

Chapter 11

INVESTMENT APPRAISAL

This chapter focuses on the capital budgeting process and methods of investment appraisal – payback and discounted cash flow.

CONTENTS

KNOWLEDGE AND UNDERSTANDING

		Reference
1	Management information requirements.	Item 2
2	Methods of project appraisal: payback and discounted cash flow methods (NPV and IRR).	Item 18
3	The principles of discounted cash flow.	Item 25

PERFORMANCE CRITERIA

		Reference
1	Identify information relevant to estimating current and future revenues and costs.	A (element 6.3)
2	Prepare estimates of future income and costs.	B (element 6.3)
3	Calculate the effects of variations in capacity on product costs.	C (element 6.3)
4	Analyse critical factors affecting costs and revenues using appropriate accounting techniques and draw clear conclusions from the analysis.	D (element 6.3)
5	State any assumptions used when evaluating future costs and revenues.	E (element 6.3)
6	Identify and evaluate options and solutions for their contribution to organisation goals.	F (element 6.3)
7	Present recommendations to appropriate people in a clear and concise way and supported by a clear rationale.	G (element 6.3)

LEARNING OUTCOMES

At the end of this chapter you should be able to.

- explain the issues involved with capital investment decisions

- determine the payback period for a project

- explain the principles of discounted cash flow

- appraise an investment by using the NPV method of DCF analysis

- appraise an investment by using the IRR method of DCF analysis.

---

1 INVESTMENT APPRAISAL

1.1 CAPITAL INVESTMENT

Most businesses have to spend money from time to time on new fixed assets. Spending on fixed assets is capital expenditure. There are various reasons why capital expenditure might be either necessary or desirable, and these can be categorised into the following types.

(a) **Maintenance** – This is spending on new fixed assets to replace worn-out assets or obsolete assets, or spending on existing fixed assets to improve safety and security features.

(b) **Profitability** – This is spending on fixed assets to improve the profitability of the existing business, to achieve cost savings, quality improvement, improved productivity, and so on.

(c) **Expansion** – This is spending to expand the business, to make new products, open new outlets, invest in research and development, etc.

(d) **Indirect** – This is spending on fixed assets that will not have a direct impact on the business operations or its profits. It includes spending on office buildings, or welfare facilities, etc. Capital spending of this nature is necessary, but a businesses should try to make sure that it gets good value for money from its spending.

In contrast to revenue expenditure, which is normally continual spending but in fairly small amounts, capital expenditure is irregular and often involves large amounts of spending. Because of the large amounts of money involved, it is usual for decisions about capital expenditure to be taken at a senior level within an organisation.

1.2 CAPITAL BUDGET

Large organisations will spend much more money on capital expenditure items, and much more regularly, than smaller organisations. Some organisations might have a long-term programme of capital spending that is reviewed and updated every year.

A capital budget is a programme of capital expenditure for the next few years, updated every year that sets out details of:

- Capital investment projects that have been authorised but not yet undertaken.

- Projects that likely to occur in the next few years, but that have not yet been authorised.

Before any individual investment project goes ahead, it should be authorised by an appropriate manager or committee within the organisation (or perhaps by the board of directors).

Basic stages in the capital budgeting cycle for a large organisation might be as follows:

Step 1   The requirements for capital expenditure in the business are forecast.

Step 2   Projects that might meet those requirements are identified.

Step 3   Alternative projects for meeting the requirements are appraised.

Step 4   The best alternatives are selected and approved.

Step 5   When a project has been approved, the capital expenditure is made.

Step 6   Actual spending is compared with planned spending, and the actual benefits obtained are monitored over time against the expected benefits. Deviations from estimates are examined.

1.3   THE FEATURES OF CAPITAL EXPENDITURE APPRAISAL

Before any capital expenditure is authorised, the proposed spending (or 'capital project') should be evaluated. Management should be satisfied that the spending will be beneficial.

- If the purpose of a capital project is to improve profits, we need to be convinced that the expected profits are big enough to justify the spending. Will the investment provide a reasonable return?

- If the capital expenditure is for an essential purpose, such as to replace a worn-out machine or the acquire a new office building, we need to be convinced that the spending decision is the best option available, and that there are no cheaper or more effective spending options.

When a proposed capital projects evaluated, the costs and benefits of the project should be evaluated over its foreseeable life. This is usually the expected useful life of the fixed asset to be purchased, which will be several years. This means that estimates of future costs and benefits call for long-term forecasting.

A 'typical' capital project involves an immediate purchase of a fixed asset. The asset is then used for a number of years, during which it is used to increase sales revenue or to achieve savings in operating costs. There will also be running costs for the asset. At the end of the asset's commercially useful life, it might have a 'residual value'. For example, it might be sold for scrap or in a second-hand market. (Items such as motor vehicles and printing machines often have a significant residual value.)

A problem with long-term forecasting of revenues, savings and costs is that forecasts can be inaccurate. However, although it is extremely difficult to produce reliable forecasts, every effort should be made to make them as reliable as possible.

- A business should try to avoid spending money on fixed assets on the basis of wildly optimistic and unrealistic forecasts.

- The assumptions on which the forecasts are based should be stated clearly. If the assumptions are clear, the forecasts can be assessed for reasonableness by the individuals who are asked to authorise the spending.

1.4   METHODS OF CAPITAL EXPENDITURE APPRAISAL

When forecasts of costs and benefits have been made for a capital project, the estimates must be analysed to establish whether the project should go ahead. Should the business spend money now in order to earn returns over a number of years into the future?

Capital investment appraisal is an analysis of the expected financial returns from a capital project over its expected life.

There are several methods of carrying out a capital expenditure appraisal. The methods that will be described in this chapter are:

- Payback

- The net present value method of discounted cash flow

- The internal rate of return method of discounted cash flow.

A common feature of all three methods is that they analyse the expected *cash flows* from the capital project, not the effects of the project on reported accounting profits.

Before describing the three techniques in detail, it will be helpful to look at the 'cash flow' nature of capital investment appraisal.

2 INVESTMENT APPRAISAL AND CASH FLOWS

2.1 ACCOUNTING PROFITS AND CASH FLOWS

An investment involves the outlay of money 'now' in the expectation of getting more money back in the future. In capital investment appraisal, it is more appropriate to evaluate future cash flows – the money actually spent, saved and received - rather than accounting profits. Accounting profits do not properly reflect investment returns.

Suppose for example that a business is considering whether to buy a new fixed asset for £80,000 that is expected to increase profits before depreciation each year by £30,000 for four years. At the end of year 4, the asset will be worthless.

The business should assess whether the expected financial return from the asset is sufficiently high to justify buying it.

(a)   If we looked at the accounting returns from this investment, we might decide that annual depreciation should be £20,000 each year (£80,000/4 years). Annual profits would then be £10,000. We could then assess the project on the basis that it will add £10,000 each year to profit for the next four years. (We could estimate an expected average return on capital employed, or 'accounting rate of return'. Since the average balance sheet value of the asset over its useful life will be £40,000 after depreciation, we could say that the project will provide an average return on capital employed, in accounting terms, of 25% (£10,000/£40,000).

(b)   If we looked at the investment cash flows, the analysis is different. Here we would say that to invest in the project, the business would spend £80,000 now and would expect a cash return of £30,000 each year for the next four years.

Capital investment appraisal should be based on cash flows, because it is realistic to do so. Capital spending involves spending cash and getting cash back in return, over time.

2.2 CASH FLOWS AND RELEVANT COSTS

The only cash flows that should be taken into consideration in capital investment appraisal are:

*   cash flows that will happen in the future, and

*   cash flows that will arise only if the capital project goes ahead.

These cash flows are direct revenues from the project and relevant costs. Relevant costs are future costs that will be incurred or saved as a direct consequence of undertaking the investment.

*   Costs that have already been incurred are not relevant to a current decision. For example, suppose a company makes a non-returnable deposit as a down-payment for an item of equipment, and then re-considers whether it wants the equipment after all. The money that has already been spent and cannot be recovered and so is not relevant to the current decision about obtaining the equipment.

*   Costs that will be incurred anyway, whether or not a capital project goes ahead, cannot be relevant to a decision about investing in the project. Fixed cost expenditures are an example of 'committed costs'. For the purpose of investment appraisal, a project should not be charged with an amount for a share of fixed costs that will be incurred anyway.

- Non-cash items of cost can never be relevant to investment appraisal. In particular, the depreciation charges on a fixed asset are not relevant costs for analysis because depreciation is not a cash expenditure.

ACTIVITY 1

A company is evaluating a proposed expenditure on an item of equipment that would cost £160,000. A technical feasibility study has been carried out by consultants, at a cost of £15,000, into benefits from investing in the equipment. It has been estimated that the equipment would have a life of four years, and annual profits would be £8,000. Profits are after deducting annual depreciation of £40,000 and an annual charge of £25,000 for a share of fixed costs that will be incurred anyway.

Task

What are the cash flows for this project that should be evaluated?

This activity covers performance criteria A and B in element 6.3.

For a suggested answer, see the 'Answers' section at the end of the book.

3 PAYBACK METHOD OF APPRAISAL

3.1 INTRODUCTION

Definition   **Payback** is the amount of time it is expected to take for the cash inflows from a capital investment project to equal the cash outflows.

It is the time that a project will take to pay back the money spent on it. It is based on expected cash flows form the project, not accounting profits.

The payback method of appraisal is used in one of two ways.

- A business might establish a rule for capital spending that no project should be undertaken unless it is expected to pay back within a given length of time. For example, a rule might be established that capital expenditure should not be undertaken unless payback is expected within, say, five years.

- When two alternative capital projects are being compared, and the decision is to undertake one or the other but not both, preference might be given to the project that is expected to pay back sooner.

Payback is commonly used as an initial screening method, and projects that meet the payback requirement are then evaluated using another investment appraisal method.

3.2 CALCULATING PAYBACK: CONSTANT ANNUAL CASH FLOWS

If the expected cash inflows from a project are an equal annual amount, the payback period is calculated simply as:

$$\text{Payback period} = \frac{\text{Initial payment}}{\text{Annual Cash Inflow}}$$

It is normally assumed that cash flows each year occur at an even rate throughout the year.

Example

An expenditure of £2 million is expected to generate cash inflows of £500,000 each year for the next seven years.

What is the payback period for the project?

Solution

$$\text{Payback} = \frac{£2,000,000}{£500,000} = \textbf{4 years}$$

The payback method provides a rough measure of the liquidity of a project, in other words how much annual cash flow it earns. It is not a measure of the profitability of a project over its life. In the example above, the fact that the project pays back within four years ignores the total amount of cash flows it will provide over seven years. A project costing £2 million and earning cash flows of £500,000 for just five years would have exactly the same payback period, even though it would not be as profitable.

A pay back period might not be an exact number of years.

Example

A project will involve spending £1.8 million now. Annual cash flows from the project would be £350,000.

What is the expected payback period?

Solution

$$\text{Payback} = \frac{£1,800,000}{£350,000} = \textbf{5.1429 years}$$

This can be stated in any of the following ways.

- Payback will be in 5.1 years.

- Payback will be in just over 5 years (or between 5 and 6 years).

- Payback will be in 5 years 2 months.

Payback in years and months is calculated by multiplying the decimal fraction of a year by 12 months. In this example, 0.1429 years = 1.7 months (0.1429 x 12 months), which is rounded to 2 months.

ACTIVITY 2

An investment would cost £2.3 million and annual cash inflows from the project are expected to be £600,000.

Task

Calculate the expected payback period in years and months.

State an assumption on which this estimate is based.

This activity covers performance criteria D and E in element 6.3.

For a suggested answer, see the 'Answers' section at the end of the book.

3.3   CALCULATING PAYBACK: UNEVEN ANNUAL CASH FLOWS

Annual cash flows from a project are unlikely to be a constant annual amount, but are likely to vary from year to year.

Payback is calculated by finding out when the cumulative cash inflows from the project will pay back the money spent. Cumulative cash flows should be worked out by adding each year's cash flows, on a cumulative basis, to net cash flow to date for the project.

The simplest way of calculating payback is probably to set out the figures in a table.

An example will be used to illustrate how the table should be constructed.

Example

A project is expected to have the following cash flows.

Year	Cash flow
	£000
0	(2,000)
1	500
2	500
3	400
4	600
5	300
6	200

What is the expected payback period?

Solution

Figures in brackets are negative cash flows. In the table below a column is added for cumulative cash flows for the project to date. Figures in brackets are negative cash flows.

Each year's cumulative figure is simply the cumulative figure at the start of the year plus the figure for the current year. The cumulative figure each year is therefore the expected position as at the end of that year.

Year	Cash flow	Cumulative cash flow
	£000	£000
0	(2,000)	(2,000)
1	500	(1,500)
2	500	(1,000)
3	400	(600)
4	600	0
5	300	300
6	200	500

The payback period is exactly 4 years.

Payback is not always an exact number of years.

Example

A project would have the following cash flows.

Year	Cash flow
	£000
0	(1,900)
1	300
2	500
3	600
4	800
5	500

The payback period would be calculated as follows.

Year	Cash flow	Cumulative cash flow
	£000	£000
0	(1,900)	(1,900)
1	300	(1,600)
2	500	(1,100)
3	600	(500)
4	800	300
5	500	800

Payback is between the end of year 3 and the end of year 4 – in other words during year 4.

If we assume a constant rate of cash flow through the year, we could estimate that payback will be three years, plus (500/800) of year 4. This is because the cumulative cash flow is minus 500 at the star of the year and the year 4 cash flow would be 800.

We could therefore estimate that payback would be after 3.626 years or 3 years 8 months.

ACTIVITY 3

Calculate the payback period in years and months for the following project.

Year	Cash flow
	£000
0	(3,100)
1	1,000
2	900
3	800
4	500
5	500

This activity covers performance criteria D and E in element 6.3.

For a suggested answer, see the 'Answers' section at the end of the book.

3.4 MERITS OF PAYBACK METHOD AS AN INVESTMENT APPRAISAL TECHNIQUE

The payback method of investment appraisal has some advantages.

(a) **Simplicity**

As a concept, it is easily understood and is easily calculated.

(b) **Rapidly-changing technology**

If new plant is likely to be scrapped in a short period because of obsolescence, a quick payback is essential.

(c) **Improving investment conditions**

When investment conditions are expected to improve in the near future, attention is directed to those projects which will release funds soonest, to take advantage of the improving climate.

(d) **Payback favours projects with a quick return**

It is often argued that these are to be preferred for three reasons:

(i) Rapid project payback leads to rapid company growth – but in fact such a policy will lead to many profitable investment opportunities being overlooked because their payback period does not happen to be particularly swift.

(ii) Rapid payback minimises risk (the logic being that the shorter the payback period, the less there is that can go wrong). Not all risks are related to time, but payback is able to provide a useful means of assessing time risks (and only time risk). It is likely that earlier cash flows can be estimated with greater certainty.

(iii) Rapid payback maximises liquidity – but liquidity problems are best dealt with separately, through cash forecasting.

(e) **Cash flows**

Unlike the other traditional methods it uses cash flows, rather than profits, and so is less likely to produce an unduly optimistic figure distorted by assorted accounting conventions which might permit certain costs to be carried forward and not affect profit initially.

3.5 WEAKNESSES OF PAYBACK METHOD

(a) **Project returns may be ignored**

Cash flows arising after the payback period are totally ignored. Payback ignores profitability and concentrates on cash flows and liquidity.

(b) **Timing ignored**

Cash flows are effectively categorised as pre-payback or post-payback – but no more accurate measure is made. In particular, the time value of money is ignored.

(c) **Lack of objectivity**

There is no objective measure as to what length of time should be set as the minimum payback period. Investment decisions are therefore subjective.

(d) **Project profitability is ignored**

Payback takes no account of the effects on business profits and periodic performance of the project, as evidenced in the financial statements. This is critical if the business is to be reasonably viewed by users of the accounts.

Conclusion Payback is best seen as an initial screening tool – for example a business might set a rule that no project with a payback of more than five years is to be considered.

It is an appropriate measure for relatively straightforward projects e.g. those which involve an initial outlay followed by constant long-term receipts.

However in spite of its weaknesses and limitations the payback period is a useful most initial screening method of investment appraisal. It is normally used in conjunction with another method of capital investment appraisal, such as the NPV or IRR methods of discounted cash flow analysis.

4 TIME VALUE OF MONEY

Money is invested to earn a profit. For example, if an item of equipment costs £80,000 and would earn cash profits (profits ignoring depreciation) of £20,000 each year for four years, it would not be worth buying. This is because the total profit over four years (£80,000) would only just cover its cost.

Capital investments must make enough profits to justify their costs. In addition, the size of the profits or return must be large enough to make the investment worthwhile. In the example above, if the equipment costing £80,000 made total returns of £82,000 over four years, the total return on the investment would be £2,000, or an average of £500 per year. This would be a very low return on an investment of £80,000. More money could be earned putting the £80,000 on deposit with a bank to earn interest.

If a capital investment is to be justified, it needs to earn at least a minimum amount of profit, so that the return compensates the investor for both the amount invested and also for the *length* of time before the profits are made. For example, if a company could invest £80,000 now to earn revenue of £82,000 in one week's time, a profit of £2,000 in seven days would be a very good return. However, if it takes four years to earn the money, the return would be very low.

Money has a time value. By this we mean that it can be invested to earn interest or profits, so it is better to have £1 now than in one year's time. This is because £1 now can be invested for the next year to earn a return, whereas £1 in one year's time cannot. Another way of looking at the time value of money is to say that £1 in six years' time is worth less than £1 now. Similarly, £1 in five years' time is worth less than £1 now, but is worth more than £1 after six years.

DCF is an capital expenditure appraisal technique that takes into account the time value of money.

5 DISCOUNTED CASH FLOW (DCF)

Discounted cash flow, or DCF, is an investment appraisal technique that takes into account both the timing of cash flows and also the total cash flows over a project's life.

- As with the payback method, DCF analysis is based on future cash flows, not accounting profits or losses.

- The timing of cash flows is taken into account by discounting them to a 'present value'. The effect of discounting is to give a higher value to each £1 of cash flows that occur earlier and a lower value to each £1 of cash flows occurring later in the project's life. £1 earned after one year will be worth more than £1 earned after two years, which in turn will be worth more than £1 earned after five years, and so on. Cash flows that occur in different years are re-stated on a common basis, at their present value.

5.1 COMPOUNDING AND DISCOUNTING

To understand discounting, it is helpful to start by looking at compounding or compound interest.

Suppose that a business has £100,000 to invest, and wants to earn a return of 10% (compound interest). If it could invest at 10% compound, the value of the investment with interest would build up as follows.

- After 1 year $\quad$ £100,000 × (1.10) $\quad$ = £110,000
- After 2 years $\quad$ £100,000 × (1.10)^2 $\quad$ = £121,000
- After 3 years $\quad$ £100,000 × (1.10)^3 $\quad$ = £133,100, and so on.

This is **compounding**. The formula for the future value of an investment plus accumulated interest after n years is:

$FV = PV (1 + r)^n$

where $\quad$ FV is the future value of the investment with interest

$\quad$ PV is the initial or 'present' value of the investment

$\quad$ r is the compound annual rate of return or rate of interest (the 'cost of capital'), expressed as a proportion (so 10% = 0.10, 5% = 0.05 and so on)

$\quad$ n is the number of years.

FOULKS LYNCH
PUBLICATIONS

Discounting is compounding in reverse. It starts with a future amount of cash and converts it into a present value.

Definition   A **present value** is the amount that would need to be invested now to earn the future cash flow, if the money is invested at the 'cost of capital'.

For example, if a business expects to earn a (compound) rate of return of 10% on its investments, how much would it need to invest now to build up an investment of:

(a)   £110,000 after 1 year

(b)   £121,000 after 2 years

(c)   £133,100 after 3 years?

The answer is £100,000 in each case, and we can calculate it by discounting. The discounting formula to calculate the present value of a future sum of money at the end of n years is:

$$PV = FV \frac{1}{1+r^n}$$

(a)   After 1 year, $£110,000 \times \frac{1}{1.10} = £100,000$

(b)   After 2 years, $£121,000 \times \frac{1}{1.10^2} = £100,000$

(c)   After 3 years, $£133,100 \times \frac{1}{1.10^3} = £100,000$

Both cash inflows and cash payments can be discounted to a present value. By discounting all payments and receipts from a capital investment to a present value, they can be compared on a like-for-like basis.

ACTIVITY 4

Task 1

How much would you need to invest now to earn £2,000 after 4 years at a compound interest rate of 8% a year?

Task 2

What is the present value of £5,000 receivable at the end of year 3 at a cost of capital of 7% per annum?

This activity covers performance criterion B in element 6.3.

For a suggested answer, see the 'Answers' section at the end of the book.

5.2   DISCOUNT FACTORS AND DISCOUNT TABLES

A present value for a future cash flow is calculated by multiplying the future cash flow by a factor:

$$\frac{1}{1+r^n}$$

Check that you know how to do this on your calculator.

For example:

$$\frac{1}{1.10} = 0.909$$

$$\frac{1}{1.10^2} = 0.826$$

$$\frac{1}{1.10^3} = 0.751$$

However, there are tables that give you a list of these 'discount factors' without you having to do the calculation yourself.

To calculate a present value for a future cash flow, you simply multiply the future cash flow by the appropriate discount factor.

Any cash flows that take place 'now' (at the start of the project) take place in Year 0. The discount factor for Year 0 is 1.0, regardless of what the cost of capital is. Cash flows 'now' therefore do not need to be discounted to a present value equivalent, because they are already at present value.

ACTIVITY 5

The cash flows for a project have been estimated as follows:

Year	£
0	(25,000)
1	6,000
2	10,000
3	8,000
4	7,000

The cost of capital is 6%. Discount factors at a cost of capital of 6% are:

Year	Discount factor at 6%
1	0.943
2	0.890
3	0.840
4	0.792

Task

Convert these cash flows to a present value.

Add up the total of the present values for each of the years.

This activity covers performance criterion B in element 6.3.

For a suggested answer, see the 'Answers' section at the end of the book.

5.3 THE COST OF CAPITAL

The cost of capital used by a business in DCF analysis is the cost of funds for the business. It is therefore the minimum return that the business should make from its own investments, to earn the cash flows out of which it can pay interest pr profits to its own providers of funds.

For the purpose of this text, the cost of capital is assumed to be a known figure.

FOULKS LYNCH
PUBLICATIONS

6 NET PRESENT VALUE METHOD (NPV)

The **net present value** or **NPV** method of DCF analysis is to calculate a net present value for a proposed investment project. The NPV is the value obtained by discounting all the cash outflows and inflows for the project capital at the cost of capital, and adding them up. Cash outflows are negative and inflows are positive values. The sum of the present value of all the cash flows from the project is the 'net' present value amount.

The NPV is the sum of the present value (PV) of all the cash inflows from a project minus the PV of all the cash outflows.

- **If the NPV is positive**, it means that the cash inflows from a capital investment will yield a return in excess of the cost of capital. The project therefore seems financially attractive.

- **If the NPV is negative**, it means that the cash inflows from a capital investment will yield a return below the cost of capital. From a financial perspective, the project is therefore unattractive.

- **If the NPV is exactly zero**, the cash inflows from a capital investment will yield a return exactly equal to the cost of capital. The project is therefore just about financially attractive.

Example

Rug Limited is considering a capital investment in new equipment. The estimated cash flows are as follows.

Year	Cash flow £
0	(240,000)
1	80,000
2	120,000
3	70,000
4	40,000
5	20,000

The company's cost of capital is 9%.

Task

Calculate the NPV of the project to assess whether it should be undertaken.

The following are discount factors for a 9% cost of capital.

Year	Discount factor at 9%
1	0.917
2	0.842
3	0.772
4	0.708
5	0.650

Solution

Year	Cash flow £	Discount factor at 9%	Present value £
0	(240,000)	1.000	(240,000)
1	80,000	0.917	73,360
2	120,000	0.842	101,040
3	70,000	0.772	54,040
4	40,000	0.708	28,320
5	20,000	0.650	13,000
Net present value			**+ 29,760**

FOULKS LYNCH
PUBLICATIONS

The PV of cash inflows exceeds the PV of cash outflows by £29,760, which means that the project will earn a DCF return in excess of 9%. It should therefore be undertaken.

ACTIVITY 6

Fylingdales Fabrication is considering investing in a new delivery vehicle which will make savings over the current out-sourced service.

The cost of the vehicle is £35,000 and it will have a five-year life.

The savings it will make over the period are:

Cash flow:

	£
Yr 1	8,000
2	9,000
3	12,000
4	9,500
5	9,000

The firm currently has a return of 12% and this is considered to be its cost of capital.

Discount factors at 12%.

Yr 1	0.893
2	0.797
3	0.721
4	0.636
5	0.458

Tasks

Calculate the NPV of the investment.

On the basis of the NPV you have calculated, recommend whether or not the investment should go ahead.

This activity covers performance criteria F and G in element 6.3.

For a suggested answer, see the 'Answers' section at the end of the book.

6.1 ASSUMPTIONS IN DCF ABOUT THE TIMING OF CASH FLOWS

In DCF, certain assumptions are made about the timing of cash flows in each year of a project.

- A cash outlay at the beginning of an investment project ('now') occurs in year 0.

- A cash flows that occurs **during the course of a year** is assumed to occur all at once at the end of the year. For example, profits of £30,000 in Year 3 would be assumed to occur at the end of Year 3.

- If a cash flow occurs **at the beginning of a year**, it is assumed that the cash flow happens at the end of the previous year. For example, a cash outlay of £10,000 at the beginning of Year 2 would be treated as a cash flow in Year 1, occurring at the end of Year 1.

6.2 INVESTMENT IN WORKING CAPITAL

Some capital projects involve an investment in working capital as well as fixed assets. Working capital should be considered to consist of investments in stocks and debtors, minus trade creditors.

An investment in working capital slows up the receipt of cash. For example, suppose that a business buys an item for £10 for cash and resells it for £16. It has made a cash profit of £6 on the deal. However, if the item is sold for £16 on credit, the cash flow is different. Although the profit is £6, the business is actually £10 worse off for cash. This is because it has invested £16 in debtors (working capital).

An increase in working capital reduces cash flows and a reduction in working capital improves the cash flow in the year that it happens.

By convention, in DCF analysis, if a project will require an investment in working capital, the investment is treated as a cash outflow at the beginning of the year in which it occurs. The working capital is eventually released at the end of the project, when it becomes a cash inflow. (It is treated as a cash inflow because actual cash flows will exceed cash profits in the year by the amount of the reduction in working capital.)

Example

A company is considering whether to invest in a project to buy an item of equipment for £40,000. The project would require an investment of £8,000 in working capital. The cash profits from the project would be:

Year	Cash profit
	£
1	15,000
2	20,000
3	12,000
4	7,000

The equipment would have a resale value of £5,000 at the end of Year 4.

The cost of capital is 10%. Discount factors at 10% are:

Year	
1	0.909
2	0.826
3	0.751
4	0.683

Task

Calculate the NPV of the project and recommend whether or not, on financial grounds, you would recommend that the project should be undertaken.

Solution

Year	Equipt	Working capital	Cash profit	Total cash flow	Discount factor at 10%	Present value
	£	£	£	£		£
0	(40,000)	(8,000)		(48,000)	1.000	(48,000)
1			15,000	15,000	0.909	13,635
2			20,000	20,000	0.826	16,520
3			12,000	12,000	0.751	9,012
4	5,000	8,000	7,000	20,000	0.683	13,660
						+ 4,827

The NPV is positive, and from a financial perspective should therefore be undertaken.

7 INTERNAL RATE OF RETURN METHOD (IRR)

Using the NPV method of discounted cash flow, present values are calculated by discounting cash flows at a given cost of capital, and the difference between the PV of costs and the PV of benefits is the NPV. In contrast, the **internal rate of return (IRR)** method of DCF analysis is to calculate the exact DCF rate of return that the project is expected to achieve. This is the cost of capital at which the NPV is zero.

If the expected rate of return (known as the internal rate of return or IRR, and also as the DCF yield) is higher than a target rate of return, the project is financially worth undertaking.

Calculating the IRR of a project can be done with a programmed calculator. Otherwise, it has to be estimated using a rather laborious technique called the interpolation method. The interpolation method produces an estimate of the IRR, although it is not arithmetically exact.

The steps in this method are as follows.

Step 1   Calculate two net present values for the project at two different costs of capital. You should decide which costs of capital to use. However, you want to find two costs of capital for which the NPV is close to 0, because the IRR will be a value close to them. Ideally, you should use one cost of capital where the NPV is positive and the other cost of capital where the NPV is negative, although this is not essential.

Step 2   Having found two costs of capital where the NPV is close to 0, we can then estimate the cost of capital at which the NPV is 0. In other words, we can estimate the IRR. This estimating technique is illustrated in the example below.

Example

A company is trying to decide whether to buy a machine for £13,500. The machine will create annual cash savings as follows.

Year	£
1	5,000
2	8,000
3	3,000

Task

Calculate the project's IRR.

Solution

Step 1   The first step is to calculate the NPV of the project at two different costs of capital. Ideally the NPV should be positive at one cost of capital and negative at the other.

So what costs of capital should we try?

One way of making a guess is to look at the profits from the project over its life. These are £16,000 over the three years. After deducting the capital expenditure of £13,500, this gives us a net return of £2,500, or an average of £833 each year of the project. £833 is about 6% of the capital outlay. The IRR is actually likely to be a bit higher than this, so we could start by trying 7%, 8% or 9%.

Here, 8% is used.

Year	Cash flow	Discount factor at 8%	PV
	£		£
0	(13,500)	1.000	(13,500)
1	5,000	0.926	4,630
2	8,000	0.857	6,856
3	3,000	0.794	2,382
			+ 368

The NPV is positive at 8%, so the IRR is higher than this. We need to find the NPV at a higher cost of capital. Let's try 11%.

Year	Cash flow	Discount factor at 11%	PV
	£		£
0	(13,500)	1.000	(13,500)
1	5,000	0.901	4,505
2	8,000	0.812	6,496
3	3,000	0.731	2,193
			(306)

The NPV is negative at 11%, so the IRR lies somewhere between 8% and 11%.

Step 2   The next step is to use the two NPV figures we have calculated to estimate the IRR.

We know that the NPV is + 368 at 8% and that it is - 306 at 11%.

Between 8% and 11%, the NPV therefore falls by 674 (368 + 306).

If we assume that the decline in NPV occurs in a straight line, we can estimate that the IRR must be:

$$8\% = \left[\frac{368}{674} \times (11-8)\% \right]$$

$$= 8\% + 1.6\% = 9.6\%.$$

An estimated IRR is therefore 9.6%.

Formula for calculating IRR

You might find the following formula for calculating the IRR useful.

If the NPV at A% is positive, + £P

and if the NPV at B% is negative, - £N

then

$$IRR = A\% \left[\frac{P}{(P+N)} \times (B+A)\% \right]$$

Ignore the minus sign for the negative NPV. For example, if P = + 60 and N = - 50, then P + N = 110.

Another example

A business undertakes high-risk investments and requires a minimum expected rate of return of 17% on its investments. A proposed capital investment has the following expected cash flows.

Year	£
0	(50,000)
1	18,000
2	25,000
3	20,000
4	10,000

Tasks

1   Calculate the NPV of the project if the cost of capital is 15%.

2   Calculate the NPV of the project if the cost of capital is 20%.

3   Use the NPVs you have calculated to estimate the IRR of the project.

4   Recommend, on financial grounds alone, whether this project should go ahead.

Discount factors:

Year	Discount factor at	
	15%	20%
1	0.870	0.833
2	0.756	0.694
3	0.658	0.579
4	0.572	0.482

Solution

Year	Cash flow	Discount factor at 15%	Present value at 15%	Discount factor at 20%	Present value at 20%
	£		£		£
0	(50,000)	1.000	(50,000)	1.000	(50,000)
1	18,000	0.870	15,660	0.833	14,994
2	25,000	0.756	18,900	0.694	17,350
3	20,000	0.658	13,160	0.579	11,580
4	10,000	0.572	5,720	0.482	4,820
NPV			+ 3,440		(1,256)

The IRR is above 15% but below 20%.

Using the interpolation method:

The NPV is + 3,440 at 15%.

The NPV is – 1,256 at 20%.

The NPV falls by 4,696 between 15% and 20%.

The estimated IRR is therefore:

$$IRR = 15\% + \left[\frac{3,440}{4,696} \times (20 - 15)\% \right]$$

$$= 15\%\% + 3.7\%$$

$$= 18.7\%$$

Recommendation

The project is expected to earn a DCF return in excess of the target rate of 17%, so (ignoring risk) on financial grounds it is a worthwhile investment.

KEY TERMS

Maintenance costs – spending on new fixed assets to replace worn-out assets or obsolete assets, or spending on existing fixed assets to improve safety and security features.

Profitability costs – spending on fixed assets to improve the profitability of the existing business, to achieve cost savings, quality improvement, improved productivity, and so on.

Expansion costs – spending to expand the business, to make new products, open new outlets, invest in research and development, etc.

Indirect costs – spending on fixed assets that will not have a direct impact on the business operations or its profits. It includes spending on office buildings, or welfare facilities, etc.

Payback – the amount of time it is expected to take for the cash inflows from a capital investment project to equal the cash outflows.

Present value – the amount that would need to be invested now to earn the future cash flow, if the money is invested at the 'cost of capital'.

Chapter 12

WRITING REPORTS

This chapter looks at the factors that need to be considered when preparing the written elements of a report, and sets out guidelines for good report writing.matthew76

CONTENTS

KNOWLEDGE AND UNDERSTANDING

		Reference
1	Methods of presenting information in written reports	Item 14

PERFORMANCE CRITERIA

		Reference
1	Present recommendations to appropriate people in a clear and concise way and supported by clear rationale.	G (element 6.3)

LEARNING OUTCOMES

At the end of this chapter, you should be able to:

- describe reporting structures within an organisation

- describe the key features of a report

- understand the rules or guidelines for preparing a report.

---

1   CHARACTERISTICS OF GOOD INFORMATION

A report is intended to provide information to its recipient. No matter what type of report you prepare, the information you give must be:

- **Relevant**. The report should have a purpose. If it doesn't have a purpose, there is no reason for having it at all. You need to be aware what the report is for, and

---

the information put into it should then be relevant to this purpose. Anything irrelevant should be kept out.

- **Understandable**. The person who reads the report must be able to understand what you have written. This might seem obvious, but in practice, very many reports are difficult to follow, often because they are badly written and often because the information is not presented clearly enough – for example without the use of tables, diagrams or graphs.

- **Reliable**. The reader of the report needs to be able to rely on the accuracy of the information it contains. If there are doubts about the accuracy of any of the information, this should be made clear in the report.

- **In time**. If a report has a purpose, it must be available in time to be put to its intended use. If a report is provided too late for its intended use, it has no value.

The above characteristics of good information should apply to all the reports that you write.

2 TYPES OF REPORT: REPORTING STRUCTURES

Within any organisation, there are reporting structures. Information and reports are generally needed by management, and a system needs to exist whereby managers get all the reports they need.

Within a typical large organisation:

- Many reports are prepared by junior staff for their superiors.

- In addition, some departments or functions are often responsible for providing information to other departments. In particular, accountants are generally expected to provide accounting and financial information to managers throughout the business.

Most reporting is internal, to management or supervisors. However, businesses are also required on occasion to provide reports to external organisations, such as government departments. When reports are produced for an external organisation, they should be:

- written by a person who has been given the responsibility for its preparation

- approved and authorised by a n appropriate manager before submission to the outside organisation.

2.1 FORMAL AND INFORMAL REPORTS

Some reports are written as large formal documents. Formal reports are often submitted to a committee or senior manager and used as a basis for discussions and decision-making. However a report could be informal, and written simply as a one-sheet memorandum.

For example a report to the board of directors of a company analysing the potential profitability for a new product might well be in the form of a large formal document, incorporating large amounts of detail such as marketing information and competitor product details. However a report to a manager explaining how a problem customer's complaint was dealt with might simply be in the form of a one- or two-paragraph memo.

2.2 ROUTINE REPORTS AND SPECIAL REPORTS

Some reports will be produced on a regular basis at similar time intervals. These are known as routine reports. As a rule, such reports are required at say monthly, quarterly or yearly intervals. They might be required by management from such units as agencies, units, decentralised areas of the organisation or departments. They are often statistical in nature providing details of trading activities, stocks, profits or losses etc. Regular performance reports are commonly prepared on costs and profitability, and perhaps also

on productivity and resource utilisation. For example, a board of directors might expect to see a monthly or quarterly financial performance report at every regular board meeting.

Other examples of routine reports include weekly sales reports, monthly stock reports or an annual labour turnover report. Due to the statistical nature of many routine reports, they may well include some tables, diagrams or graphs.

In addition to routine reports, one-off or special reports are also produced. For example, reports on possible new products or the effect of computerisation or the level of employee wage rates could be commissioned on an *ad hoc* basis.

2.3 CONFIDENTIAL REPORTS

Some reports might be confidential and these are usually of a more formal nature and follow a more formal layout than most. Any confidential report must be clearly labelled as such.

Examples of reports

Given below are examples of some of the types of reports that might be produced.

(a) **Production reports**

- idle time reports

- machine downtime reports

- shift reports (e.g. units produced, materials used, hours worked)

- material usage reports

- maintenance reports

- rejection/scrap reports.

    These reports would be addressed to the manager of the production function responsible.

(b) **Marketing/sales reports**

- advertising reports (e.g. costs, effectiveness)

- sales orders reports

- customer complaints reports.

    These types of reports would be addressed to the marketing and sales managers.

(c) **Accounting reports**

- financial reports (e.g. balance sheets and profit and loss accounts, routine reports on product costs and profits)

- cash reports (ranging from daily to monthly).

3 PLANNING A REPORT

Like any piece of written work, a report should be properly planned. When planning a report there are a number of factors to consider.

3.1 AIM OF THE REPORT

In order to make a report effective, it is obviously important that the purpose of the report is clearly understood by the report writer. One way of ensuring that the aim is clear is to set out the following statement and then complete it:

'As the result of reading this report, the reader will...'

There are a number of possible aims that could be established such as:

- '... agree to authorise the project.'
- '... take the necessary action.'
- '... make a decision.'

3.2 CHECKLIST FOR PLANNING

The following additional points are the sort that should be considered when planning a report:

- Who commissioned the report and who is to use the report? It may be that there are a number of different users of the report with different needs, levels of knowledge and levels of understanding.

- What information does the user of the report require?

- What background information does the user of the report already have?

- What type of report would best suit the subject matter and the user?

- What is required in the report: information only or judgement, opinions and recommendations?

- What is the time scale of the report?

- What format should be used, for example should there be appendices, graphs, diagrams etc?

- What detailed points will need to be made in the body of the report?

- Is the report confidential?

3.3 PRINCIPLES OF REPORT WRITING

Once the bare bones of a report have been sketched in the planning stage, the report will need to be written in detail. When writing any type of report it is worth bearing in mind a few basic stylistic points.

The main purpose of any report is to convey information and this purpose can be advanced by taking care to follow the points considered below.

3.4 LAYOUT OF THE REPORT

Information is not only conveyed by the contents of a report but also by its design and presentation. The layout of the report and the overall impression that is made are therefore important.

Care should be taken to make the report easier to understand by the use of appropriate headings and to make the report pleasing to the eye by the sensible use of spacing and paragraphs. This can all help with the overall impression that the report gives.

More detailed guidance on layout and headings will be given in later paragraphs of this chapter.

3.5 SIZE OF THE REPORT

An early decision in planning a report should be regarding the size of the report. Any diagrammatic, tabulated or graphical illustrations might make the data seem clearer and will emphasise key facts and figures.

However the inclusion of such illustrations will often increase the size of the report. Care should be taken not to waste managers' time by making a report too long.

FOULKS LYNCH
PUBLICATIONS

3.6 LOGIC OF ARGUMENT

In planning the report, the key issues to be covered should be listed. These should form the basic structure of the report. Once the key issues have been identified then they should be arranged into a logical order and appropriate sequence.

It is important to ensure that the points that are to be made in the report are given in a logical order and that they lead to a logical conclusion. The writer of a report should be quite clear whether the purpose of the report is simply to inform or whether a conclusion or recommendations are required.

3.7 LANGUAGE

The language that is used in a formal report should be formal. Abbreviations and colloquialisms should be avoided.

In most reports other than the most informal the first person should be avoided and the third person used. So for example 'you will be able to see that...' would become 'it should now be clear that ...' etc.

If the report is being produced for the layman or non-technical user then jargon or technical language should be avoided.

3.8 OBJECTIVITY

Even if the purpose of a report is simply to inform rather than reach any conclusion it is important that the report appears to be written from an objective viewpoint. Therefore any emotive or loaded wording should be avoided at all costs. The report must appear to be unbiased and impartial.

Any bias that exists in the report writer should not be allowed to surface in the report as this could have an adverse effect on the person using the report and his view of any conclusions or recommendations that might have been reached.

4 KEY FEATURES OF A FORMAL REPORT

4.1 USER OF THE REPORT

Before thinking about the actual content of a report, you should first think about who the reader will be. You need to think about the user in order to decide on the amount of detail the report should contain.

- Who is the user?
- How much background information does the user have?
- How much technical or business knowledge does the user have?
- Why does the user want the report?
- What does the user want to get out of the report?

Once these questions have been satisfactorily answered then it is possible to consider the more detailed points of the report.

4.2 ADDRESSEE, AUTHOR AND DATE

A report should state clearly who it is being sent to. It should also state who it is from. It should also be dated.

Addressee, author and date should be the first three items on a report, even an informal memo.

4.3 SUBJECT

The report should be given a title or subject heading that is concise and also gives a clear indication of the subject matter of the report.

so as a matter of routine, always start your reports with:

To:

From:

Date:

Subject:

4.4 CONTENTS LIST

Many reports will be quite extensive and will include not only the main report but also appendices (see later in this paragraph). Therefore at the start of such a report there will usually be a summary of contents showing what elements of the report are to be found on what pages or in which paragraph numbers.

4.5 SUMMARY OF THE REPORT

If a report is long and complex, then it is common practice to include a summary of the findings, arguments etc, in the report, as the first element of the report. This ensures that busy executives can find the relevant details easily without having to work through the entire report itself.

4.6 CONCLUSIONS AND RECOMMENDATIONS

It is also common practice in a longer or more formal report to include as the next element of the report the following items:

- any conclusions reached in the report

- any recommendations made in the report regarding further actions.

4.7 MAIN BODY OF THE REPORT

The precise contents and length of the main body of the report will depend upon the type and detailed content of the report. However the following points should be borne in mind when writing this area.

- There will often be an introductory paragraph explaining the terms of reference of the report. This might include details of who commissioned the report, why it has been written, its scope and any limitations on the report such as confidentiality limitations or time limitations.

- Many reports involve some sort of investigation or research. There will usually be a paragraph that explains or identifies the methods of investigation or research used. If other sources of information have been used in the writing of the report then these will usually also be acknowledged here.

- The results or findings that have come from the commissioning of the report would then be shown.

- These results would then be analysed, discussed and interpreted. This might involve a number of paragraphs in a complex report and these paragraphs should have a logical sequence to them.

Each of the paragraphs of a report may benefit from a heading or perhaps some sort of paragraph numbering. Always remember that it is not only what is written but also how it is produced and structured that is important.

4.8 REPORT CONCLUSION

The main body of the report is then completed with a conclusion of the arguments, findings, recommendations and conclusions of the report.

4.9 APPENDICES

In many reports there are large amounts of information. Some could be very detailed, in particular graphs and tables of figures supporting the arguments, findings or conclusions of the report. However if all this detail were to be included in the main body of the report, the report might become too long and time-consuming for many readers.

Therefore detailed supporting information is usually included in appendices at the end of the report. Readers can look at it if and when they want to. This ensures that the main body of the report is concise, and deals with only the most important areas. The information contained in the appendices of the report should be referred to at appropriate places in the main body of the report.

Conclusion   The possible elements of a report can therefore be listed as follows:

- addressee
- author
- date
- title
- contents
- summary
- main body of the report
- conclusion
- appendices.

Not all reports include all these elements. Most formal, lengthy and complex reports do but other shorter or informal reports may not need all of these elements. Routine reports, such as management accounting reports, might simply be presented as tables of figures with a few introductory words of comment.

5   EXAMPLE REPORTS

The following report shows how you should try to layout your work if you are asked to prepare a simple report. Note that the language is formal.

REPORT
To: Managing Director **From**: Candidate **Date**: Dec 03 **Subject:** Net present value technique
The net present value technique relies on discounting relevant cashflows at an appropriate rate of return. It would be helpful to know: 1   Whether there are any additional cashflows beyond year five. 2   Whether the introduction of a new product will affect sales of the existing products E, C and R. On the basis of the information provided, the project has a positive net present value of £28,600 and should be carried out.

Compare this to a memo which as a similar structure, but uses less formal language.

INTERNAL MEMO
To: Bobby Forster, Accounts Assistant
From: General Manager
Date: 28 October 2003
Subject: Budgeted production costs for 2004
As you know we have begun our budgetary planning exercise for 2004.
I understand that you have been working on the analysis of budgeted production costs.
Could you please pull together all the information you have gathered and carry out the allocation and apportionment exercise for production overhead costs for 2004.
Thanks. Then we will have the necessary information that we need to calculate the pre-determined overhead absorption rates for 2004.

CONCLUSION

In this chapter you have learnt:

*   the importance of planning a report

*   the key features of a good report.

ANSWERS TO ACTIVITIES

CHAPTER 1

ACTIVITY 1

Specific order	Operation
Building contractor	Oil refining
Printer	Food processing
Specialist aircraft equipment	Power generation

ACTIVITY 2

Direct costs are all costs which are: 'physically traceable to the finished goods in an economically feasible manner. All other costs are indirect.' There are several factors which will affect whether a cost is direct or whether it is treated as being indirect. For example, as the definition suggests, certain costs may be traceable to finished goods but it may not be economically worthwhile to do so.

If the cost unit is very large, e.g. contract costing, then the majority of costs, including depreciation of plant and machinery and foreman's salary will be direct costs for a particular contract. For 'small' cost units where for example, cost units are processed on a machine, the depreciation of the machine is not traceable to individual cost units. It would, therefore, be treated as production overhead and included in unit cost via the overhead absorption rate.

Another cost which may be direct or indirect is overtime premium. It may be possible to, for example, trace which jobs are carried out during overtime hours, and charge the premium to those jobs. However, if overtime is worked to increase the overall volume of production it would not be equitable to charge the premium to certain units. The premium would therefore be treated as a production overhead unless the overtime is worked at the specific request of a customer in which case it would be treated as direct.

Conclusion   Whether costs are direct or indirect depends on the individual circumstances.

ACTIVITY 3

Annual rental £100,000 - fixed cost

Materials, labour and expenses £250 per unit - variable cost

Production level	Variable cost £	Fixed cost £
500 units (£250 × 500)	125,000	100,000
2,000 units (£250 × 2,000)	500,000	100,000

Conclusion   The fixed cost does not vary whatever the level of production. The variable costs however increase in line with any increase in production.

ACTIVITY 4

Total fixed costs = £560,000 each month.

	100,000 units	120,000 units	140,000 units	160,000 units
	£	£	£	£
Fixed cost per unit	5.60	4.67	4.00	3.50
Variable cost per unit	6.75	6.75	6.75	6.75
Total cost per unit	12.35	11.42	10.75	10.25

If output went up from 100,000 units to 160,000 units each month, the unit cost would fall from £12.35 to £10.25. This means that if the selling price of widgets is unchanged, the business will make bigger profits. Alternatively, it could reduce its selling price without reducing the amount of its unit profits.

ACTIVITY 5

		£
High	900	2,300
Low	(400)	(1,050)
	500	1,250

Variable cost = £1,250/500 = £2.50/unit

Fixed cost = £1,050 − (400 × £2.50) = £50.

FOULKS LYNCH
PUBLICATIONS

ACTIVITY 6

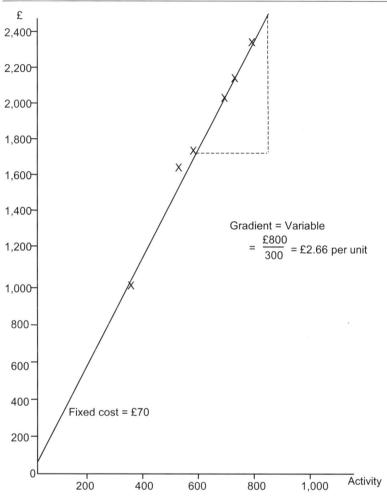

Note that because drawing the line of best fit is subjective your estimate of fixed and variable costs may differ from the suggested solution which differs from the estimate found using the high – low method.

CHAPTER 2

ACTIVITY 1

45 – 7 units = 38 units

ACTIVITY 2

$$\text{Average usage per day} = \frac{\text{Maximum usage} + \text{Minimum usage}}{2}$$

$$= \frac{500 + 300}{2}$$

$$= 400$$

Minimum stock level is therefore:

$$3,600 - (400 \times 5) = 1,600 \text{ units}$$

ACTIVITY 3

The maximum level is:

$$300 + 500 - (50 \times 4) = 600 \text{ units}$$

ACTIVITY 4

Order Quantity	Delivery cost $\dfrac{1,000}{x} \times 15$	Storage cost $\dfrac{x}{2} \times 2.70$	Ordering cost Delivery cost + Storage cost
	£	£	£
50	$\dfrac{1,000}{50} \times 15 = 300$	$\dfrac{50}{2} \times 2.70 = 67.50$	367.50
100	$\dfrac{1,000}{100} \times 15 = 150$	$\dfrac{100}{2} \times 2.70 = 135.00$	285.00
150	$\dfrac{1,000}{150} \times 15 = 100$	$\dfrac{150}{2} \times 2.70 = 202.50$	302.50
200	$\dfrac{1,000}{200} \times 15 = 75$	$\dfrac{200}{2} \times 2.70 = 270.00$	345.00
250	$\dfrac{1,000}{250} \times 15 = 60$	$\dfrac{250}{2} \times 2.70 = 337.50$	397.50

Note: from the figures calculated we can see that the order quantity of 100 units results in the lowest cost.

ACTIVITY 5

$$EOQ = \sqrt{\frac{2\,Co\,D}{Ch}}$$

where
$Co = £50$
$D = 5,000 \text{ units}$
$Ch = £575 \times 10\% = £57.50$

$$= \sqrt{\frac{2 \times 50 \times 5000}{57.50}}$$

$$= 93 \text{ units}$$

FOULKS LYNCH
PUBLICATIONS

ACTIVITY 6

ROWSON SUPPLIES LTD – DELIVERY NOTE		
Delivery to: French Products Ltd		Date: 30 July 20X1
Purchase order no: 7374		
Purchase invoice no: FP 832		
Quantity	*Description*	*Code*
200 metres	Chipboard	D35
Signed: Storeman		

ACTIVITY 7

ROWSON SUPPLIES LTD – PURCHASE INVOICE	
To: French Productions Ltd	Number: FP832
Date: 30 July 20X3	
Purchase order no: 7374	
For supply and delivery of:	**£**
200 metres chipboard D35 @ £4.35 per metre	870.00
Payment due in 30 days	

ACTIVITY 8

STOCK LEDGER ACCOUNT

| Material: | Chipboard | | | | Maximum Quantity: | | | | | | | |
| Code: | D35 | | | | Minimum Quantity: | | | | | | | |

Receipts					Issues					Stock		
Date	GRN No	Qty	Unit Price £	Amount £	Date	Stores Req. No.	Qty	Unit Price £	Amount £	Qty	Unit Price £	Amount £
30.7.X1	8737	200m	4.35	870.00								

ACTIVITY 9 – FIRST-IN-FIRST-OUT (FIFO) PRICE

Definition   The materials issued represent the earliest purchases of stock items.

Each issue is valued at the price paid for the material first taken into the stocks from which the issue could have been drawn.

The stock ledger account (in abbreviated form) would appear as below:

STOCK LEDGER ACCOUNT

| Material: | Grotom | | | | Maximum Quantity: | | | | | | | |
| Code: | | | | | Minimum Quantity: | | | | | | | |

Receipts					Issues					Stock		
Date	GRN No	Quantity	Unit Price £	Amount £	Date	Stores Req. No.	Quantity	Unit Price £	Amount £	Quantity	Unit Price £	Amount £
3 Nov		400	60	24,000						400	60	24,000
					5 Nov		200	60	12,000	200	60	12,000
11 Nov		300	70	21,000						500		33,000
					14 Nov		200	60	12,000	300		21,000
21 Nov		300	80	24,000						600		45,000
					22 Nov		200	70	14,000	400		31,000
					27 Nov					200		16,000
							100	70				
30 Nov							100	80	15,000	200	80	16,000

5 November issue - priced at £60, which is the price of the purchase on 3 November.

14 November issue - priced at £60, which is the price of the remaining purchases from 3 November.

22 November issue - priced at £70, which is the purchase price for the 11 November purchase.

27 November issue -100 tonnes of the 11 November purchase remain, priced at £70, and the final 100 tonnes comes from the 21 November purchase at £80.

LAST-IN-FIRST-OUT (LIFO) PRICE

Definition The materials issued represent the most recent purchases of stock items.

Each issue is valued at the price paid for the material last taken into the stock from which the issue could have been drawn.

STORES LEDGER ACCOUNT											
Material: Grotom							Maximum Quantity:				
Code:							Minimum Quantity:				
Receipts				Issues					Stock		
Date	GRN No	Quantity	Unit Price £	Amount £	Date	Stores Req. No.	Quantity	Unit Price £	Amount £	Quantity	Unit Price £	Amount £
3 Nov		400	60	24,000						400	60	24,000
					5 Nov		200	60	12,000	200	60	12,000
11 Nov		300	70	21,000						500		33,000
					14 Nov		200	70	14,000	300		19,000
21 Nov		300	80	24,000						600		43,000
					22 Nov		200	80	16,000	400		27,000
					27 Nov		100	80		200	60	12,000
							100	70	15,000	200	60	12,000
30 Nov bal												

Note: The columns in this table do not align perfectly with the header. The Date, GRN No, Quantity, Unit Price £, Amount £ are the five Receipts columns; Date, Stores Req. No., Quantity, Unit Price £, Amount £ are the five Issues columns; and Quantity, Unit Price £, Amount £ are the three Stock columns.

5 November issue - priced at £60, the price of the previous purchase on 3 November.

14 November issue - priced at £70, the price of the previous purchase on 11 November.

22 November issue - priced at £80, the price of the previous purchase on 21 November.

27 November issue - 100 tonnes can be priced at £80, the amount remaining of the 21 November purchase. The balance of 100 tonnes is priced at £70, the purchase on 11 November.

WEIGHTED AVERAGE PRICE

Definition The materials issued are priced at an average price of the items in stock at that time.

Each time a consignment is received a weighted average price is calculated as:

$$\frac{\text{Stock value} + \text{Receipt value}}{\text{Quantity in stock} + \text{Quantity received}}$$

The price so calculated is used to value subsequent issues until the next consignment is received.

STORES LEDGER ACCOUNT												
Material:	Grotom						Maximum Quantity:					
Code:							Minimum Quantity:					
Receipts					Issues					Stock		
Date	GRN No	Quantity	Unit Price £	Amount £	Date	Stores Req. No.	Quantity	Unit Price £	Amount £	Quantity	Unit Price £	Amount £
3 Nov		400	60	24,000						400	60	24,000
					5 Nov		200	60	12,000	200	60	12,000
11 Nov		300	70	21,000						500	66	33,000
					14 Nov		200	66	13,200	300	66	19,800
21 Nov		300	80	24,000						600	73	43,000
					22 Nov		200	73	14,600	400	73	29,200
					27 Nov		200	73	14,600	200	73	14,600
										200	73	14,600
30 Nov bal												

5 November issue - priced at £60, the price of the only purchase to date.

14 November issue - priced at weighted average price at that date.

$$\frac{£33,000}{500} = £66 \text{ per tonne}$$

22 and 27 November issues - priced at weighted average price on both those dates.

$$\frac{£43,800}{600} = £73 \text{ per tonne}$$

ACTIVITY 10

FIFO results in later purchases remaining in stock.

		Units
Opening stock		50
Purchases	(60 + 70)	130
Sales	(40 + 60)	(100)
Closing stock		80
		£
Comprising		
1 April	70 × £9 =	630
1 February	10 × £8 =	80
		710

CHAPTER 3

ACTIVITY 1

<table>
<tr><td colspan="8" align="center">ATTENDANCE RECORD</td></tr>
<tr><td colspan="8">Name: Thomas Yung
Employee number: Y4791</td></tr>
<tr><td>Month</td><td>Work</td><td>Sick leave</td><td>Holiday</td><td>Training</td><td>Unpaid leave</td><td>Other</td><td></td></tr>
<tr><td>January</td><td>14</td><td>2</td><td>5</td><td></td><td></td><td></td><td>21</td></tr>
<tr><td>February</td><td>11</td><td></td><td>4</td><td>3</td><td></td><td></td><td>18</td></tr>
<tr><td>March</td><td>19</td><td>2</td><td></td><td></td><td></td><td></td><td>21</td></tr>
<tr><td>April</td><td></td><td></td><td></td><td></td><td></td><td></td><td></td></tr>
<tr><td>May</td><td></td><td></td><td></td><td></td><td></td><td></td><td></td></tr>
<tr><td>June</td><td></td><td></td><td></td><td></td><td></td><td></td><td></td></tr>
<tr><td>July</td><td></td><td></td><td></td><td></td><td></td><td></td><td></td></tr>
<tr><td>August</td><td></td><td></td><td></td><td></td><td></td><td></td><td></td></tr>
<tr><td>September</td><td></td><td></td><td></td><td></td><td></td><td></td><td></td></tr>
<tr><td>October</td><td></td><td></td><td></td><td></td><td></td><td></td><td></td></tr>
<tr><td>November</td><td></td><td></td><td></td><td></td><td></td><td></td><td></td></tr>
<tr><td>December</td><td></td><td></td><td></td><td></td><td></td><td></td><td></td></tr>
<tr><td></td><td colspan="7">Reasons for 'other' leave:</td></tr>
</table>

ACTIVITY 2

31.5 hours × £5.86 = £184.59

ACTIVITY 3

Total weekly wage

	£
Monday (12 × £3)	36
Tuesday (14 × £3)	42
Wednesday (9 × £3)	27
Thursday (14 × £3)	42
Friday (8 × £3)	24
	171

As the weekly earnings are above £140, the guaranteed amount is not relevant to the calculations in this instance.

Conclusion   The payment of any guaranteed amount is not a bonus for good work but simply an additional payment required if the amount of production is below a certain level.

ACTIVITY 4

The amount the employee will be paid will depend upon the exact wording of the agreement. Production of 102 units has taken the employee out of the lowest band (up to 99 units) and into the middle band (100 – 119 units). The question now is whether **all** his units are paid for at the middle rate (£1.50), or only the units produced in excess of 99. The two possibilities are as follows:

(a)   102 × £1.75 = £178.50

(b)   (99 × £1.50) + (3 × £1.75) = £153.75

Most organisations' agreements would apply method (b).

ACTIVITY 5

	£
Basic pay (40 × £5)	200.00
Overtime (5 hours × (£5 × 1.5))	37.50
Weekly wage cost	237.50

Alternatively this could be shown as:

	£
Basic pay (45 × £5)	225.00
Overtime premium	
(5 hours × (£5 × 0.5))	12.50
	237.50

Conclusion   This second method is the only one that shows the overtime premium separately. The premium is the additional amount over the basic rate that is paid for the overtime hours rather than the total payment. This method is preferred because it provides the information needed for costing products.

ACTIVITY 6

Annual salary	£19,500
Standard hours to be worked in the year	
(52 weeks × 38 hours)	1,976 hours
Salary rate per hour	$\dfrac{£19,500}{1,976}$
	= £9.87 per hour
Overtime rate (1.5 × £9.87)	= £14.81 per hour

ACTIVITY 7

Managing director's bonus

(£48,000 × 0.016) = £768

Chris Roberts's bonus

(£18,000 × 0.016) = £288

ACTIVITY 8

		£
Basic rate	$\frac{36}{60} \times £4.80$	2.88
Bonus	$\frac{36}{60} \times (60 - 36) \times \frac{£4.80}{60}$	1.15
Total payment for job A		4.03

ACTIVITY 9

$$\text{Bonus} = \frac{40 - 25}{60} \times 35\% \times £5.00$$

$$= £0.4375$$

ACTIVITY 10

TIME SHEET						
Name: Brendan McCullough				**Clock Number:** 59275		
Department: Factory						
Week commencing: 28 March 20X4						
To be completed by employee				For office use		
Date	Start	Finish	Job	Code	Hours	£
28/3	8.00	12.00	Cutting			
	12.30	5.30	Cutting			____
29/3	9.00	12.00	Machining			
	1.00	3.00	Cutting			____
30/3	10.00	1.00	Machining			
	1.30	4.30	Polishing			
31/3	8.00	12.00	Polishing			
	1.00	7.00	Polishing			
1/4	7.00	2.00	Machining			
Basic pay						
Overtime premium						
Gross wages						
Foreman's signature:						
Date:						

There might also be an additional column on the time sheet to record any bonus that might be payable to employees.

ACTIVITY 11

JOB CARD - 28/3JN	£
Materials	X
Labour	
- making icing (3 hours × £5.30)	15.90

JOB CARD - 28/3KA	£
Materials	X
Labour	
- making icing (5 hours × £5.30)	26.50

ACTIVITY 12

Cost of machine breakdown

(3 × 2 hours × £6.00)   £36

This would be written off to the profit and loss account as an idle time cost that is not part of normal product costs.

ACTIVITY 13

The cost to the employer is the full seven hours per day at £5.50 per hour, £38.50 per employee.

As the tea and rest breaks are a necessary cost of production and are therefore described as unavoidable idle time they should be included as part of the cost of the products on which the employees work.

ACTIVITY 14

(a) **Basic rate**

The basic hourly rate for this employee is £6 per hour. This will be charged to products not only for the 48 weeks in the year when he is working on them but also in the four weeks when he is on holiday.

(b) **Inflated hourly rate**

Some organisations however prefer to inflate the basic hourly rate to reflect the paid holiday period and only charge the employee's hours during the 48 weeks that he actually works.

In this instance the total holiday pay is £840 (4 weeks × £210). This £840 is then spread across the actual hours that the employee is expected to work in the year.

Actual hours expected to work

48 weeks × 35 hours   1,680

Holiday pay spread over these hours

$$\frac{£840}{1,680 \text{ hours}}$$ £0.50 per hour

Inflated basic hourly rate   £6.50 per hour

Conclusion   When an employee is on holiday in most cases he will be paid although he will not be producing any products.

CHAPTER 4

ACTIVITY 1

	£
Cost	15,000
Estimated residual value	5,140
	9,860

Annual depreciation charge $= \dfrac{9,860}{3}$

$= £3,287$

ACTIVITY 2

	£
Cost	15,000
Year 1 depreciation charge	
(£15,000 × 30%)	4,500
Net book value	10,500
Year 2 depreciation charge	
(£10,500 × 30%)	3,150
Net book value	7,350
Year 3 depreciation charge	
(£7,350 × 30%)	2,205
Net book value	5,145

ACTIVITY 3

Depreciation charge $\quad = \quad \dfrac{2{,}000 \text{ hours}}{15{,}000 \text{ hours}} \times £10{,}000$

$\qquad\qquad\qquad = \quad £1{,}333$

Conclusion   Whatever the method of calculating depreciation it is an expense of the business that should appear in the financial accounting profit and loss account. The treatment of the expense of depreciation for cost accounting purposes will be as for any other expense incurred by the business.

CHAPTER 5

ACTIVITY 1

(a)   Fixed (paid regardless of the level of output).

(b)   Variable.

(c)   Fixed.

(d)   Variable.

(e)   Fixed.

(f)   Fixed.

(g)   Variable (could be said to be semi-variable - see earlier chapter).

(h)   Variable.

(i)   Fixed.

(j)   Fixed.

ACTIVITY 2

(a)   Direct.

(b)   Indirect or overhead (direct if by customer request).

(c)   Indirect or overhead.

(d)   Direct.

(e)   Indirect or overhead.

(f)   Indirect or overhead.

(g)   Indirect or overhead.

(h)   Indirect or overhead.

(i)   Indirect or overhead.

(j)   Indirect or overhead.

Conclusion   Whilst most of the material and labour costs in an organisation will tend to be direct costs, in most cases the majority of expenses will fall into the category of indirect costs or overheads.

ACTIVITY 3

	£	Allocate to
Labour costs in department S	6,500	Service department S
Direct labour costs in department P	4,700	Don't allocate. These are a direct production cost, not an overhead.
Costs of supervision in Department Q	2,100	Production department Q. Supervision costs are generally treated as an overhead rather than a direct labour cost.
Material costs of widgets	10,300	Don't allocate. These are a direct production cost, not an overhead.
Machine repair costs, Department Q	800	Production department Q
Materials consumed in department S	1,100	Service department S
Depreciation of machinery in department S	700	Service department S
Indirect materials consumed in department P	500	Production department P
Lighting and heating	900	Cost centre for general costs
Cost of works canteen	1,500	Cost centre for general costs. Canteen costs are incurred for the benefit of all employees. The canteen could be made a separate service cost centre if required.

ACTIVITY 4

Direct method

With the direct method, the costs of the canteen should be apportioned to the production departments only.

Canteen costs	£22,880
Total number of employees (33 + 27)	60
Apportionment rate (£22,880/60)	£381.33/employee

	£
Apportion to department X	12,584
Apportion to department Y	10,296
	22,880

Step-down method

With the step-down method, the costs of the canteen should be apportioned to the service departments as well as the production departments.

Canteen costs	£22,880
Total number of employees (33 + 27 + 8 + 14 + 6)	88
Apportionment rate (£22,880/88)	£260/employee

	£
Apportion to department X	8,580
Apportion to department Y	7,020
Apportion to stores department	2,080
Apportion to engineering department	3,640
Apportion to production control department	1,560
	22,880

ACTIVITY 5

(a)   Number of actual machines or number of machine hours per cost centre.

(b)   Value of machinery in each cost centre.

(c)   Number of vehicles used by each cost centre or mileage of vehicles used by each cost centre.

ACTIVITY 6

Task 1

Neither service department does work for the other.

	Total	Dept P1	Dept P2	Dept S1	Dept S2
	£	£	£	£	£
Allocated costs/share of general costs	550,000	140,000	200,000	90,000	120,000
Apportion:					
S1 costs (60:40)		54,000	36,000	(90,000)	
S2 costs (1:2)		40,000	80,000		(120,000)
		234,000	316,000		

Task 2

Department S2 does some work for Department S1.

Start by apportioning the costs of Department S2.

	Total	Dept P1	Dept P2	Dept S1	Dept S2
	£	£	£	£	£
Allocated costs/share of general costs	550,000	140,000	200,000	90,000	120,000
Apportion:					
S2 costs (25: 50: 25)		30,000	60,000	30,000	(120,000)
				120,000	
				(120,000)	
S2 costs (60:40)		72,000	48,000		
		242,000	308,000		

FOULKS LYNCH
PUBLICATIONS

ACTIVITY 7

Machining:

$$\frac{\text{Cost centre overhead}}{\text{Machine hours}} = \frac{£65,525}{7,300}$$

$$= £8.98 \text{ per machine hour.}$$

Finishing:

$$\frac{\text{Cost centre overhead}}{\text{Direct labour hours}} = \frac{£36,667}{6,250}$$

$$= £5.87 \text{ per direct labour hour.}$$

Packing:

$$\frac{\text{Cost centre overhead}}{\text{Direct labour hours}} = \frac{£24,367}{5,200}$$

$$= £4.69 \text{ per direct labour hour.}$$

ACTIVITY 8

		£
Machining	3 machine hours @ £8.98	26.94
Finishing	0.9 direct labour hours @ £5.87	5.28
Packing	0.1 direct labour hours @ £4.69	0.47
Overhead absorbed in one unit of "pot 3"		32.69

ACTIVITY 9

Task 1

	Department X	Department Y
Budgeted overheads	£840,000	£720,000
Budgeted activity	40,000 machine hours	60,000 direct labour hours
Absorption rate	£21 per machine hour	£12 per direct labour hour

Task 2

	Department X		Department Y	
		£		£
Absorbed overhead	(41,500 x £21)	871,500	(62,400 x £12)	748,800
Actual overhead		895,000		735,000
Over-/(under-)absorbed		(23,500)		13,800

ACTIVITY 10

Workings

The overhead absorption rate is £12 per direct labour hour (£960,000/80,000 hours).

	£
Overheads absorbed into production costs (81,000 hours x £12)	972,000
Actual overheads incurred	955,000
Over-absorbed overhead	17,000

Profit and loss account for the year ended 31 December 20X3

	£	£	£
Sales			4,090,000
Opening stock		201,000	
Production costs			
Direct materials	1,642,000		
Direct labour	1,200,000		
Production overhead (absorbed)	972,000		
		3,814,000	
		4,015,000	
Less: Closing stock		(172,000)	
Production cost of sales			3,843,000
			1,247,000
Over-absorbed overhead			17,000
			1,264,000
Administration overhead		420,000	
Selling and distribution overhead		719,000	
			1,139,000
Profit			125,000

ACTIVITY 11

Workings

The overhead absorption rate is £15 per machine hour (£600,000/40,000 hours).

Production overheads absorbed were £585,000 (39,000 hours x £15 per hour).

Production overheads account

	£		£
Stores account	25,000	Work in progress a/c	585,000
Wages control account	375,000		
Indirect expenses	220,000	Under-absorbed overhead	35,000
	620,000		620,000

Work-in-progress account

	£		£
Opening stock	64,000	Finished goods	1,255,000
Stores	416,000		
Wages control	272,000	Closing stock	82,000
Production overhead	585,000	(balancing figure)	
	1,337,000		1,337,000

There is under-absorbed overhead.

Under-/over-absorbed overhead account

	£		£
Production overhead account	35,000	Profit and loss account	35,000
	35,000		35,000

ACTIVITY 12

Task 1

		£
		£
Total overhead cost of:	42,000 hours	
		153,000
Total overhead cost of:	37,000 hours	145,500
Variable overhead cost for:	5,000 hours	7,500

Variable overhead cost per hour (£7,500/5,000)	£1.50

This should be the absorption rate for variable overheads.

	£
Total overhead cost of 42,000 hours	153,000
Variable overhead cost of 42,000 hours (x £1.50)	63,000
Therefore fixed costs	90,000

The absorption rate for fixed overhead, given a budget of 40,000 direct labour hours, should therefore be £2.25 per direct labour hour (£90,000/40,000 hours)

Task 2

	Fixed overhead	Variable overhead
	£	£
Absorbed overheads:		
Fixed (41,500 hours x £2.25)	93,375	
Variable (41,500 x £1.50)		62,250
Overheads incurred	91,000	67,400
Over-/(under-)absorbed overhead	2,375	(5,150)

Task 3

Production overheads account

	£		£
Expenses incurred:		Work in Progress:	
Fixed overheads	91,000	Fixed overheads absorbed	93,375
Variable overheads	67,400	Variable overheads absorbed	62,250
Over-absorbed (fixed)	2,375	Under-absorbed (variable)	5,150
	160,775		160,775

Under-/over-absorbed overhead account

	£		£
Production overhead account	5,150	Production overhead account	2,375
		Profit and loss account	2,775
	5,150		5,150

ACTIVITY 13

Overhead recovery rates:

	Finishing	Packing
$\dfrac{\text{Overhead}}{\text{direct labour hours}}$	$\dfrac{£74,000}{12,750}$	$\dfrac{£49,000}{10,500}$
	= £5.80	= £4.67

January 20X4

	Finishing	Packing
Overhead absorbed	1,100 direct labour hours × £5.80 per hr	900 direct labour hours × $4.67 per hr
	£6,380	£4,203
Incurred	£6,900	£4,000
Over-(under) absorbed	£(520)	£203

Overhead control a/c

	£		£
Overhead incurred	6,900	Overhead absorbed W-I-P	
Balance c/d	4,000	Finishing	6,380
		Packing	4,203
		P/L a/c	317*
	£10,900		£10,900

*This £317 net under-recovery comprises:

Finishing	£(520) under-absorbed
Packing	£203 over-absorbed
	£(317)

CHAPTER 6

ACTIVITY 1

EDSP

ACTIVITY 2

Stock ledger account A

	£			£
3 May	2,000	7 May	WIP	1,000
24 May	9,000	27 May	WIP	7,000

Stock ledger account B

	£			£
6 May	5,000	8 May	WIP	3,000
10 May	3,000	10 May	WIP	4,000
21 May	7,000			

Stock ledger account C

	£			£
1 May	4,000	2 May	WIP	3,000
7 May	4,000	8 May	WIP	3,000
28 May	4,000	29 May	WIP	3,000

Work in progress

	£		£
2 May Material C	3,000		
7 May Material A	1,000		
8 May Material B	3,000		
8 May Material C	3,000		
10 May Material B	4,000		
27 May Material A	7,000		
29 May Material C	3,000		

ACTIVITY 3

Wages control account

	£		£
31 May Cash/PAYE/NI	43,000		
NI	3,700		

Cash account

	£		£
		31 May Net wages	37,000

NI and PAYE creditor account

	£		£
		31 May Employee's NI and PAYE (£43,000 – (£37,000)	6,000
		Employer's NI	3,700

ACTIVITY 4

Overhead absorption = 1,600 units × £10

= £16,000

Production overhead account

	£		£
Indirect wages	11,700	Work in progress overhead absorbed	16,000
Rent	2,000		
Rates	600		
Power	800		16,000
Insurance	500		
Over absorption (bal fig)	400		
	16,000		

Work in progress

	£		£
2 May Material C	3,000		
7 May Material A	1,000		
8 May Material B	3,000		
8 May Material C	3,000		
10 May Material B	4,000		
27 May Material A	7,000		
29 May Material C	3,000		
31 May Direct wages	35,000		
31 May Production overhead absorbed	16,000		

ACTIVITY 5

	£
200 units @ £16.27	3,254
100 units @ £17.46	1,746
	5,000

CHAPTER 7

ACTIVITY 1

JOB COST CARD

Job number: 3867
Customer name: OT Ltd
Estimate ref:
Quoted estimate:
Start date: 1 June
Delivery date: 17 June
Invoice number:
Invoice amount:

COSTS:

Materials

Date	Code	Qty	Price	£
1 June	T73	40 kg	£60	2,400
5 June	R80	60 kg	£5	300
9 June	B45	280m	£8	2,240
				4,940

Labour

Date	Grade	Hours	Rate	£
1 June	II	43	5.80	249.40
2 June	II	12	5.80	69.60
	IV	15	7.50	112.50
5 June	I	25	4.70	117.50
	IV	13	7.50	97.50
9 June	I	15	4.70	70.50
				717.00

Expenses

Date	Code	Description	£

Production overheads

Hours	OAR	£

Cost summary:	£
Direct materials	
Direct labour	
Direct expenses	
Production overheads	
Administration overheads	
Selling and distribution overheads	
	———
Total cost	
Invoice price	
	———
Profit/loss	
	———

ACTIVITY 2

As the machinery is used in equal proportions on three different jobs then only one third of the hire charge is to be charged to job 3867 (£1,200 × ⅓ = £400).

JOB COST CARD

Job number: 3867
Estimate ref:
Start date: 1 June
Invoice number:

Customer name: OT Ltd
Quoted estimate:
Delivery date: 17 June
Invoice amount:

COSTS:

Materials

Date	Code	Qty	Price	£
1 June	T73	40 kg	£60	2,400
5 June	R80	60 kg	£5	300
9 June	B45	280m	£8	2,240
				———
				4,940
				———

Labour

Date	Grade	Hours	Rate	£
1 June	II	43	5.80	249.40
2 June	II	12	5.80	69.60
	IV	15	7.50	112.50
5 June	I	25	4.70	117.50
	IV	13	7.50	97.50
9 June	I	15	4.70	70.50
				———
				717.00
				———

Expenses

Date	Code	Description	£
1 June	85	Machine hire	400
			———
			400
			———

Production overheads

Hours	OAR	£
		———
		———

Cost summary:

	£
Direct materials	
Direct labour	
Direct expenses	
Production overheads	
Administration overheads	
Selling and distribution overheads	
	‾‾‾
Total cost	
Invoice price	
	‾‾‾
Profit/loss	
	‾‾‾

ACTIVITY 3

JOB COST CARD

Job number: 3867
Estimate ref:
Start date: 1 June
Invoice number: 26457

Customer name: OT Ltd
Quoted estimate:
Delivery date: 17 June
Invoice amount: £7,800

COSTS:

Materials

Date	Code	Qty	Price	£
1 June	T73	40 kg	£60	2,400
5 June	R80	60 kg	£5	300
9 June	B45	280m	£8	2,240
				‾‾‾
				4,940

Labour

Date	Grade	Hours	Rate	£
1 June	II	43	5.80	249.40
2 June	II	12	5.80	69.60
	IV	15	7.50	112.50
5 June	I	25	4.70	117.50
	IV	13	7.50	97.50
9 June	I	15	4.70	70.50
				717.00

Expenses

Date	Code	Description	£
1 June	85	Machine hire	400
			400

Production overheads

Hours	OAR	£
123	4.00	492
		492

Cost summary:

	£
Direct materials	4,940
Direct labour	717
Direct expenses	400

Production overheads	492
Administration overheads	156
Selling and distribution overheads	78
Total cost	6,783
Invoice price	7,800
Profit/loss	1,017

CHAPTER 8

ACTIVITY 1

Expected output = 1,900 units less normal loss of 2% = 1,900 – 38 = 1,862 units.

Actual output = 1,842units.

Abnormal loss = 1,862 - 1,842 = 20 units.

Total costs of production = £31,654 (£28,804 + £1,050 + £1,800).

Cost per unit of expected output = $\dfrac{£31,654}{1,862 \text{ units}}$ = £17 per unit

Both good output and abnormal loss are valued at this amount.

These transactions should be recorded in the cost accounts as follows.

Process A

	Units	£		Units	£
Direct materials	1,900	28,804	Finished goods	1,842	31,314
Direct labour		1,050	Normal loss	38	-
Process overhead		1,800	Abnormal loss	20	340
	1,900	31,654		1,900	31,654

Abnormal loss a/c

	Units	£		Units	£
Process A	20	340	Prift and loss a/c	20	340
	20	340		20	340

Finished goods

	Units	£		Units	£
Process B	1,842	31,314			

FOULKS LYNCH
PUBLICATIONS

ACTIVITY 2

We start by calculating the equivalent units of production. This is simply the expected units of output, allowing for the unfinished closing stock.

	Total units	Equivalent units	
		Materials	Added materials and conversion costs
Finished output	4,000	4,000	4,000
Closing stock in progress	1,000	1,000	400
	5,000	5,000	4,400

We can now calculate a cost per equivalent unit, and use these costs to work out the value of finished output and closing work in process.

	Materials from Process X	Added materials and conversion costs
Cost	£27,500	£14,080
		(£2,080 + £4,000 + £8,000)
Equivalent units	5,000	4,400
Cost per equivalent unit	£5.50	£3.20

		Materials from Process X		Added materials and conversion costs	Total
		£		£	£
Finished output	(4,000 x £5.5)	22,000	(4,000 x £3.2)	12,800	34,800
Closing WIP	(1,000 x £5.5)	5,500	(400 x £3.2)	1,280	6,780
		27,500		14,080	41,580

The process account would be drawn up as follows:

Process Y a/c

	Units	£		Units	£
Process X materials	5,000	27,500	Output	4,000	34,800
Added materials		2,080			
Direct labour		4,000			
Process overhead		8,000	Closing WIP	1,000	6,780
	5,000	41,580		5,000	41,580

CHAPTER 9

ACTIVITY 1

	Product A	Product B	Total
	£	£	£
Sales	120,000	150,000	270,000
Variable cost of sales			
Direct materials	18,000	20,000	38,000
Direct labour	24,000	30,000	54,000
Variable production overhead	6,000	7,500	13,500
Variable selling costs	9,000	12,500	21,500
Total variable costs	57,000	70,000	127,000
Contribution	63,000	80,000	143,000
Fixed costs			
Fixed production costs			50,000
Administration costs			18,000
Fixed selling costs			35,000
Total fixed costs			103,000
Profit			40,000

ACTIVITY 2

Absorption costing

The absorption rate per unit for fixed production overhead = Budgeted fixed production overheads/budgeted production = £30,000/20,000 units = £1.50.

Absorption costing
Operating statement for quarter ended 31 March

	£	£
Sales (19,800 units at £20)		396,000
Production costs (22,000 units)		
Direct material (£4)	88,000	
Direct labour (£3)	66,000	
Variable overhead (£2)	44,000	
Fixed overhead absorbed (at £1.50)	33,000	
	231,000	
Closing stock: 2,200 units at £10.50	(23,100)	
Production cost of sales		207,900
		188,100
Fixed production overhead absorbed	33,000	
Fixed production overhead incurred	30,000	
Over-absorbed fixed overhead		3,000
		191,100
Administration and selling costs		100,000
Profit for the period		£91,100

Marginal costing

	£
Sales (19,800 units at £20)	396,000
Variable costs of production (22,000 units)	
Direct materials (£4)	88,000
Direct labour (£3)	66,000
Variable production overhead (£2)	44,000
	198,000
Closing stock: 2,200 units at £9	(19,800)
Variable production cost of sales	178,200
Contribution	217,800
Fixed production costs incurred	30,000
Administration and selling costs	100,000
Total fixed costs for the period	130,000
Profit for the period	£87,800

FOULKS LYNCH
PUBLICATIONS

The difference in profit between the two costing methods is £3,300 (£91,100 - £87,800). There was no opening stock, so the difference in profit is attributable to the different valuations of closing stocks. In absorption costing, the closing stock of 2,200 units includes £3,300 of fixed overheads (at £1.50 per unit), which are therefore carried forward as a cost of sale in the next period.

CHAPTER 10

ACTIVITY 1

$$\text{Break-even point in units} = \frac{\text{Fixed costs}}{\text{Contribution per unit}}$$

$$= \frac{£5,000}{£20} = 250 \text{ units}$$

ACTIVITY 2

Task 1

Unit variable cost = £24 - £18 = £6. Fixed costs = £800,000.

$$\text{Break-even point} = \frac{£800,000}{£6 \text{ per unit}} = 133,333 \text{ units}$$

Task 2

Budgeted sales	140,000 units
Break-even sales	133,333 units
Margin of safety	6,667 units
Margin of safety as a percentage of budgeted sales	100% x (6,667/140,000)
	= 4.8%

Task 3

Memo

To: Manager

From: Accountant

Subject: **Margin of safety in the budget**

Date: XXXXXX

On the basis of the estimates available to us, the business must sell 133,333 units of product next year to break even, and the budgeted sales volume is 140,000 units. The margin of safety is therefore just 6,667 units or 4.8% of budgeted sales volume.

This suggests that there is a fairly high risk of making a loss, because actual sales might not reach the budgeted amount.

To reduce the risk in the budget, measures should be taken if possible to reduce the risk by increasing the margin of safety.

Measures should be taken to try to reduce costs. If the unit variable costs or if the fixed costs can be reduced, the break-even point will be lowered, and the margin of safety increased.

ACTIVITY 3

	£
Target profit	400,000
Fixed costs	
Production	350,000
Administration	110,000
Selling	240,000
Target contribution	1,100,000

Contribution per unit = £25 - £10 - £4 = £11

Target sales volume

$$= \frac{\text{Target contribution}}{\text{Contribution per unit}}$$

= £1,100,000/£11 per unit

= **100,000 units**

ACTIVITY 4

Workings

	£	£
Sales price	11	12
Variable cost	8	8
Unit contribution	3	4
Expected sales demand	200,000	160,000
	£	£
Annual contribution	600,000	640,000
Annual fixed costs	550,000	550,000
Annual profit	50,000	90,000
Breakeven point (units)	183,333	137,500
Margin of safety (units)	16,667	22,500
Margin of safety (% of budget)	8.3%	14.1%

Memo

To: Manager

From: Accountant

Subject: Selling price for product ZG

Date: XXXXXX

Of the two sales prices under consideration for product ZG, product ZG appears to be preferable.

On the basis of the estimates for variable costs, fixed costs and sales demand at each price, the annual profit would be £90,000 at a price of £12 and only £50,000 at a price of £11.

The higher price also appears to offer the lower risk with regard to sales demand falling short of the expected levels. The margin of safety would be about 14% at a price of £12, but only about 8% at a price of £11.

ACTIVITY 5

Task 1

Assumptions

1.   Each product has the same unit variable cost at all output and sales volumes.

2.   Fixed costs are constant regardless of the volume of production and sales.

3.   The three products will be sold in a constant ratio, which is in this case a constant ratio of 30: 2.4 : 3.

    C/S ratio = 12,400/35,400 = 0.35028 or 35.028%

$$\text{Break-even point in sales value} \quad = \quad \frac{\text{Fixed costs}}{\text{C/S ratio}}$$

$$= \quad £5,000/0.35028 = £14,274$$

Thus, the business must sell a volume in sales, in the same mix as budget that yields £14,274 sales value, in order to break even.

Task 2

To achieve a profit of £10,000, total contribution must be (fixed costs + target profit) = £15,000 (£5,000 + £10,000).

Sales required = £15,000/0.35028 = £42,823.

ACTIVITY 6

(a)   Break-even point in units

$$\frac{\text{Fixed costs}}{\text{Contribution per unit}}$$

$$\frac{£650,000}{£35}$$

= **18,572** tonnes

= **37.14%**

Margin of safety **62.86%.**

(b)   Break-even point in sales value:

$$\frac{\text{Fixed costs}}{(\text{Contribution}/\text{Sales})}$$

$$= \frac{£650,000}{(175,000/375,000)}$$

= **£1,392,857**

(c)

Shireoaks Feeds Ltd
Budgeted operating statement

	£
Sales	3,750,000
Less variable costs	2,000,000
Contribution	1,750,000
Less fixed costs	650,000
Profit	1,100,000

(d)   **Break-even chart**

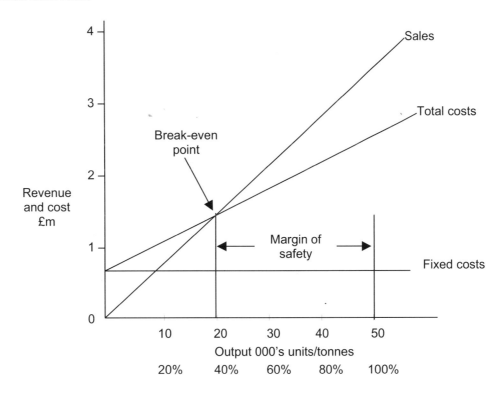

Break-even point approx 18,500 tonnes

Margin of safety

Approx 31,500 tonnes

Approx 63%

(e) **Profit volume graph**

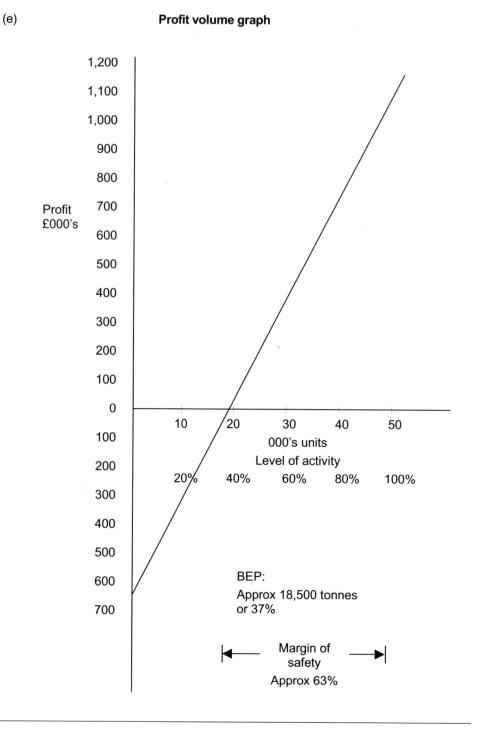

Profit
£000's

BEP:
Approx 18,500 tonnes
or 37%

Margin of
safety
Approx 63%

ACTIVITY 7

(1)   The first step is to calculate a variable cost per unit using the high-low method.

	£
Total costs of 70,000 units	675,000
Total costs of 55,000 units	607,500
Therefore variable costs of 15,000 units	67,500

Variable cost per unit = £67,500/15,000 = £4.50 per unit.

We can now calculate fixed costs, in either of the ways shown below.

	70,000 units	55,000 units
	£	£
Total costs	675,000	607,500
Variable costs at £4.50 per unit	315,000	247,500
Therefore fixed costs	360,000	360,000

Contribution per unit = Sales price – Variable cost = £10 - £4.50 = £5.50.

Breakeven point = £360,000/£5.50 per unit = 65,455 units.

(2) **Margin of safety** = 68,000 – 65,455 = 2,545 units. As a percentage of budgeted sales, this is 3.7%.

(3) To achieve a **target profit** of £40,000, total contribution must be £400,000 (£360,000 fixed costs + £40,000 profit). Required sales =

£400,000/£5.50 contribution per unit = 72,727 units.

This is a higher sales volume than the 'high' level of costs used in the high-low analysis. This must raise doubts as to whether a sales volome of nearly 73,000 units and a proofit of £40,000 are achievable at the current sales price and cost levels.

ACTIVITY 8

Task 1

Production is restricted as follows:

Machine hours	200/5	=	40 units of X; or
	200/2.5	=	80 units of Y
Materials	£500/£10 =		50 units of X; or
	£500/£5	=	100 units of Y

Therefore machine hours are the limiting factor since X's and Y's production are most severely limited by machine hours.

Task 2

Benefit per machine hour:

Product X	£20/5 hours	=	£4/hour
Product Y	£15/2.5 hours	=	£6/hour

Product Y should be made.

ACTIVITY 9

Product	A	B	C
Contribution per labour hour	$\frac{£25}{5} = £5.00$	$\frac{£40}{6} = £6.66$	$\frac{£35}{8} = £4.375$
Rank order	2nd	1st	3rd

Firstly make 200 units of product B (maximum demand) and then with the remaining 300 hours make 60 units of product A.

ACTIVITY 10

Product	X	Y	Z
Contribution per machine hour	$\frac{£15}{3} = £5.00$	$\frac{£9}{2} = £4.50$	$\frac{£12}{4} = £3.00$
Rank order	1st	2nd	3rd
Machine hours for minimum demand	300	100	600

The total machine hours for the minimum demand is 1,000 (300 + 100 + 600).

Machine hours available for additional units:

Product X:	$(300 - 100) \times 3$ hours	=	600 hours
Product Y:		=	100 hours
			———
			700
			———

The additional units of product Y $\quad = \quad \dfrac{100 \text{ hours}}{2 \text{ hours/unit}} \quad = \quad$ 50 units

The optimum production plan is:

Product X: 300 units (maximum)

Product Y: 100 units (minimum + 50)

Product Z: 150 units (minimum only).

CHAPTER 11

ACTIVITY 1

The £15,000 already spent on the feasibility study is not relevant, because it has already been spent. (It is a 'sunk cost'.) Depreciation and apportioned fixed overheads are not relevant. Depreciation is not a cash flow and apportioned fixed overheads represent costs that will be incurred anyway.

	£
Estimated profit	8,000
Add back depreciation	40,000
Add back apportioned fixed costs	25,000
Annual cash flows	73,000

The project's cash flows to be evaluated are

Year		£
Now (Year 0)	Purchase equipment	(160,000)
1 - 4	Cash flow from profits	73,000 each year

ACTIVITY 2

$$\text{Payback} = \frac{£2,300,000}{£600,000} = 3.8333 \text{ years}$$

0.8333 years = 10 months (0.8333 x 12)

Payback is therefore after 3 years 10 months.

It is assumed that the cash flows each year occur at an even rate throughout the year.

ACTIVITY 3

The payback period would be calculated as follows.

Year	Cash flow	Cumulative cash flow
	£000	£000
0	(3,100)	(3,100)
1	1,000	(2,100)
2	900	(1,200)
3	800	(400)
4	500	100
5	500	600

Payback is between the end of year 3 and the end of year 4 – in other words during year 4.

If we assume a constant rate of cash flow through the year, we could estimate that payback will be three years, plus (400/500) of year 4, which is 3.8years.

0.8 years = 10 months (0.8 x 12)

We could therefore estimate that payback would be after 3 years 10 months.

ACTIVITY 4

Task 1: $\quad £2,000 \times \dfrac{1}{1.08^4} = £1,470$

Task 2: $\quad £5,000 \times \dfrac{1}{1.07^3} = £4,081$

ACTIVITY 5

Year	Cash flow	Discount factor	Present value
	£	at 6%	£
0	(25,000)	1.000	(25,000)
1	6,000	0.943	5,658
2	10,000	0.890	8,900
3	8,000	0.840	6,720
4	7,000	0.792	5,544
			+ 1,822

+ £1,822 is in fact the net present value of the project.

ACTIVITY 6

DCF Schedule (NPV method)

Discount rate 12%

Year	Outflow	Inflow	Discount factor at 12%	NPV
	£	£		£
0	(30,000)		1.000	(35,000)
1		8,000	0.893	7,144
2		9,000	0.797	7,173
3		12,000	0.712	8,544
4		9,500	0.636	6,042
5		9,000	0.568	5,112
			NPV	(985)

Recommendation

At the cost of capital of 12%, the NPV is negative, showing that the investment would earn a return below 12% per annum. On financial considerations, the recommendation is that the project should not be undertaken.

INDEX